UNBOUNDED

Praise for the book

Abhayanand, the famous Director General of Police who was the brain behind Nitish Kumar's successful campaign for speedily trying and convicting criminals in Bihar.

—**S.A. Aiyar**, *The Economic Times*

Abhayanand has not used his licensed service revolver even once in his 36 years of service as an IPS officer. He led 22 encounters, but never used his weapon even when he was SP of Naxal-infested districts.

—*Deccan Herald*

Told with an elegiac ferocity, unadulterated impartiality and unsettling forensic memories of policing, Abhayanand's *Unbounded* is a compelling and gripping tale of a supercop's daring deeds to fix a dystopian Leviathan without blood or gore. He also inspired poor students to pursue their dreams of joining IITs through his conceptualization of Super 30.'

—**Ashwani Kumar**, Professor, Tata Institute of Social Sciences, Mumbai, and author of *Community Warriors: State Peasants and Caste Armies in Bihar*

A lot has been written about Bihar's crime and law and order, but only by journalists and academicians. This will be the first book by a man who was at the helm of affairs. While talking about the importance of integrity, especially in relation to the police service, the book talks about the innovations and experiments Abhayanand tried and tested during his service period.

—**Prakash Jha**, Award-winning Filmmaker

He has an air of power and moral authority that he carries with him wherever he goes.

—**Alexander Lee,** Assistant Professor, Political Science, Rochester University, USA

His ideas on management, policing and broader social change carry important lessons for public officials not just in India but around the world.'

—**Rohan Mukherjee**, Assistant Professor, Political Science, Yale-NUS College, Singapore

Rather than going for aggressive action against crime violators, Abhayanand conceived a strategy to concentrate upon successful prosecution of serious offenders.

—**Arvind Verma**, Criminal Justice, Indiana University, USA

His understanding of problems of policing is deep and incisive. Is unattached to issues and yet deeply involved with policing, to the extent that he declined to be recommended for various medals. Perhaps he believes in working as a karma yogi.

—**R.R. Prasad**, DGP, Bihar, 2003

Quiet by nature, Shri Abhayanand is one of the most outstanding officers of the state. He has a pleasant manner and razor-sharp intellect. His contribution to the restoration of law and order, and re-enforcement of rule of law has been substantial. He played a key role in drafting the Bihar Police Act, 2007. His concern for SC/ST and other weaker sections is well known. A new leaf has been added to the police department, as it has succeeded in getting 1,84,986 schoolgoing children enrolled in schools.

—**A.K. Chaudhary**, Chief Secretary, Bihar, 2007

UNBOUNDED

My Experiments with Law, Physics,
Policing and Super 30

ABHAYANAND

RUPA

First published by
Rupa Publications India Pvt. Ltd 2022
7/16, Ansari Road, Daryaganj
New Delhi 110002

Sales Centres:

Allahabad Bengaluru Chennai
Hyderabad Jaipur Kathmandu
Kolkata Mumbai

Copyright © Abhayanand 2022

The views and opinions expressed in this book are the author's own and the facts are as reported by him which have been verified to the extent possible, and the publishers are not in any way liable for the same.

All rights reserved.
No part of this publication may be reproduced, transmitted, or stored in a retrieval system, in any form or by any means, electronic, mechanical, photocopying, recording or otherwise, without the prior permission of the publisher.

ISBN: 978-93-5520-449-3

Second impression 2022

10 9 8 7 6 5 4 3 2

The moral right of the author has been asserted.

Printed in India

This book is sold subject to the condition that it shall not, by way of trade or otherwise, be lent, resold, hired out, or otherwise circulated, without the publisher's prior consent, in any form of binding or cover other than that in which it is published.

To the constables of Bihar Police, in whose lap I spent my childhood, and the people of Bihar, who protected me from the whims and fancies of politicians in power

CONTENTS

Career Trajectory	ix
Introduction	xi
Prologue	xv

1.	I Remember, I Remember...	1
2.	A Firm and Ample Base	18
3.	The More the Storm, the More the Strength	39
4.	Be a Hero in the Strife	61
5.	Stick to the Fight When You're Hardest Hit	75
6.	Round Pegs in Square Holes	97
7.	The World Will Not Be Destroyed by Those Who Do Evil	115
8.	A Cog in a Giant Machine	139
9.	Criminal Justice System	151
10.	The Man Must Furnish the Will to Win	158
11.	The Man in the Arena	177
12.	Economics of Crime	182
13.	A Problem Well-Stated Is a Problem Half-Solved	190
14.	What Makes a Great Leader	204
15.	Limitations of the Legislature	211
16.	Change the Way You Look at Things	217
17.	My Powers Are Ordinary	224
18.	I Am the Master of My Fate	227

20.	The Interregnum Called Super 30	239
21.	The Elections of 2005	246
22.	The Road Less Travelled By	252
23.	Brave Hearts Dare to Climb the Steep	278
24.	O Captain! My Captain!	283
25.	A Story That Was Never Told...	306

Epilogue   309
Acknowledgements   315
Law Lexicon   316

CAREER TRAJECTORY

Posting	From	To
Training – Sardar Vallabhbhai Patel National Police Academy, Hyderabad	13 November 1977	31 December 1978
Probationer Ranchi	1 January 1979	20 April 1980
ASP Sasaram	21 April 1980	6 May 1981
SP Madhepura	7 May 1981	30 March 1982
Training at Lal Bahadur Shastri National Academy of Administration, Mussoorie		
SP Aurangabad	24 July 1982	23 November 1983
SP Sahibganj	28 November 1983	21 April 1984
SP CBI, Ranchi	14 August 1984	14 August 1988
SRP Dhanbad	16 August 1988	14 January 1989
SP Nalanda	16 January 1989	24 December 1989
SP (Special Branch)	25 December 1989	22 April 1992
SP Bettiah	23 April 1992	13 June 1993
DIG (BMP)	15 June 1993	12 June 1996
DIG/IG (Wireless)	13 June 1996	17 February 1999
IG (Special Branch)	18 February 1999	23 March 1999
IG (Training)	23 March 1999	6 March 2000
IG (Prashasan)	6 March 2000	12 March 2000
IG (Training)	13 March 2000	23 November 2000
IG (Provisions)	23 November 2000	22 December 2003
IG (EOW)	22 December 2003	31 March 2005
Zonal IG	1 April 2005	21 May 2005
ADG (Special Branch)	17 December 2005	9 April 2008
ADG (HQ)	17 February 2006	9 April 2008
ADG (BMP)	10 April 2008	8 March 2010
ADG (Training)	8 March 2010	31 October 2011
ADG (Wireless)	19 April 2010	31 August 2011
DGP	31 August 2011	24 June 2014
DG, Home Guards	25 June 2014	31 December 2014

INTRODUCTION

What is the necessity for the police?
Who will police the police?
Why are crimes committed at all?
Why is there so much mistrust between the people and the police?
Can the human dynamics, which we see around us every moment, be explained by some unifying theory?

Such questions motivated me to steer through 37 years in the police, almost entirely in Bihar. Seeking answers to these and many such similar questions helped me find my way through the 'slush and muck' of human life that crimes portray. The pace at which life moves in the world of crime, and the darkness that envelopes it, is scary by any standard. More so, for a person who, in his student life, was destined to be a 'man of physics', such questions had never even been within his purview. Someone who gets trained in physics observes things in his surroundings, applies the principles hitherto known and moves on in the choppy seas of life till he reaches the frontiers of the subject, where his training helps him ask questions that have not been asked earlier. If he is able to answer his own questions, and at the same time, is able to assimilate everything else that history knows, he is considered to be a physicist worth his name.

My story is of someone whose journey certainly began as a man of physics, who was almost on the path, just picking up speed on the runway, when destiny made him change track. Such sudden and violent changes often result in crashes.

I was lucky that I survived this change. In fact, I not only survived but was able to use the speed of the first track to power the second run. In the language of mathematics, I never let my life's 'function' become discontinuous at any point.

This story is about seeking answers to simple but revealing questions, applying those answers to real-life situations and finding out the effectiveness of the solutions hence found.

However, the questions never stopped. They came up with regularity, challenging my capacity to reach new horizons, every single time. I would indeed say the quality of these questions only became better with age. My scientific mind knew that with every solution I unearth, nature is bound to show me another layer waiting to be peeled, bringing me one step closer to the truth.

The story is, therefore, a quest that never ends. Maybe it needs another change of track.

The concept that ignited my mind most in the police was: can the police service be 'marketed'? I had tried to use this word, which is used in managerial science, in my earlier days when I ventured onto paths where angels fear to tread. I realized that I couldn't stray far because law defines the hard boundaries of policing. This story is also of how innovations were made by a fertile mind, which was locked within limits and yet how it created solutions to ever-changing police problems.

Realization of the mistrust between people and police is painful for the leadership of the police—the Indian Police Service (IPS). We are meant to serve the people through an instrument called police, but at the same time, we are painfully aware that people hate this instrument. This story tries to bring out ways and means of resolving this conflict, within the ambit of law. This challenge has to be accepted, and solutions have to be sought tirelessly, while being fully aware that society will always peel the next layer, one after another.

Standing on the frontiers of this quest, I saw at a distance, people's acceptance of the police becoming the more dominant force than the State's control over it. I can see glimpses of this already on the horizon. It's hazy, but keen eyes can discern it. It will be defined by the struggle between State and society, which is more clear than the picture of the police, but the bearings of one on the other are too obvious to be missed.

I wish I could see this struggle emerging and taking shape, though from the sidelines.

The intriguing part of the story is that the politicians, as part of the legislature, who contribute least to solving any issue confronting society, including the acrimony between people and police, take all the credit.

The power of the people is much bigger than the powers of the so-called powerful. It can move mountains. Society is a powerful agency capable of solving its own problems. Agencies such as the State and the police seem to only add to the problems.

People of Bihar remain intrigued that the innovations that worked a few years ago don't seem to work any longer, though the political dispensation seems to be largely the same, including the top players. This seems to be reason enough to take a relook at the answers that people thought they had found.

The journey continues…

PROLOGUE: LAW VS LATHI

Year 2008. Month January.

Police firing in a law and order situation had resulted in a few deaths at Kahalgaon in Bhagalpur district of Bihar. Tension had been brewing for close to three days.

It was a holiday, and I was teaching my students when I suddenly got a call on my mobile from the chief minister (CM) himself. Quite succinctly, he informed me that the state government had directed a helicopter to take me to Kahalgaon to handle the situation. I had to leave immediately.

As per the protocol, the additional director general (ADG) (Law and Order) is supposed to handle such situations; I could not understand why I, as ADG, Headquarters (HQ), was being asked to look into this. Nonetheless, I left immediately, since the orders came from the CM himself, and landed on Kahalgaon National Thermal Power Corporation (NTPC) premises. I didn't even get time to change into my uniform. There was no policeman to receive me at the landing ground; it seemed as if nobody was informed about my arrival. I requested the chief of NTPC to drop me at the local police station, which was about 4 kilometres away. He gave me a rickety jeep for my ride. There was hardly a soul to be seen on the roads. The driver alerted me that the situation was especially tense, and the local people were furious with the police. He dropped me at the police station and drove off. The chopper that had brought me to Kahalgaon had also taken off.

I arrived at the police station to find that all police officers, up to the rank of inspector, were not on duty; they had all been suspended. The superintendent of police (SP) was not present, the deputy superintendent of police (DSP) was not present, the range deputy inspector general (DIG) was perhaps on leave, and the zonal inspector general (IG) Bhagalpur was also not to be seen. Only about 25 armed men and a few press reporters were huddled together in a corner, fear writ large on their faces. When I checked on the policemen present there, they told me that they hadn't even had a meal for the entire day because the people of Kahalgaon had instructed all the hotels to not serve any food to any policeman. I asked the journalists, and they said, 'We dare not move out of the police station for fear of being thrashed by the locals.' I enquired if there was any way of having a dialogue with the local populace, but I was told that the gap between the police and the people had become so wide that a dialogue at this stage seemed next to impossible.

I sat down in the police station, not understanding what to do next. I was sure that if I did not establish communication fast enough, the situation might escalate within a few hours. If that happened, and the people attacked the police station out of vengeance, I would be left with no option but to order firing. The use of lathi, which I loathed throughout my policing career, would become inevitable.

I do not know what prompted me, but almost impulsively, I came out of the police station with folded hands and started walking towards a house with an open window, right across the road. I could see a person peeping out of the window. I went up to him and said, 'My name is Abhayanand, and I have come from Patna to talk to the people of Kahalgaon.' He did not say a word and closed the window. Within about half a minute, I saw him coming out of the house. He came up to me and said, 'Come along with me.'

The two of us started walking on the roads and went to one

house after another. In the next five minutes, there was a group of about 25 people accompanying us. I was leading this group on the roads of the Kahalgaon market, where about seven armed policemen had been held captive for a ransom. The crowd behind me had started to swell. On the way, I could see four-five police jeeps that had been overturned and burned, and there I was, a man from the same police department, leading a crowd of angry local people.

I reached Ganguly maidan, next to the Kahalgaon railway station. It had become dark by then. All I could see was a sea of people that had already gathered there from before. A local leader was standing on a slightly raised platform that looked like a makeshift stage and was addressing them. I went up to him, introduced myself and expressed my desire to move around the town and talk to the people. I received an abrasive reply, 'No need. If you want to talk to the people, come to the stadium, and we will have a meeting there.'

I accepted that proposal instantly. I reached the stadium and stood in front of around 10,000 angry people, all by myself. Somebody got a battery and a microphone was arranged. The people started shouting at the police officers, and their demand was to hang the district magistrate (DM) and the SP of Bhagalpur. I was at my wit's end about what I could do in that situation. I knew that I did not have any police support and I was facing an extremely violent crowd. I quickly made up my mind on how I wanted to handle this.

A chapter from the principles of physics, called forced harmonic oscillator, rushed to my mind: *In the steady-state, the oscillator loses its initial memory and starts to oscillate with force from outside.* My thoughts were suddenly disrupted by a sudden voice, 'We have someone who has come from Patna. Let us hear what he has got to say.' The mic was handed over to me, and I started off by saying, 'Let us first bow our heads in silence for the four people who have been martyred in the police firing in the last three days.' The crowd fell silent immediately. I realized that a door for communication had been opened.

The conversation started. I was being bombarded with all types of demands, from all sides. A few shots were being relayed live by a news channel, and people in Patna could see the scene I was in. I got a call from the CM, instructing me to accept no demand under any circumstance. I replied, 'Since I am physically present here, I will have to take decisions according to how the situation evolves.'

After about four-and-a-half hours of discussion, the temper of the crowd cooled down. Finally, at around 11 in the night, they agreed to pull back and disperse. I started walking back to the police station. I was trying to let the transients die down till a steady state was reached.

Laws of physics proved to be mightier than the lathi of the police.

A small group of about 25 young men eagerly wanted to escort me back to the police station. I allowed them to do so. On the way, they talked to me excitedly. At one point, they said that they were quite disheartened that I had come to Kahalgaon in such circumstances. If I had visited them during normal, peaceful times, they would have liked to discuss academics with me. It was then that I realized that I could win my way through and get the support of the people there not just through my skills as a policeman but also due to my image as a man who was furthering the cause of education and helping the younger generation of Bihar through his efforts—as the man who had founded Super 30.

When I returned to Patna the next day, I met the CM and narrated the entire episode to him personally. He appeared nonchalant. When I reached my office, I saw a written order from the home secretary to the effect that I have been directed to proceed to Kahalgaon to tackle the law and order situation there. The government issuing written orders to me was an absolute rarity. Even today, I wonder who had done this and under whose order, when the verbal orders had come from the CM himself. I also wonder why the CM was monitoring the progress of the situation personally?

I shall remember this as an incident that tested me and left too many questions unanswered. Such events in life compel one to believe in that ultimate invisible power that protects us all and ensures that there is justice in the universe.

I REMEMBER, I REMEMBER...

> *I remember, I remember,*
> *The house where I was born,*
> *The little window where the sun*
> *Came peeping in at morn;*
> *He never came a wink too soon,*
> *Nor brought too long a day,*
> *But now, I often wish the night*
> *Had borne my breath away!*
>
> —Thomas Hood

Situated on the banks of a sandy, seasonal, shallow river Morhar is a village named Chitap Khurd, in the district of Gaya in Bihar. Although history has never been one of my chosen subjects, I searched for the origin of my ancestors who had settled in this village. The farthest I could trace back to was to a district called Monghyr in Bihar. So, I was convinced that I am a pure Bihari, with no mix from either side.

Chitap is a small sleepy village with hardly 30 families. Even today, they all live as one big family. Sans cut-throat competition, the residents of this village can boast of living in peaceful coexistence, with agriculture being their primary source of livelihood. At some point in the past, school education gained currency in this village, and most families started believing that it paved the way to prosperity. After finishing primary education in the village, families shifted to neighbouring towns in search of high school and college education. Families that moved earlier supposedly 'prospered' more than the others.

My great-grandfather, late Ram Bharosa Singh, was a man of average means and not 'educated' in the modern sense. Spiritually, he was an elevated soul, quiet and sedate, always eager to help others. Wealth never attracted him, and he remained devoted to the Almighty.

Sanyasa dharma at the age of 40

'These are the keys to the household. Today I am handing over all responsibilities of the house to you.' These were the words of my great-grandfather to my grandfather, who was then just 20 years old. My grandfather received this as his reward on the day he joined the Bar Association of Gaya, after completing his study of law. Before he realized it, he was shouldering the complete responsibility of the house and the family. His father left for the holy city of Benares immediately and never returned.

My great-grandfather lived in an ashram at Benares, dedicating himself to the Almighty. My grandfather would visit him once in a couple of months with some money and food for his livelihood, and bring back his blessings for the family. The only memory I have of him is through a photograph, that too in samadhi.

I strongly believe that it is his blessings that have helped our family reach wherever we are today. I shall always carry the regret of not locating his ashram in Benares, which would have been a place of worship for me.

On the contrary, my grandfather, late Shri Goverdhan Prasad Singh, took the lead in this race of prosperity and moved to Gaya, where my father got his high school education. Born in

1896, my grandfather certainly had a vision, which I thought was singularly bright for his time.

He had inherited little in terms of property and lived the life of a karma yogi[1]. If there is one person who laid the base of education in our lineage, it is him.

In 1835, Lord Macaulay's education policy had consciously replaced the traditional gurukul system of education in India. Roots of English had been sown in the Indian subsoil. My grandfather realized that only if he adapted to this change, could he lift himself, and his not-so-well-off family, up the rungs of the ladder of prosperity. He would travel on foot to reach his school in Gaya, which was 16 kilometres from our village.

He also ensured that my father strived for the best academically and pushed him to build a strong and respectable career of his own.

First lesson in administration

Year 1950, the results of the Union Public Service Commission (UPSC) examination had been declared. The son of an advocate in the district Bar of Gaya had been selected for the IPS. My grandfather's joy knew no bounds. My father, late Shri Jagadanand, who later became the 28th Director General of Police (DGP) of Bihar, had qualified.

My grandfather took him to the sprawling residence of the district judge of Gaya to seek his blessings for the new journey. My father, who had played small roles in the independence movement, did not like the ambience that had the stamp of British authority. Yet, he chose to keep an open mind and not feel repulsed by it.

After the exchange of pleasantries, at the request of my grandfather, the district judge shared a valuable learning with

---

[1] According to the Bhagavad Gita, a karma yogi treads the path of salvation through right action and no expectation.

my father, a tip which both of us practised to great advantage in our professional lives.

He said that in a courtroom, everyone except the presiding officer sits at the same level. The presiding officer sits on an elevated platform at one end of the room. He can oversee all activities except that of his peshkaar[2]. The officer is confident that nothing is happening behind his back but does not know what is happening under his nose!

He further said, 'Son, in the service that you are going to join, all types of situations will arise. Always be aware of the limitations of your position and never try to overreach them. A senior officer must work within the mandate demanded by the situation.'

My father and I both stuck to this principle.

My grandfather struggled his way up the socio-economic order. He worked in the fields, studied diligently and was focused intently on his mission in life. He became a lawyer and earned enough money to reach some level of prosperity. This he translated into agricultural lands in villages around Chitap.

My grandmother, late Lakhpati Devi, was a lady with a religious bent of mind, a strict disciplinarian who had a complete grip over family matters. She had a soft interior and an aura that commanded respect. In a sense, she was the architect of the family. On a few occasions as a child, I had seen her empathize with clients who would request her for fee waivers. She would ask my grandfather to forgo his fees in such matters, to which he would agree.

I am convinced that these three were the strong roots of my family tree, who laid the foundations of the sanskaar[3] in our family for generations to come.

---

[2]Court clerk
[3]Sanskrit word 'saṃskāra' refers to a person's behaviour, thought and action.

The prestige of the village was at stake!

Chitap Khurd is situated on the bank of Morhar River, and our ancestral house is the first building, right at its entrance.

It was that time of the year which is considered auspicious for marriages. My grandmother was sitting in the verandah of the house, gazing at the river, which had only ankle-deep water in that season. My grandfather had gone to Gaya for some work.

She saw that a bride's family from the neighbouring village was coming over to perform the tilak ceremony of a young man living next door. Tilak is a pre-wedding ritual where the male members of the bride's family visit the groom's house, anoint his forehead and offer gifts and cash to him and his family as a token of acceptance of the groom into their own family. Unfortunately, this ritual has lost its original significance over time and has morphed into a dowry-giving ceremony.

Suddenly, she saw that this family was returning much sooner than one would expect. She suspected something was wrong. She quickly summoned one of her servants to go and find out. The servant came back, saying that the marriage had been called off due to a dispute regarding the tilak amount.

On knowing this, my grandmother immediately stopped the family from returning. She offered her eldest son in marriage to measure up to the reputation of our village. The bride's family instantly accepted the offer. The tilak was performed with my uncle.

My grandfather endorsed this decision upon his return. He, too, thought that the village's name would have been tarnished otherwise.

The history of my mother's side of the family takes me to a village named Rahimpur, located in the proximity of the Khagaria district of Bihar. Both my maternal grandfather, late Pramod Narain Singh, and grandmother belonged to typical traditional land-owning zamindar families, where the power of education had not shown its strength as yet. Female education used to be an unknown concept, but the women had strong values, which strengthened the families from within.

My mother, late Smt Krishna, had attended school only for a day in her life. Her educational training happened with my father after she got married to him at the age of 13. The way she interacted with people and her quips on issues surprised me. She was a beacon and a source of strength for all of us. I vividly remember how every year, during Dussehra, a mela would descend onto our home premises to receive food and clothes from her. She used to collect old, outgrown clothes from all our relatives, carry the huge bundle to Chitap and distribute them amongst those who needed them.

My father, Shri Jagadanand, was a hard-working and bright student. He was exceptionally good at mathematics at school but forsook it for humanities later in college. I remember he would discuss history with me, using intriguing words like 'historical forces' that brought about sociological changes. Unfortunately, my school teachers never used such concepts in class that could attract me towards this subject.

I recall one incident from his college days. One of his classmates woke him up from sleep the night just before his graduation examinations. He had brought the question paper for the next day's exam and needed my father's help. My father would never sacrifice his sleep for anything. Half-awake, he quickly pointed to the relevant sections of the book and went back to sleep. The next day, identical questions appeared. My father wrote the answers in his own words and ended up scoring lower than his friend who had memorized every word from the book. Nonetheless, he topped the class in the final exams. It seems that academic brilliance has been passed on genetically in our family.

Even in the police, my father valued those subordinates who applied their minds in solving a problem more than those who mechanically followed orders.

SHO accuses the SP of stealing a rifle

'Sir, you have taken a rifle from my police station last night.' The officer-in-charge of Ekma Police Station accused my father, the SP of Saran district.

As a mandatory activity, an SP needed to go on rounds and patrol his district during the darkest nights of the month. On one such night, my father reached Ekma Police Station in his district. He saw that the armed constable on duty was sleeping with his rifle by his side. He switched off his car's engine and stealthily went into the police station to find that even there, no one was awake. He then quietly picked up the rifle and came back to his residence in Chhapra.

The next day, when my father was having his morning tea in his garden, the station house officer (SHO) of Ekma arrived at his residence and made this accusation against him. My father was intrigued and asked him how he could say so. The SHO replied that when he started looking for the missing rifle in the morning, he saw broad tyre marks of a car just outside the police station, which were suggestive of an imported car. He knew that there was only one such car in the entire district—my father's Chevrolet.

My father was extremely impressed with this answer. The SHO was rewarded instead of being punished.

My father was the assistant superintendent of police (ASP) of Deoghar, now in Jharkhand, where I was born. It was a matter of great joy in the family. My grandfather, who was then in Gaya, became impatient to know the sex of the newborn. So much so that he went to the local PCO and booked a call to Deoghar immediately. Such were the days, a decade into our country's independence.

I was the eldest son, preceded only by my sister, who is three years elder to me. My early life was marred by ill health, so much so that my family had lost all hope of my survival. When I was two years old, I fell really unwell. I was standing quite at the edge of life and death. It was a miracle that I survived. My father was the additional superintendent of police (Addl. SP) Monghyr at that time, and he called upon the best of doctors there to treat me. They all came, examined me and each threw up his hand.

Just then, my nani and nana came to my rescue. My nani had come with her troupe of female househelp to look after me. She would take care of all my requirements, every moment. My nana would camp at Monghyr, in the absence of my father, to help us all.

On this scene, appeared an old homoeopath, Dr Kalipada Sarkar, to try his hands at treating my undiagnosed ailment. He took charge of my health and finally cured me. He prescribed a list of extremely unconventional, unthinkable medicines that nobody in his sane mind would ever consume. I would have preferred to die instead. The excreta of a young horse had to be squeezed along with the pulp of a freshly killed housefly and mixed with goat's milk. This had to be fed to me twice a day. Today, the mere thought of this makes me nauseous. Miraculously, these medicines, which were devoid of modern-day scientific techniques, worked, and I survived.

As I grew up, I didn't have much association with children of my age. The SP's bungalow used to be a sprawling campus, from where a small child could only feel like the master of all that he surveys. It was too guarded for access to any friends. The best that I had was a group of constables who lived inside the campus for security duties. I spent a lot of time with them. During lunchtime, on holidays, my mother would keep looking for me, and I wouldn't be found. 'Look for him in the tents,' my mother would cry. Sure enough, I would always be found with the constables, sitting on a low wooden seat called *pidhia*, having lunch with them. This would be my favourite place on holidays. I loved the ambience of the tents. At times, I would climb on the top to see everything far and beyond. It was such a pleasant experience.

Two constables need special mention here. Ram Sundar ji and Pradeep Singh ji. During afternoons, I would go to Ram Sundar ji and sit next to him on the floor. He would tell me stories from the Ramayana. I loved to hear those stories. I remember having learnt all of them from him. Pradeep Singh ji would carry me to school every single day despite all my tantrums and violent protests.

What immense contribution these 'illiterate' constables could make to the development of a growing mind like mine! I can never forget the affection that I got from the constabulary during my childhood, affection that I carried through my career in the police.

༄༅

Interpersonal relationships should not be made commercial

No child wants to leave the canopy of his parent's love and the comfort of his home to go to school every day. I was no exception. Every morning, I would stir up a storm in the house and just refuse to go to school. My parents were unable to handle this, and the job was delegated to one of the police constables, Pradeep Singh.

He would put me on his shoulders and walk down to

school, which was only about half a kilometre from home. All along the way, I would cry, scratch his head, pull his hair and show my rebellion in all possible ways. It used to be an early morning entertainment for the passers-by. Yet, like a dutiful policeman, he would obey the orders given to him.

In spite of all the torture that I unleashed upon him, I never felt that he hated me for any of it. I could still feel his love and care towards me through his words and actions. He would fondly call me Baua ji.[4] The fact that a person who is not even related to me showed so much care amazed me. Not just him, but almost every constable who was on duty with my father, behaved similarly towards me.

I grew up with a lot of respect for constables. However, when I joined the police service myself, I realized that this relationship had disappeared in the newer generation. It bothered me, and I used to wonder why. The only possible reason I could lay my fingers on was the commercial relationship that today's SPs have with their constables—that had changed this equation completely. In fact, this change, I figured, had many more facets to it.

My good feeling towards the constabulary kept increasing with time and manifested itself in many ways.

※

In the year 1962, my father got posted as assistant to inspector general (AIG) at the police headquarters. He was allotted a flat in Patna, and I got admission in Class 2. A school bus would pick me up and drop me back every day. Things had begun to settle down. I finally had what I could call a neighbourhood. I started making some friends, though very few. School brought in a disciplined routine for the first time in my life. This was a significant change.

---

[4]Affectionate way of addressing children in Bihar

The biggest guru of my life, my Dost ji[5]

'Chaliye sab log baith jaaiye, main tayyar hokar aa raha hoon. Padhai shuru hogi. (Everyone take a seat. I will get ready and be back. We will start studying),' Dost ji's voice would ring like an unfailing alarm in the ears of all the children in the house at around 6 p.m. every day. We had got trained to bring our school boxes onto the chowkis laid out for us, begin our homework and discuss our academic issues for the day. The person who continued to do this for us for 10 long years was the late Shyam Kishore Sharma. He was my first academic teacher who initiated me into education right at the start by teaching me the alphabet.

Our parents could hardly get involved in our day-to-day academic activities, so Dost ji took on this critical responsibility. He worked as a teacher in Sir G.D. Patliputra High School in Patna, which was more than 10 kilometres from our house. He would go to his school every day, riding a bicycle. Returning home after a long day at work, he would gather all the brothers and sisters for studies without losing a moment. No wonder he had so much respect in the entire family. I still remember how he treated us as his wards, not only in terms of academics but also in our health, nourishment and the way we lived. At every stage in life, he was there as a guiding light.

One of the saddest moments of my life was when, towards the end of my career in the police, I received a call from his son to inform me of his sudden demise at the Jhajha railway station. This unfortunate incident happened while he was en route to attend the marriage of his granddaughter. The least I could do at that moment was to arrange for the transport of his mortal remains from Jhajha to Patna, and pay my last

---

[5] A friend, addressed respectfully

respects to him. Great are these men who light the candle of education in families and leave an indelible contribution in setting their foundations. My pranam to Dost ji and my blessings to his family.

※

St Xavier's High School, Patna, was where my serious academic journey began. In the half-yearly exam, I stood second in my class and was promoted to Class 3 in the middle of the academic session itself. Here, too, I put in my best and cemented my place in the top bracket. I got into the 'academic vortex' at the cost of everything else and, consequently, was branded as a 'no extra-curricular' boy.

Multiple facets of life had started opening up to me. My first tryst with the reality of death was in Class 3 when I lost my nani. Before beginning school, my life had revolved around her. My first experience of love stemmed from her—love that she gave to me in abundance. I felt, for the first time, the painful pangs of separation from a person whom I loved intensely.

I was never deprived of the bare essentials of life, typically called roti, kapda aur makaan.[6] Yet, I did not seem to have a surfeit of anything. My father never let me feel that I was, in any way, more privileged than the others and kept reminding me that he did not have anything to offer to me in life except an opportunity to decent education. In fact, this reminder from him grew more and more frequent as I progressed in school. I realize now that he probably wanted to shake me up from any slumber I chose to slip into.

He was particular about how we needed to keep our personal needs separate from the position he held in his career. We were never allowed to use government vehicles; we had access only to his personal car. Once in Class 4, I pleaded with the driver of the police jeep to teach me how to drive. He was a little diffident, as

---

[6]Food, clothes and shelter

he thought he would face the wrath of my father. Well, he was not quite wrong. We chose the afternoons for this adventure, as my father would be away. In just a couple of days, I gained confidence to drive on my own. That very day, my father was returning home early, and our vehicles crossed each other, with me in the driver's seat. All hell broke loose. That was the end of my driving excursions. But I had learnt driving, nonetheless.

Things went on smoothly till Class 7. School for me was confined to English, Hindi, Arithmetic, with a sprinkling of History, Sanskrit and some similar subjects. I got into a groove, so to say. Come Class 8, and changes could be seen. I moved to senior school. Two sections got merged into one. The dress code had also changed—navy blue shorts were replaced by white flannel pants. Science was split into physics, chemistry and biology. A course in higher mathematics appeared, which students entered through a selection process. I found a place in that elite group of about 10 students. Too many changes in one go! One of these had a major impact on my life.

I had accompanied my father on one of his trips to Delhi. We happened to visit a bookshop where I spotted three hard-bound, big-sized, red colour books with 'Physics' written on them. I flipped through the first volume and could understand some words. Volumes two and three went over my head. Out of curiosity, I read the name of the author. It read Richard P. Feynman. I had never heard this name before but somehow felt drawn to the books. Hesitatingly, I requested my father to buy me all three volumes. While the bookseller was packing the books, I saw another set of three paperbound problem set along with it. Greed took over me, and I bought them too.

I was the proud owner of *Lectures on Physics* by Richard Phillips Feynman. The way he talks about physics and its understanding, helped me to learn ways of looking at every aspect of life, not just the subject. I am indebted to him for teaching me how to think differently. If he could do so much through written words, I can only imagine what he could have done if I had had a chance of being his student. My salute to this man!

When I started teaching my children for IIT-JEE, I bought two volumes of Resnick and Halliday, which are still my companions. Problem-solving is an art I learnt from these two books.

With devotion shifting towards problem-solving, language subjects like Hindi took a back seat. I remember an incident when in Class 8, I showed my father an essay I had written in Hindi. As with all students, I, too, used to collect quotations from multiple sources and insert these meaninglessly, mainly to show off knowledge. He patiently read through it. In the end, he said that in the entire essay, he kept looking for my views on the topic, but he got everyone else's instead. I learnt an important lesson in my life.

Around the same time, my elder sister, Vibha didi, was in Class 12, when my parents decided to get her married; quite early by today's standards. I had no clue what it means when a woman gets shipped to her husband's house after marriage. The happiness of the occasion and the sadness of separation—both on an even keel. Such feelings go a long way in understanding the pleasures and pains of life.

Life moved on, and before I could realize it, I was writing my board exams. While I was waiting for the results, my father asked me to go to our village and assist my grandfather in agricultural activities. During my childhood, I don't remember seeing more than a few rupees in cash in our house. Whatever was our requirement, was provided to us in that form. We were never given money to go and buy things on our own.

I had to buy tickets from the railway counter and travel all alone by train, and partly by bus, to reach my village. It was an experience that I cherish to date. In the village, I lived with the impoverished and uneducated farm labourers, which opened up an entirely new paradigm of life's story in front of me. My respect for them heightened after I witnessed their lives so closely.

The theatre of life shifted from Patna to Delhi after school. I set out on my journey into the mysteries of physics and was enrolled at the Ramjas College, University of Delhi. The faculty was exceptionally good; the peer group was competitive; and the laboratories were of high standards. My gaze was getting fixed and my heart got stuck on mathematical physics as a tool to lift me into the world of theoretical physics.

Unfortunately, all this dream was not meant to be. The result of the first year of the university examination saw me at the top of my class. I applied for my transfer to another college in the university itself, but my teachers at Ramjas were not willing to let me go. I was upset at this irrational behaviour. I finally told them, in a counselling session conducted by the faculty to dissuade me from leaving the college, that I was not prepared to study such a rational subject as physics under people who were behaving so irrationally. I applied for my college leaving certificate and said goodbye to the University of Delhi.

This was the turning point in my life.

My decisions were usually impulsive. If something did not appeal to logic, I would not think twice before taking a decision, even if it hurt me. This was one of them. Quitting my passion for theoretical physics for practical policing was another such decision that followed.

When I came back and joined the Patna Science College, I realized that the syllabus in this university was not updated. I walked up to the head of department (HOD) of the physics department with a request to introduce mathematical physics as a part of the course. The reply I got left me crestfallen. He said, 'If you are so keen, go and join the mathematics department.' I decided to buy my own books and learn the topics of this course by myself.

I got noticed by the laboratory-in-charge of the university as a student who preferred to watch experiments rather than do them himself. I would try to find out the 'why' of each step and figure out alternate ways of getting to the same result. He felt that I was different, that I was of a 'thinking type'. He would keep advising me to get the hang of the practical training of the equipment too, because, on the day of the examination, I would have to go through the process all by myself.

His concern was right. On the day of the examination, I got a difficult and long experiment to perform. I was shaky and knew that I had not done it well. I stood in the queue for my viva voce. I heard the examiner enquiring from a student at the front of the queue, 'What is a fringe?' The student was giving all types of answers except perhaps the one that he was looking for. While waiting for my turn, I suddenly discovered a mathematical answer to this physics question. I immediately shot up my hand. When he heard my answer, the examiner's face gleamed with joy. He took my answer sheet, patted me and asked me to leave. I secured the highest marks on this practical paper.

Dr R.B. Singh, our quantum mechanics teacher, was particularly impressed by my answers in the graduation exam, as I was the only one who could solve a challenging problem that he had set. He was so impressed that he wanted to give me full marks on that paper, but hesitated because a perfect score was unheard of back then. I ended up securing 90 out of 100 on that paper. When I qualified for the IPS, he felt it was a loss for physics.

Statistics was one of my subsidiary papers, in which I secured 99 out of 100. After the results were out, the HOD called me to personally congratulate me for achieving near perfection.

I topped in the examinations and was adjudged the 'Best Graduate' with record-breaking marks. However, by the time I finished my graduation, I realized that I wouldn't be able to survive on the frontiers of physics and live my dream. At this point in time, I decided on the UPSC instead. This is where the course of my life changed completely. My degree in academics stopped at a simple graduation in physics, albeit studded with a gold medal.

The laws of nature had been replaced by the laws of legislature.

Physics and statistics saw me through at my hustings in

the Civil Services Examinations of the UPSC. Trained to think mathematically, precision and brevity became my hallmark. English, therefore, became my weak link. A relative of mine put me through to a professor of English, K.M. Tiwari. In his first assignment, he asked me to write an essay on a topic. I wrote one and showed it to him. After reading it thoroughly, he wrote at the bottom of the paper, 'Constipated'. 'Your basics are right,' he said, 'You have to generate a flow in your writing.' I would give all credit to him for pointing out my flaws and straightening them, which helped me overcome this challenge.

It was 1975—the year of JP agitation in Bihar. Colleges shut down and life came to a standstill. My father was posted as the DIG Kosi range at Saharsa. While preparing for the UPSC, I accompanied him to Saharsa, where he lived alone. About 40 kilometres away is a renowned Shiva temple at Singheshwar, which boasts of a long history. My father and I used to visit this temple intermittently. Before I left for Patna to take the written test for UPSC, I had visited Singheshwar Sthan and sought the blessings of Shiva. Results came on time, and I had qualified for the interview. All through my life, at all important and critical junctures, I have sought the blessings of Lord Shiva at Singheshwar.

In the year 1981, I was promoted to the rank of SP from ASP. On the same day, Madhepura was notified as a district carved out of Saharsa. Singheshwar was a part of this newly formed district. I was convinced that this was way beyond coincidence. I knew that I was chosen by Shiva as his servant.

As an embryo in an amniotic sac, I had started to get groomed into a policeman. After being brought up in a sterile environment for so long, I had to get exposed to the toxic state of society and try to mitigate it without becoming a part of the toxicity. A long, arduous journey stared dauntingly at me.

A FIRM AND AMPLE BASE

Build today, then strong and sure,
With a firm and ample base;
And ascending and secure
Shall tomorrow find its place.

—Henry Wadsworth Longfellow

Training, Sardar Vallabhbhai Patel National Police Academy (13 November 1977 to 31 December 1978)
Probationer, Ranchi (1 January 1979 to 20 April 1980)

The train chugged into Nagpur railway station. I picked up my luggage and was more than ready to alight. I was greeted by a travelling ticket examiner (TTE) as I was about to cross the platform, who told me that I was carrying more than the permissible luggage limit and motioned me to the weighing machine. I was in a hurry; I could not afford to reach late on the first day. Some people around advised me to 'settle' the matter. Acknowledging my ignorance about the rules, I paid the demanded sum to be able to leave on my journey to the IPS. I literally bribed my way to join the service. What irony!

The sojourn at Nagpur was more fun than I expected—well-arranged accommodation and good food, punctuated by a few classes at the National Fire Service College. We had the evenings entirely to ourselves. We roamed around, not only in the town but also into the peripheral areas. I would keep reminding myself that the carefree life of college was over and I would need to prepare myself for the disciplined life of a policeman.

Those 15 days just flew by and soon we were boarding the train to our next destination—the Sardar Vallabhbhai Patel National Police Academy at Hyderabad, where a year-long professional training awaited us.

We woke up early morning to an extraordinary reception at the Nampally railway station. Police personnel of various ranks were present there to receive us, and arrangements had been made to visibly convey that we were now in the folds of an elite class.

On reaching the campus of the National Police Academy, realization dawned upon us that we were in for a tough, disciplined life. We were asked to fall in line immediately. We assembled on the ground and danced to the tune of the instructors.

Life of a policeman had begun.

It was the wee hours of the morning. The moon was still up in the sky. We all lined up on the parade ground. I suddenly saw R.D. Singh, the director of the Academy, arriving on horseback, in his uniform. He was barely visible in the feeble moonlight. We were made to stand at attention to report to him. He did not say anything. It appeared as if he had stopped by only for a salute from the newcomers before proceeding to his morning riding exercise.

I had started to get the feel of the aura of the police. The stern ambience of the campus created awe for the director. As I discovered more about him, I realized that he had a soft interior, and I developed a lot of respect for him.

I remember our first swimming class. Our director, who was a great swimmer, was diving from the diving board, and those who knew swimming were also having a really good time. On the other hand, there were people like me, standing in the shallow end of the pool, flailing our hands and legs as an apology for swimming. When he noticed this, he approached me and called me by my name. He stretched his hands out and encouraged me to take his support to float on water. This was my first lesson in swimming.

The exterior of R.D. Singh was tough, in stark contrast to his interior, which surfaced on rare occasions. I was so impressed by his personality as a policeman that I decided to imbibe as much of it as I could. He was the 'best probationer' of his batch of 1949 and later went on to become director of the Central Bureau of Investigation (CBI).

The campus was still in the process of adding facilities. Once every week, we would contribute to the beauty of the campus through our shramdaan[1]. R.D. Singh would gather us in a group and talk to us like a mentor. One day, he compared us to the lotus plant. He told us how we, as policemen, have to live in the filthy world of crime and yet how important it is for us to remain detached. This was one of those lessons from my training days that I would never forget.

Policemen should be like the lotus in a filthy pond

Year 1979, district training at Ranchi, a city that was communally sensitive back then. I was just four months into practical policing, with no experience of communal situations.

One evening, I drove down on my government motorcycle to the central market area of the city, near Firayalal chowk. While I was in a shop, I felt the movement on the roads outside suddenly dampening down. Shutters of all the shops were closing down; people were trying to take shelter; and the roads suddenly got bereft of people. A self-imposed curfew descended within no time.

I peeped outside the shop to find a man, hardly 50–70 yards away, stabbing another man. I had no support with me in terms of either firepower or policemen. I was not even in my uniform. Yet, I gathered courage and rushed towards the

---

[1]Shram (labour) + Daan (donation). Shramdaan is the voluntary donation of physical labour.

spot. I started chasing the aggressor. On the way, I picked up a couple of bricks and threw them at him in an attempt to slow him down, but he kept running, with a knife in his hand. Just then, I saw a few traffic constables huddled at one place. I beckoned to them to come to my support, but they were too terrified.

The aggressor took a turn and ran into a densely populated locality. I continued my chase, but then suddenly, a probationer sub-inspector (SI), who was on patrol duty, ran towards me, caught hold of my arm and pulled me back. I got slightly agitated, but he immediately warned me that if I entered that locality without a police force, the district administration might not even be able to locate my dead body. I stuttered to a stop.

I then rushed back to the victim and got him shifted to the Ranchi Medical College and Hospital (present-day Rajendra Medical College and Hospital) with the help of the traffic constables. I went to the nearest shop and called the senior superintendent of police (SSP) and narrated the incident to him. The SSP, along with the DM, came down in no time and started appealing to the people to resume normalcy. I noticed that this methodology worked.

The shops started opening up and traffic resumed. The police force took some time to gather and start patrolling. The investigation got underway. The victim was saved, and the aggressor was arrested later.

This way of handling communal situations impressed me a lot, and all through my career, I stuck to the principle of swift and transparent action without getting attached to any case, however gruesome.

∞

Back in the Academy, we had started learning our first lessons in policing. Hierarchy, discipline and carrying out commands were

the first few things. I realized that my old ways of questioning things would no longer be appreciated when, on a particular day on the parade ground, my drill instructor made us run to a post for exercise and made it competitive. I protested with a logical argument that if it is a race, each should be made to run the same distance. He was cross with this behaviour of mine, and I sheepishly followed the instructions. Outside the parade ground, I tried to reason it out with him. He taught me an important lesson: in operational situations, questioning the commander is prohibited. No difference of opinion is allowed.

During the entire training, there was more emphasis on the outdoor components than the indoor ones. This took a heavier toll on my physical capacity than I had bargained for. Doing everything at breakneck speed converted us into man-machines, with almost no time to stand and stare.

At one stage, I had almost decided to throw up my hands and call it a day. I thought I was not fit enough to be in the police. Seeing me in despair, my drill instructor, Havildar Vasudev Singh, came to me saying, '*Sahab, latke raho* (sahab, hang in there).' These words became etched deeply in my mind forever. They planted me firmly on the terra of life.

∞

My first guru in police refused gurudakshina[2]

I heard a strong, loud voice, 'Squad *savdhaan* (Stand at attention).'

This was the first command that I received as a policeman. The training had started. We were split into squads, each headed by our assistant drill instructor, who would teach us physical exercises and drills.

In the early days of my training, during one of those

---
[2]Sanskrit word dakshinā—what a student gives to his teacher (guru) on the completion of education or learning.

pull-up exercises, I somehow managed to hang by my hands but could not pull my heavy body up with my weak arms. I dropped like an apple from a tree and stood under the bar. There were many such occasions when I embarrassed myself due to my poor physical fitness.

After feeling depressed about this for around a couple of months, I decided to go and meet my assistant drill instructor, Havildar Vasudev Singh, at his residence on a Sunday, to seek his advice. When I reached his house, I saw a different man altogether. He was an institution in himself. He not only taught us parade and drill but guided us when we would go astray.

I laid a lot of store by all he said to me that day. In spite of the fact that my father himself was an IPS officer, I held my assistant drill instructor as my first guru, as his command on the parade ground was the first command that I had followed as a policeman. When I became the DGP, I requested him to come to Patna to be felicitated formally as my gurudakshina to him. He blessed me but politely declined my request. Probably he had reached that stage in life where he had risen above the material world.

Out of the entire gamut of outdoor activities, only horse riding and shooting interested me. These two interests remained kindled in me all through my career. Controlling an animal that was physically far stronger than me boosted my confidence, and hitting the bull's eye in firing exercises literally meant success of the highest order.

Horses have played a significant role in my life as a policeman. As strange as it may sound, they taught me that true strength is not just muscular but comes from within. They inspired me to understand the softer skills in the tough job I was in, something that could not be taught to me in any of our classes. I thank my father for introducing me to them even before I reached the Academy for my training.

My first adventure with a horse

I had just completed my graduation. The UPSC results had arrived, and I had qualified for the IPS. Everyone in the family was quite happy. My father advised me to take a course on horse riding to get familiar with the new sport before I reach the Academy. From his experience, he knew that every year in the Academy, there were numerous stories of trainees falling off the horses. So, I started visiting the Mounted Military Police (MMP) centre in Patna one month before I was to leave for Hyderabad.

The horses in the police department were quite sturdy and tall. In my first meeting with them, I felt quite intimidated. The riders on the campus would lead me from the ground while guiding the horses. This happened for nearly 10 days, after which I was taught my first lesson: horses are controlled from over the horseback and not led from the ground. This freed me of all fear.

One day, I managed to get permission from the chief to allow me to take the horse outside the campus. He sent one of his riders to go along with me on another horse. We left the campus in the morning and trotted and cantered to a place near the Patna airport.

On our way back, I found that my horse had started picking up speed on the empty roads. I was loving the cold and refreshing breeze on my face. Perhaps this was the fastest that I had experienced on horseback till now. As we kept getting closer to the base, the horse picked up more and more speed. The rider who was accompanying me was left far behind. I was thoroughly enjoying my ride.

Along the way, there was a railway gumti[3], which was

---

[3]Barricade at a rail-road crossing

closed. I tried to stop the horse, but to my shock, he just jumped over the first hurdle as well as the next. I was totally aghast. This was my first jump on horseback, unintentional and uncontemplated. The pleasure ride was now turning into an adventure that I had not planned.

My horse finally jumped over the wicket gate of the MMP campus and galloped straight to the water tank. It was a sight for the whole campus, and everyone ran towards us, gathering around me. I was scared out of my wits. I somehow got down from horseback and stood on the ground. The horse, unaware of his surroundings, was drinking water merrily while the chief of the campus was waiting for me with a stern look in his eyes.

∞

When I reached the Academy for my training, the stakes went up. There was so much more to learn, and we were mostly all by ourselves. On top of that, not only was I expected to learn the nuances of the sport but also excel at it as a mandatory subject in the training curriculum.

Our horse riding instructor, Hanuman Singh, was a national figure in this field. While teaching us how to handle horses, he would also give us the rationale behind every step of the process. During one galloping training, my horse decided to stop listening to me. I was using the reins with all my might but kept failing continuously in my attempt to control his speed. Our riding instructor, who was watching all this, called me and gave me a lesson. 'sahab,' he said, '*Ghoda aapse kai guna shaktishali jaanwar hai. Woh taakat se nahi chalta hai. Usko buddhi se chalaana padta hai* (Sir, the horse is a strong animal. It is many times stronger than you are. You will not be able to control it through your muscular strength, use your brains).' I had started learning the nuances for use in police life.

∞

Lesson of compassion from a horse

One day, the director of the Academy announced that he would like a group of good riders to accompany him on a cross-country ride to a far-off village. I was one of the few selected in the group.

Somewhere in the middle of the ride, my horse began to slow down and finally stopped. I nudged him all I could, but all efforts to speed him up proved futile. Just then, the director came by and asked what had happened. When I explained the matter to him, he gave me only one line of advice. He said, 'If any individual who always obeyed your commands suddenly refuses to do so, try to find out the reason behind it. Try to understand what discomfort changed this behaviour.'

Following this advice, I got down from horseback and started examining the horse. When I lifted his left rear leg, I found that the horseshoe was missing, and the horse was bleeding. I realized that my horse had continued trying until his body gave up due to this injury. I could now understand everything.

Not just in the police, but even otherwise, I realized that getting angry or frustrated when someone disobeys you is not the right thing to do. Subordinates should not always be mistrusted. There may be valid reasons for their non-performance. An effort to find the real cause must always be made.

∞

The Academy really prepared us mentally and physically for the tough life ahead. On many occasions, I found that my body was giving way. It couldn't cope with the stress. Yet, we were taught that we couldn't forgo our routine and discipline as police officers under any circumstance. This helped me in attending to law and order situations, whatever be the physical condition I found myself in. The Academy taught us how important it is to be true to ourselves and to the service that we as policemen provide to the country, even when no one is watching.

Why should you be honest?

'Why should you be honest?' This was a simple question asked by the then CBI director, C.V. Narasimhan, the first batch of IPS, who passed out from the Academy as the best probationer of the batch. He was literally the number one in the IPS civil list of the country.

Each of us gave all sorts of bookish answers to his question. The final answer that came from him quietened everyone. He turned towards the board, picked up a chalk and wrote: 'It satisfies me.' He turned around to face the class and said, 'If there is any other reason, gentlemen, you better become dishonest.' He added, 'Your honesty does not help anyone. It may satisfy only you. If you decide to live a life of honesty, never feel that you are doing a favour on anyone other than yourself.'

I practised this all through my life as a policeman. Now when that life is over, and I am six years into my post-retirement life, I feel that there cannot be a higher truth than those three words that answered the most difficult question faced by a government servant every moment.

How life had changed all of a sudden! From a student who forever remained drowned in academics, pushing his mental capabilities to solve complex problems in physics and mathematics, I was now trying my best to push my physical limits on a completely unfamiliar terrain.

The redeeming feature of this world was that there was an intellectual component here too—law, as it is generally known. I was exposed to the Constitution and the various major and minor laws. Principles of law, called Interpretation of Statutes, became my favourite. The faculty was quite competent.

We were made to study cases taken from the *All India Reporter*, and then discuss these with the rulings given by the Supreme Court. I thought this really helped us to see and feel the way judges operate on disputed matters. It gave me a lens to see policing in its rational form. My thinking ability in the law lexicon grew abundantly and helped me immensely in analysing evidence in criminal matters.

Books will never judge you for your ignorance

'Sir, what is raid?' I asked the SSP Ranchi on my first day of practical training under him.

After the formal salute, I was asked to take a seat. SSP sahab was going through his daily dak, and there was silence in the room. Just then, he pushed a paper towards me which read, 'ASP U/T organize and conduct a raid to recover the idols.' It appeared to be an order I was supposed to carry out. I had no clue what that sentence meant. At the risk of making a fool of myself, I asked him the brave question out of sheer ignorance.

The SSP looked at me with disbelief. He said, 'You have joined the police, and you do not know what a raid is?' I could feel the disappointment and irritation in his tone. I thought it wouldn't be a good idea to ask more questions. So I apologized, assured him that I would comply with his orders and left the room.

During lunchtime, I met my father, who was a DIG back then, and decided to get the answer from him. I looked at

A FIRM AND AMPLE BASE

my father expectantly and asked him the same question. The answer I got from him was even more disconcerting. He asked me, 'Did you clear the UPSC examination using your brains or mine?' This was enough indication that I was entirely on my own, with no one, not even my father, to handhold me.

I withdrew from his presence too. My last resort was my books. After giving the matter some thought, I felt I might be able to find an answer to this question in the 'Search and Seizure' chapter of the book The Code of Criminal Procedure, 1973, also called Criminal Procedure Code (CrPC). To confirm my assessment, I gathered the courage to cross-check with an assistant sub-inspector (ASI), hoping that I would not get snubbed for my ignorance by him at least.

I read through the chapter, carried out the search and seizure exactly as laid out by the law and felt quite satisfied at my first ever practical application. I also prepared a zimmanaama[4] quite methodically. I could very well find my ways to sail through the problems I faced in the police.

∞

Forensic science was an area that evoked intense interest in me because of my science background. Although, what we were taught at the Academy was mostly theoretical in nature. In the one year of training, I understood that forensic science did matter a lot in an investigation. Cases appeared to be jigsaw puzzles that needed clues to be decoded. These clues could best be provided by forensic science.

Comparison microscope, fingerprints, serological examination of body fluids and neutron activation analysis had caught my imagination as a probationer and continued all along. I had to wait for the entire span of my service, till I became the DGP, to

---

[4]The document with details of seized property to be left in the custody of a responsible person for producing before court when needed.

see the 'flowers' of forensic science in full bloom.

I devoted my time to the study of this subject. I did well in the final exam, which helped me improve my inter se ranking. What I lost in the outdoors, I gained in the indoor subjects. Forensics had taught me that there is more to policing than just brute force. Problems require the application of the mind where muscles may not work.

∞

Inventions are born in a scientific mind

I remember one day, during the district training in Ranchi, I was sitting in the office of the city SP Ranchi and discussing policing issues with him while he was going through his routine morning dak.

He suddenly looked up at me and said, 'There is a problem in the city. There has been a huge traffic jam for the last three days on the Ratu road, which is one of the major outlets of Ranchi town to the rural parts of the district. Traffic is not flowing at all. You have to ensure that the situation is restored to normal.' I was aware that there was a petrol pump on this road where trucks would have to line up and wait for their turn to get diesel. This would create a traffic jam, such that not even a bicycle could cross through the web of trucks, which spread to a distance of about 2 kilometres.

I went to the site, and when I saw the traffic jam, I realized that no number of traffic constables and no amount of 'force' would be able to manage the situation. I told the truck owners that I would make an arrangement for them to queue up in the big Morabadi ground in Ranchi while they wait for their turn. This would ensure that not more than five trucks were on the campus of the petrol pump at any given point in time.

To facilitate real-time communication in an age of archaic landline telephones, I had put up two wireless sets, one at the

Morabadi ground and the other at the petrol pump. It took me about 24 hours to get the system galvanized into action, and thereafter the road was absolutely free of traffic, and things were moving as smoothly as ever. The city SP came to inspect the place when he heard that the ASP probationer had freed the Ratu road of its four-day-long traffic jam.

We were nearing the end of our training. The final phase was army attachment in Gangtok and then in Nathu La during the freezing month of December. In only 15 days, I realized that army life was physically many times more demanding than that of police. Additionally, I got a glimpse of few other aspects of the 'uniform life', which I would need to wade through in the coming years, consciously and cautiously.

A debate with a colonel

December 1978. It was extremely cold. At the end of the army attachment, we were invited for a farewell dinner at the unit's headquarters. Alcohol, as a befitting drink for the weather and the occasion, was being served lavishly. Being a teetotaller, I had opted for cold drinks and was also enjoying my drink. A colonel came to me and gave me a quizzical look. He said, 'This is a woman's drink. It doesn't look good in the hands of an IPS officer. I am ordering a man's drink for you.'

I politely said, 'If you have a couple of minutes, please allow me to debate with you on this.' He promptly agreed and said, 'Yes, I am prepared.'

In my characteristic style, I asked him, 'What is the most precious organ in your body?' He thought for a while and answered, 'My brain.' Then I asked him how would he feel if someone took away his brain, and he said that such a situation would be unacceptable to him. So I asked, 'Doesn't alcohol numb your brain? Don't we end up surrendering our most precious organ to this drink?'

The colonel had got my point and slowly disappeared in the crowd.

I didn't consume alcohol throughout my service and even before or after it. I wasn't willing to give control of my mind to anyone or anything.

∞

By this time, my parents had started thinking about getting me married. For this, two parameters were non-negotiable: the girl had to be a doctor, and there was no question of dowry. After doing their research, they found a family who checked all their boxes, and my marriage was fixed. The wedding was to be conducted in Ranchi in 1979. My father-in-law, late Dr Triveni Roy, had left for his heavenly abode about six years before my marriage. My mother-in-law had had a difficult time looking after the family all alone. She hardly had any support to make arrangements for the marriage in her small house in a locality called Bariatu in Ranchi. I, therefore, offered help and did the running around for my own marriage.

My father-in-law had been a professor of pathology at the Ranchi Medical College Hospital. In his time, he was well-liked and well-loved by his students. My wife, Dr Nutan Anand, too, was a student of this medical college. I was touched by the kind of support I got from the students of the college in arranging for things during the marriage. I got quite emotional when I saw that the students, who were actually invited as guests for the marriage, were clearing used plates and doing similar chores during the function.

Soon after, the training began, and I was sent to Mandar Police Station for my practical training as SHO. It was the largest police station in the district, comprising two blocks—Mandar and Chanho. There was no place for me to stay during the three months of the training, so I got a Swiss cottage tent pitched for myself and put up in it. I took this training extremely seriously because I knew that a police station was the most fundamental unit of the department, and therefore, I needed to understand every nuance of this unit if I wanted to understand the department.

I woke up the next day to be greeted by a road accident case where a truck had capsized, resulting in the death of a labourer, whose name I still remember as Jatru Oraon. I tried to get his body sent to a hospital for post-mortem. No vehicle on the highway was willing to oblige. I was trying my gentlemanly ways when the subordinates suggested that we use our 'power' to get this done. They demonstrated it, and within no time, we were able to dispatch the body. It made me realize that a strong arm has its place in practical policing. And also that the government doesn't provide for sundry expenditure in police stations.

Within a week of my joining as the SHO of Mandar, I was told that a dreaded criminal under the jurisdiction of this police station, named Furkan Ansari, had fired a few blank rounds in the local market with an intent to introduce himself to me. I was too naive and new in the police to understand all such tactics. I tried to discuss this with the subordinates to understand what it all really meant. Suddenly, a bulb in my head lit up. He was perhaps challenging me in the open!

I drove down to the district jail and talked to the jailor to gather more information about him. I got to know that he was a known criminal and that his number two man was in jail. For this reason, he used to visit the jail quite often. The jailor promised to inform me about his next visit. As soon as I got the information, I reached the jail gate and arrested this criminal there and then. A few years later, I came to know that he had become the pramukh[5] of that block.

---

[5]Head of the administrative unit

This was the first glimpse of things to come.

I had picked up a habit of thoroughly going through the records kept in the police stations. No one ever told me about any interconnections between each of these records. I went through the previous inspection notes of the senior IPS officers who cared to pen down their observations during their visits. I decided to delve deeper into the police station's responsibility of keeping professional criminals under surveillance, and I noticed that many of these criminals were untracked, according to their dossier entries. Out of sheer curiosity, I picked up one of them and went through his history. I found that about eight years ago, this criminal had been sent to jail in a case of burglary. I contacted the court staff for his records and got to know that he was convicted. When I checked up with the jail authorities, I found that he had completed the sentence and, towards the end of it, had applied for transfer of his jail to Buxar under provisions of the Police Manual. I checked up from his address at Buxar to find that he was alive and living with his relatives.

I could see that our criminal justice system (CJS) clearly has too many branches and too many agencies with very little exchange of information amongst them. No wonder it looks so chaotic.

Then came my first case—a murder case that I investigated myself as a probationer. A six-year old child was smothered to death with a pillow. I thought I had done a good job of tracking down the movements of the accused before and after the murder, as well as the motive. As per my investigation, the child's uncle was the accused, and the motive was identified as the inheritance of property. I filed a charge sheet against him in the court at Ranchi.

The following month, I was attached to the court. I called on the judicial commissioner of Ranchi, who functioned as the district judge. I gathered the courage to request him to try the case I had investigated. He accepted my request. I appeared as a witness, got myself cross-examined and followed every bit of the trial procedure mentioned in the law books.

However, the accused got acquitted. The judge, who behaved in a fatherly way, called me to explain the rationale behind his judgement. He said, 'You should read the post-mortem report. It says the cause of death cannot be ascertained. The factum of offence needs to be proved first before fixing the liability of the offender.' This gave me such a jolt, as I realized that I had applied everything I had learnt under the head of admissible evidence, without proving the murder itself.

One day, I received an order from the Range DIG of Ranchi with a list of names of three police stations, asking me to inspect those and personally show him all the three inspection notes. I felt elated at the prospect and knew that I would get to learn something new at the end of this exercise. I made a mental note of the list of things that needed to be inspected.

When I reached the first police station, I received a grand welcome from the SHO. As soon as I sat down to begin my inspection, he laid out a ready-made report in front of me, taking pride that he had reduced my workload to just a signature on that document. I was bowled over. I looked askance at his face.

I told him that I was there to learn inspection and asked him why he was not letting me do so. The SHO was contrite, and I was able to carry on with my inspection in my own non-traditional style. The Range DIG was quite impressed with my inspection notes, which showed my understanding of the functioning of the police station. This was my first experience of the weight that SI rank officers carry.

Up until the district training, all modes of learning were through people who were more experienced and senior to me, or through books. During the district training, I got exposed to the dynamics with the subordinates that remained an integral part of my entire policing career. I had started to understand that there was a lot to learn from them. My first experience of this was during a raid in Ranchi.

One morning, I got the news that the chairman of Heavy

Engineering Corporation Limited (HEC)[6], Ranchi, had been waylaid in the night. Apart from cash, his wristwatch was also looted. It was a high-profile case and was receiving huge media attention. The top brass of Ranchi police was closely involved in the progress of the investigation. The investigation officer, through his human sources, had zeroed in on a person and located his house. All IPS officers planned to accompany the search team for this particular raid. I, too, was ordered to be present.

The raid started in the evening. The police only knew the name of the suspect and couldn't identify him by face. We enquired about his whereabouts from the only person who was present at the house. He very cleanly told us that the person we were looking for was his elder brother who had gone to Patratu, a place more than 50 kilometres from Ranchi. He even offered to take us to him.

We were crestfallen, as we comprehended that he was only biding his time and we might not be able to find him there too. All four of us IPS officers, who were searching that small house for two long hours, were at our wits end. Suddenly I heard the sound of a tight slap. A constable had slapped the man in our custody and was shouting that this person was the suspect we were looking for. There was no elder brother. The man broke down and confessed, and we could recover the wristwatch, which was the only identifiable property of the loot.

I later asked that constable about how he had come to that conclusion. He said that every time he would ask the man about the various household articles, he would always say that it belonged to his brother, which made him suspect that the man was faking his identity. The speed with which he confronted that man and the strong practical sense of his analysis did the trick. Where big brains fail, small ones succeed.

---

[6]Heavy Engineering Corporation Limited is a public sector undertakings (PSU) in India dealing with sectors like steel, mining, power, etc.

I understood more about the dynamics of subordinates in the police through the Ranchi Rural SP, Ranjit Sinha. He was once discussing with me reasons why petitions relating to integrity get filed by police personnel from different police stations and offered a practical explanation for this. His logic was that no petitions would ever come from a police station where the distribution of bribes amongst the ranks is equitable. Complaints against one another indicate the inequitable distribution of illegal money in the police station.

In my district training, I got to see the ceremonial obligations and the strategic responsibilities of the police while maintaining law and order, for the first time. It was also my first view of the overlaps and boundaries of the police department with the political lobby.

Each year, the Rama Navami[7] procession in Ranchi is a big event from a law and order perspective. In 1979, I saw it being handled so deftly by the SSP who I was training under that I developed my own model of handling such problems. This model had least dependence on police personnel and complete reliance on boosting the confidence of the common man through prompt communication. The sooner the trust is restored, the faster normalcy returns. I tried this technique umpteen times and found that it succeeded without fail.

In undivided Bihar, the two days of national importance, i.e. Republic Day and Independence Day, were divided between Patna and Ranchi for flag hoisting by the CM and the governor of Bihar. As an IPS probationer, I was asked to command the parade of 15 August at Ranchi for the CM. Later one day, as SP Aurangabad, when I was working on a holiday in my residential office, I received a slip with the name Ram Sunder Das, ex-CM Bihar, written on it. Out of respect, I politely ushered him inside, and listened to him patiently. All this while, the memory of the

---

[7]Hindu festival celebrating the birth of Lord Rama

ceremonial parade in Ranchi flashed in front of my eyes when he had taken my salute on the dais.

Hail democracy!

The first year of practical training taught me a wide array of lessons to set the base for the years that lay ahead of me.

I was now headed towards my first posting as ASP Sasaram. I felt happy, as my father had also been posted there in the past. Incidentally, he, too, was trained at Ranchi. My wife and I boarded a bus to Sasaram and started our journey into a life of responsibility, with mixed feelings of happiness and humility.

THE MORE THE STORM, THE MORE THE STRENGTH

Good timber does not grow with ease,
The stronger wind, the stronger trees,
The further sky, the greater length,
The more the storm, the more the strength.
By sun and cold, by rain and snow,
In trees and men good timbers grow.

—Douglas Malloch

ASP Sasaram (21 April 1980 to 6 May 1981)

It was early evening when my wife and I reached Dehri-on-Sone. I had asked my police vehicle to pick us up from the station for our further journey to Sasaram. I had also sent a message to all my SHOs and inspectors asking them to be present in the headquarters for a brief meeting.

By the time we reached our official residence at Sasaram, it was dark. The building was a sprawling one with a huge campus. I arranged for some food from a roadside dhaba, went to the office and came back in an hour to tell my wife that I would be leaving on a night round, possibly a raid too. She was somewhat upset with the idea of spending the night all alone in such a big house in a new, unfamiliar place. I assured her that one sentry would be left to guard the house, while the rest of the troop would accompany me.

The first meeting itself made me realize that this subdivision would leave my hands full. I thanked God for posting me to a place that would keep challenging me and bring out the best in me. I went around a few villages in the jurisdiction and talked to the villagers. I ventured into the most difficult terrains, the hills and the forests of this area that were known to be the habitats of organized gangs armed with sophisticated firearms, who could take on the police for hours. It was a running battle that ensued. I was yet to understand the genesis of the problem, but I knew I had my task cut out.

Days rolled by. I soon realized that catching up with the routine tasks and responsibilities of my post was quite challenging. Supervising roughly about 40 cases per month, after visiting the places of occurrence, inspecting about 70 posts and conducting raids on outlaws and gangs of dacoits was by itself herculean. To top that, there were also miscellaneous tasks, such as attending to VIPs and their likes, which only made the load heavier.

House dacoities and road hold-ups were frequent in this region. A good percentage of these offences ended in detection. The looted property would get recovered, and criminals would get arrested. This did give me some satisfaction yet left behind sharp, edgy, unanswered questions. The criminals who looted lakhs could never become rich. Why? The rich people in town did not have an ostensible means of livelihood. How was this possible?

In the Academy, we had learnt about an Act passed during the British rule called the Criminal Tribes Act, 1871, which categorized social or ethnic communities of certain types as habitual criminals (this Act was later repealed as being unconstitutional). In Sasaram, I found that a few villages were still being treated as such. I raided those villages on a few occasions and observed that the villagers lived in abject poverty. The police used to pat its back by recovering some utensils and getting them identified by the inmates of the aggrieved family, but I hardly found this impressive. I put a stop to frequent police raids and arrests in those villages unless there was sharp and incisive evidence.

Many of the dacoities would be committed either on the highway or in the houses of wealthy people in urban areas. I remember one such case of a house dacoity in the official residence of a civil servant at the prakhand[1] level. This had stirred up a public issue almost immediately. The concerned associations of the government reared up and galvanized themselves to put pressure on the police to detect the case. On the other hand, I was myself undergoing a feeling of guilt to such an extent that, at times, I felt as if I was personally at fault. I felt that I had failed in my duty to prevent crime.

Overwhelmed with this guilt, I promptly supervised the case. The news of this dacoity had reached me in the dead of the night, sometime around 2 a.m. I had just come back from a night round and was lying on the bed, still in my uniform. I suddenly heard voices of people from outside, telling my on-duty sentry about a dacoity; I was up in a flash. I immediately jumped into my jeep, taking the informer with me. I was still tying the laces of my shoes when we started driving down to the place of occurrence. I gathered more details on the way, and when I reached there, I decided that I would rather first follow the path of the retreat taken by the dacoits and talk to the inmates of the house later. By 8 a.m., I was able to conduct the first raid and recover some clothes from the house of some criminals. I felt satisfied. My alacrity had paid off. In police language, the case was detected.

The next day, the media was ablaze. If I had not acted promptly, I knew there would have been no end to the criticism of the police. However, the thought that there were more unanswered questions than what I had unearthed made me restless. I took time off to visit the place of occurrence again. I learnt that the civil servant did not hold a good reputation, in terms of financial integrity, in that area. It worried me to realize that we, in uniform, were

---

[1]Smallest administrative unit in a district subdivision

duty-bound to protect property accrued through white-collared crime while having to shut our eyes to the crime itself. I was haunted by the thought that white-collared crime was not seen as a cognizable offence.

The second fact that struck me was that the police could hardly recover costly articles like jewellery and cash. Where did all this go? Can we pat our backs for recovering possessions of the least material value from the huts of poor criminals?

I kept thinking about the constant transfer of wealth from one group of persons to another in our society. Society defined legally acceptable ways to regulate this transfer process. As a policeman, I was often confronted with offences where this transfer happened outside this definition of 'legally acceptable'. I categorized such cases, which were mostly devoid of any form of violence, into things like forgery, cheating, embezzlement and corruption.

The presence of wealth in all types of crimes and the boundaries that were drawn for white-collared crimes kept provoking my mind. I started thinking about the role of the police in this context; who were we really protecting? These thoughts kept working within me till the end of my career and finally led me to develop my own path of policing, which I could explain through a concept called 'economics of crime'.

Crimes pertaining to family feuds also pointed in the same direction. These crimes in families and between neighbours would result in criminal cases ranging from maar-peet[2] to murders. In the police framework, such cases are called offences against persons and are not given as much importance as offences against property. As a result, some of these feuds had continued since time immemorial, passed on from one generation to another.

This caught my interest from a sociological perspective. Questions arose: what is the role of the police department in such disputes? What do we really do to mitigate such problems

---

[2]Scuffles

in society? One thing, though, was sadly true. We did not play any role in getting to the root of the tussle between the warring groups, yet we were held responsible for the consequential breach of law and order.

∽

One cannot see the details when in a hurry

'Why should you not be in a hurry while examining the scene of a crime?' This was a question raised to the probationers by the director during our training at the National Police Academy. He then turned around and wrote the answer, 'Because you may be in a hurry, but the judge who decides that case will be at leisure to do it.' This stayed in my mind throughout my career.

I could only understand its full import when I was supervising a particular murder case as ASP Sasaram. The case involved two brothers who were embroiled in a land dispute. Their houses were adjacent to each other. One was double-storeyed, plastered and painted from outside, while the other was a single-storeyed house with the bricks on its walls visible.

One day, the brother living in the double-storeyed house was on his terrace, having a heated exchange of words with the other brother, who stood on the ground. The brother on the terrace, in the midst of the argument, fired from his gun. The other brother dropped dead. A first information report (FIR) was registered. The accused, as a counter, tried to make a case of private defence in the police station, saying that his brother had taken out his weapon and had shot at him first. It was just a matter of chance that he missed the shot.

I went to the village and spent a good amount of time at the place of occurrence. I was investigating the house of

- the deceased. I observed that the bricks of the un-plastered walls were studded with pellet marks. I took out a couple of bricks as physical exhibits, without foreseeing that they would become the most critical piece of evidence and give this case a turning point.

I completed my investigation and forgot all about this case. About a month later, while I was working in my office, a public prosecutor came to visit me.

He started talking about this particular case. He told me that when the accused argued his case of self-defence, the prosecutor pointed out to the court that the ASP (me) had observed the place of occurrence keenly, diligently collected physical exhibits and had also been careful enough to have them produced before the chief judicial magistrate (CJM) the very next day to establish credibility. So it was quite obvious that a careful observation of the house of the accused would also have been undertaken, and it didn't seem like any similar evidence could be recovered there. This only meant that the claims of the accused were false. When I got to know about this, I could understand clearly what our director in the Academy meant.

∞

I observed that the subordinate police officers tended to take sides in family disputes. Incidents of violence would either be overplayed or underplayed. They would give too many flawed arguments to justify their wrong actions, which could do any young IPS officer in.

One such argument that was often raised in simple cases like forcible harvesting of crops was that, in police context, such incidents are not taken to be heinous. Such cases would get registered under sections 144 and 379 of the Indian Penal Code (IPC). I perused the reports of the inspectors who supervised these cases and case diaries of the investigating officers only to find that they would write treatises on the disputes relating to the property sharing between the family members. They would go ahead and establish that these disputes were civil in nature and would conveniently close the case under the same pretext.

I decided to call a meeting of all my police officers, everyone who investigated cases. I specifically wanted to address the ingredient of 144 and 379 IPC. Through a series of questions, I was able to drive home the point that in such offences, the title of the property was not relevant, its possession was. Police should, therefore, investigate possession of the crop rather than the title of the land. After a long day of discussions, the officers could see reason, and things changed thereafter. Police investigations now veered nearer to the truth than meandering into legal fallacies that did more harm than good.

Another section that was abundantly being abused and misused in such feuds was Section 307 IPC. The thana would apply this section at the very first stage of an FIR. Later, they would drop the section in favour of the accused. I used to be amused at this behaviour of my subordinates. It appeared like the story of the monkey settling a dispute between cats.[3]

I tried to delve into the rulings on 307 IPC to help me resolve this problem through a practical approach. Browsing through piles of *Criminal Law Journal of India* and *All India Reporter* showed me the way. I had developed a habit of going through these journals that contained Supreme Court judgements on all types of cases, lending wonderful insights. I figured out that specifically for this section, three main factors had to be considered.

1. Site of injury
2. Type of injury
3. Type of weapon

---

[3] An ancient Indian fable with a moral which says that if you fight amongst yourselves, someone else will take advantage of the situation.

If two or more of these factors were grievous, this section could be applied, otherwise, not.

I again called a meeting of all my investigating officers (IOs), and at the end of a grilling discussion, the application of this section could be defined quite precisely. I realized that the role of the police is to 'transfer the venue of dispute from the place of occurrence to the local court, in the most objective and truthful manner possible.'

I kept making attempts to clearly define my role in society. Coming from a family of advocates and policemen, I was fortunate to get inspiration from their wisdom and experiences in my early days of policing. Interactions with my grandfather and my father initiated my mind and helped me think clearly. I started answering many questions that arose in my mind as a young policeman.

Government property does not belong to you

Chitap Khurd is hardly about 150 kilometres from Sasaram. I had started functioning in my new role as the ASP in right earnest when, one day, my grandfather, then an advocate in the bar of Gaya district, arrived at Sasaram for a weekend. I was so happy to receive him because he was the first family member to visit me in my place of posting.

I was excited to narrate to him all my experiences. He, too, took a lot of interest, recalling the days when he had visited the same house when my father had held the same post. The residence of ASP Sasaram perhaps is the same even today—a traditional house situated right on the national highway, then called the GT Road. We both enjoyed each other's company over the weekend.

When his trip came to an end and he had to return to his village, I offered to drop him till Sherghati, from where he could take a rickshaw to the village. Sherghati was not within my jurisdiction, so he flatly refused my offer. But what he quoted as the reason meant a lot to me. He said, 'No, son, it will not be proper if you cross your jurisdiction in your official vehicle for a personal reason. Never commit the mistake of considering government property as our own.'

Although Sasaram was on railhead, there was no train connecting it to my village. A large number of trucks used to ply on the GT Road. My grandfather requested my help in boarding a truck to drop him at Sherghati, from where he could reach his village easily. I got a truck stopped on the GT Road and fulfilled his request. The driver and the khalasi were quite eager to oblige. My grandfather somehow managed to climb onto the truck and sat beside the khalasi. I packed him some food for his journey and bid him goodbye.

∞

It was the first time in my policing life that I came across writs filed in the high court. I had read about these in our law lessons but never got the chance, until now, to see them in practical use. I soon realized that I was on the other side of the fence and would have to reply to the allegations made by the people who had been accused in criminal cases. This would involve filing counter-affidavits on all facts given in the writ application.

I had serious objections to this. My rebellious mind said that it was the job of the person who made the allegations in the first place to establish it. Why should I provide facts, that too on an affidavit? And even if I was required to do so, why didn't we apply the same principle to police investigations? It would become so easy to arrive at conclusions in matters of dispute. Obviously, I knew none of this could happen, but these questions lingered and would pop up every now and then in my mind.

I always felt that the job of the judges of the high court and Supreme Court was being rendered easy by the affidavits of both sides, reducing their task to adjudication on issues of law only. The police, on the other hand, had to collect facts, that too without the participation of the accused, making their task so much more difficult.

Since my office was situated on the civil court campus, I had the privilege of watching proceedings of the courts at leisure and understanding their nuances. In fact, I spent time with both public prosecutors and defence lawyers to learn how to relate my theoretical knowledge from the Academy to the practical tips I got in the courts. Few occasions made me realize how beneficial these learnings could be for the police, especially in critically tense situations.

I learnt that the place of occurrence was of utmost importance during trials. Even though the IO investigates many aspects of a case, he is cross-examined only on this one. In those days, the evidence against the accused veered mostly around the test identification parade (TIP) of suspects and recovered property. One question stuck in my mind: what does the word 'test' mean in TIP? What is being tested? I could get answers to all such questions due to my stay within the court campus.

Law is a weapon that does not get stained with blood

In Rohtas district, there is a block named Chenari. A no-confidence motion had been filed against its block pramukh. This had started manifesting itself as a caste conflict and was slowly emerging as a potentially violent struggle.

The block development officer (BDO) fixed a date, and his office conference hall as the venue for the voting. The mukhiyas of all the panchayats were to assemble and cast their votes. According to all reports and speculations, a bloody scene was expected at the venue immediately after the declaration of the results. The DM called the sub-divisional officer (SDO) and the ASP, and directed us to camp there to ensure that nothing untoward happens. We reached just as the mukhiyas were entering the hall. A huge crowd was raging against each other, each side with about 100 licensed rifles with them. They had taken a threatening position, and the tension was palpable.

Looking at the situation, the SDO wanted to clamp Section 144 CrPC. I realized that we were not in a position to enforce it because of the paucity of force and our distance from the district headquarters.

I had a different plan. I asked the BDO to put up a table and a chair for the SDO and make it his camp office. Meanwhile, I ordered the SHO to prepare an impromptu report of Section 107 CrPC with 10 names of the top leaders—five from each side. These leaders were called upon to appear before the SDO in his newly formed camp court. They signed on the report there itself, signifying that the court notice had been served to them. The SDO then held the proceedings, and in view of the volatile situation, he ordered for an interim bond under Section 116(3) CrPC for maintaining peace. These bonds were executed, and everyone was made aware that any violence would entail the execution of distress warrants against the offenders, which would mean an adverse financial implication on them.

While all this was underway, the voting was completed. After the declaration of the results, the crowd dispersed peacefully. Law can be used creatively if only senior police officers apply their minds to the situations at hand.

∞

Another issue that fell into my lap without warning was that of communal sensitivity. Sasaram had an ignominious past on the communal front. I tried to find its history by talking to the elders in the area, and I got to know that in the olden days, the rural part of Sasaram subdivision housed Muslims in sizeable numbers, who were financially well-off. However, they had vacated the villages to settle in towns in small ghettos. My tenure was teaching me more than I had bargained for. I tried to define what communal tension meant for a policeman.

Coercion without discretion is avoidable

Born and raised in a well-educated family and having been a student deeply involved in academics, I remained aloof from the ills of society throughout my student life. These issues were never discussed at home either.

During my first posting at Sasaram, I not only got exposed to them but was also responsible for tackling them.

A religious procession was to take place, and I had to make the necessary security arrangements. I checked the prescribed protocol. I was expected to initiate routine Section 107 CrPC proceedings, make preventive arrests and deploy police pickets at strategic points. I wondered why all this was necessary.

At my own level, I decided to not do any of these and maintain communal harmony during the procession using other measures. Since I had taken this decision all by myself, I wanted to get a sense check done with the senior officers in the police headquarters. One of them encouraged me by saying, 'If your intentions are good, you should be able to succeed.' I was happy and felt confident about going ahead with my plan.

I called a meeting of both the communities that were to be a part of the procession. I clearly told their leaders that I would like to trust both sides and had no intention of following the regular police methodologies this year. My expectation from them was that they be present to receive the procession at the three critical points on the route of the procession. They agreed to this and assured cooperation.

The procession began at midnight. Men, women and children were all decked up in their best clothes and were enjoying themselves. Someone whispered in my ears, 'We could have never imagined seeing this procession from the place we are standing (at) right now because these are the points where explosions could take place any moment on such occasions.' I kept my fingers crossed and moved along with the crowd in my uniform. I felt happy to see that my methods had worked, and people from both communities had a good time.

∞

One day, I got the news that a piece of cow meat was found floating in a well in a Hindu locality in Sasaram town. The SHO requested that I start patrolling the town and deploy enough force to ensure peace and order. I assessed the situation and found that only a few people had come to know of this incident. I instructed the SHO to register a case against 'unknown' and not create any fuss beyond this. In fact, I even asked the SDO to not start patrolling. No one in the administration agreed with my point of view. They almost threatened that I would have to shoulder all responsibility if anything went wrong. I accepted all this and held my ground. The cow meat was quietly taken out of the well. A few constables, not in uniform, were placed in the market to gather rumours, if any. The issue went unnoticed, and the local media came to know of it only four days later.

Supervising cases was a daily affair, with no holidays, not even a reprieve for a few hours. I never carried a paper or a pen with me while on tours. I would walk kilometres on foot to go to the place of occurrence, observe the place minutely, hear the witnesses and record all the details in my memory. On an average, I would supervise a case or two per day, depending on the distance of the site of the incident from my headquarters. Late in the night, after raids, I would request my stenographer to come to my residence with his typewriter and type my dictation directly. By the time I was over with my dinner, my supervision note would be ready for signature. In this way, I would ensure that there was no scope left for anyone to approach me directly or influence me through others.

One day, I was called upon by the most powerful and prominent politician of my jurisdiction. After spending a couple of minutes singing odes to his own prominence and his acquaintances in the right quarters of the state capital, he came down to his agenda. He started narrating a story of the plight of a poor Brahmin. When I asked him where that poor person was, he pointed towards my office door. I ordered my constable on duty to bring him inside and offered him a chair right beside the politician. The man felt a little diffident sitting at the same level but eventually did so on my insistence. I asked him in an indulgent tone to narrate his woes. The issue with which he had come to me was simple, and I sorted it out in no time there itself. I then told him that the politician was a busy person and henceforth he should straightaway come to me with his problems. The message was conveyed unambiguously.

Another powerful politician of my jurisdiction was frequently visited by my subordinates. I knew that he used to closely interact with them regarding various cases registered in the police stations. He showed up in my office one fine day with his hangers-on. He started talking to me about a case where an accused was arrested with an illegal firearm in a nakabandi[4] operation right in my presence. This politician wanted me to help the accused. I told him that this was not possible. He kept on insisting. I naively asked him to suggest some way through which I could help the accused. He was elated as he thought I was ready to

---

[4]Blockade operation by police to stop and search vehicles

give in to his request. He brazenly suggested that this weapon could be shown as recovered from the possession of some other person. I immediately quipped back, saying if he was willing, it could be shown as recovered from his possession. The hangers-on laughed heartily as if I had cracked a joke. I had communicated what I desired to and reached a rational end to the irrational conversation. After this episode, the politician didn't come to me again, and my subordinates, too, understood the message loud and clear.

In the eyes of the law, all men are equal. As a policeman, I was clear that I should never have qualms in applying this fact to any person, irrespective of his position in society. Back in those days, there weren't any commissions in place to guide and audit the ways of functioning of public bodies in the country, either at a state or at a national level. Yet, I always felt the responsibility of protecting not only the people but also their mandates. As civil servants, we should always abide by the spirit of the Constitution, whatever levels we are at, in whichever way we can.

∞

A young local officer can also facilitate justice

Year 1980, Assembly by-election of Sasaram constituency. As the ASP of the subdivision, I successfully performed my duties of ensuring that the elections were peaceful and violence-free. For counting the votes, the returning officer, in collaboration with the district administration, decided to make the collectorate at Sasaram the venue for counting. I was supposed to make all the arrangements for security and allied matters, which I did almost perfectly. The counting began in the morning and went on quite peacefully through the day. We were nearing the last round, and the results had started indicating that the ruling party was going to lose.

The supporters of the ruling party began to leave the venue, while those of the opposition party had strengthened themselves and had almost started shouting slogans. Late in the evening, the ballot boxes from the strongroom were placed at the counting tables for the final leg. It had been a long day with no time to even eat. I was feeling hungry. Seeing that everything was in order, I decided to take a 10-minute break to rush back home, which was only about 500 yards away, for a quick dinner. No sooner had I reached home that I heard the phone bell ringing. I hurriedly picked up the call, and the voice from the other end said, 'Sir, come fast. There is a problem at the counting venue.'

I skipped my plans of having dinner and immediately went back. When I got there, what I saw was incredible. Ballot boxes were upturned all across; ballot papers had been torn; the counting agents and others were injured and bleeding. The SDO was hiding under his table in a terrified state. I pulled him out from underneath the table, calmed him down and asked what had suddenly happened in the last few minutes. He said, 'The moment you left, the counting agents of the ruling party started creating a ruckus in the counting hall, which led to a lathicharge by the police, and what you see is the result of it.'

Just then, he got a call from the DM who was sitting on the uppermost floor of the same building. The SDO came back in a bewildered state of mind after meeting him. He told me that had he been rebuked badly by the DM in the presence of the candidate of the ruling party. He had also been dictated to conduct a re-election in the constituency. He was quite depressed with the turn of events.

I made a suggestion to him. I told him that as the returning officer, he was not a subordinate to the DM, and therefore, he should take his own decision according to his assessment. He was unable to think clearly and asked for help. I advised that all the torn ballot papers be collected and counted in favour of the ruling party, and the rest should be counted as usual. Then, if the results can still be declared convincingly, it should be done.

He happened to like this suggestion and executed it. The results came out and were declared categorically; the opposition had won.

∞

On one occasion, when I was out on tour, a murder took place quite close to my office, in broad daylight. Upon return, when I came to know of the horrendous incident, I supervised the case and found the incident as well as the allegation to be true. One of the accused turned out to be a politician, who was quite close to the highest political executive. I had submitted my supervision note instructing the IO to arrest the accused. Even after a month's time, the IO, for obvious reasons, had not arrested him. When questioned, he replied that he had executed attachment[5] processes, which, upon inspection, I found to be nominal.

The victim's family came to me with a plea to intervene. I was sitting in my office on a holiday when they came to tell me that the accused was present at his house at Sasaram. I summoned the IO and told him to inform the accused that I wanted to meet him in my office. Within an hour, the accused arrived. I had instructed my IO that while my meeting was on, he should go to the CJM and get the production warrant for the accused. In this way, the accused could be sent to judicial custody directly without being taken to the police station.

This drill was followed. I talked to him in my office politely and finally sent him to jail. After about 70 days, he came out on bail granted by the high court. He came to meet me to ask

---

[5]Movable and immovable property of absconders are deprived by government under orders of court for forcing surrender of absconders.

why I behaved the way I did. I told him that he was a respected member of society, so I treated him so. But since he was the accused in a murder case, it was also my duty to ensure that he was arrested and put on trial. The two actions did not militate against each other.

Politicians of the ruling party had declared me a renegade. Those of the opposition were waiting in the wings to test me. Some debates regarding a few incidents in my subdivision were raised in the Assembly by Members of Legislative Assembly (MLAs) of the ruling party. Then came the group of opposition MLAs to promptly offer their support in the Assembly. I was facing and witnessing such situations for the very first time and was trying to grapple with it. I sensed that they were attempting to toss me from one lap into another. Without batting an eyelid, I told them that I did not need any support from anyone, that I would submit my reply based on the facts and that I could take care of myself. I later realized that this decision proved to be quite helpful throughout my career.

Meanwhile, a world-famous incident had shaken Bihar Police and had become a matter of serious discussion in society. This incident was known as the Bhagalpur Blinding Case. A distorted idea had taken shape in the district police of Bhagalpur. They were blinding criminals as a solution to check crime. This idea gained fast popularity in the police of that area, and many such cases took place in a short span. Within no time, this misdeed came to light, and the media, which did not boast of such speed as today, flashed it all over the world.

It made me wonder: why would the police resort to such measures outside the books of law?

The preventive sections of CrPC, which we had read in great detail in the Academy, were being used by Bihar Police in a routine manner, having little effect on the law and order situation. I set myself the task of trying to understand where the fault lay. An executive magistrate, S.N. Singh, who was really competent and knowledgeable, became my companion in this journey. He subscribed to law journals, which is a rarity amongst officers. He would try to answer my questions by showing me the rulings and also taking me along to watch court proceedings. He showed me how flawed the traditions of the Bihar Police and the executive were in matters relating to sections 107 to 110 CrPC.

I took these learnings to conduct a training programme of policemen. My intention was to rectify all these traditional faults that were making these sections ineffective. I wanted to apply Section 110 CrPC and found that it had a more salubrious impact than preventive detentions. In all these efforts, Singh was a constant aid. He really taught me how to apply the simpler laws for prevention instead of the draconian ones. I recall one case where I got the opportunity to implement Section 110 CrPC in practicality and was amazed by its impact on the minds of the criminals.

Law can never become archaic

Even during my district training, I got to see the roles of executive magistrates only in law and order problems. Most of the court work remained confined to the judicial officers.

Sasaram was a difficult subdivision by any policing standard. I hit upon the idea of introducing and implementing Section 110 CrPC proceedings against a notorious criminal, who had gained some social standing, in a place called Nokha. This section of CrPC hadn't been implemented in the state for the last almost 40 years. I started creating a proposal to be submitted to the SDM against this criminal. It turned out to be a difficult task because the subordinate police officers did not know how to create such a proposal. The magistrate, who had a deep understanding of the law, was allotted this task by the SDO. He came to my rescue.

The criminal was already in judicial custody booked under a few cases. Once the proposal was submitted, I got the notice served to him in the jail itself. The date of the proceedings was fixed, and an irrigation inspection bungalow on a canal near Nokha was chosen as the venue. This place was intentionally chosen as it was open to public view. The magistrate and I headed towards the venue with the criminal in my jeep. On the way, the criminal pointed out that he spotted his advocate on the road, looking for a bus to get to the venue. I picked him up too.

When we reached there, I found that the officer-in-charge of Nokha had gathered some people to depose before the magistrate about the bad character of this criminal. It was a special experience for me to witness the practical process of a theoretical concept that I had learnt only inside a classroom. I remember distinctly that the proceedings were held over three dates and the witnesses provided elaborate details about the character of the accused. Upon completing the third day, we were to hand him over to judicial custody on our way back from the venue.

The criminal sheepishly asked me whether he would be awarded a sentence in this matter. I told him that in these proceedings, he could not be convicted as per law. He would only need to sign a bond saying that he would not behave in this manner in the future. He immediately replied, 'Sir, please do not demoralize me further in the presence of the people of my area. I will sign the bond, but please help me in getting out of this ignominy.'

The bond was signed and the proceedings ended. Such is the effect of Section 110 CrPC on notorious criminals. It hits them with humiliation right in front of the people on whom they exercised their power for so long.

Bihar was infamous for the many massacres it saw for decades. When the first one took place in 1980, somewhere in rural Patna, a huge furore rose all over the country. Union Home Minister Zail Singh went to the place of occurrence, where a huge crowd had already gathered. He was accompanied by all the top police and civil authorities. A battery of journalists went with him to cover the incident.

At one point during his visit, he lost his cool and made a remark while motioning towards the Patna SSP, saying that he should be stripped off his uniform. Of all the senior officers present there, only L.V. Singh, the Range DIG at Patna, raised a bold voice and said that if stripping the SSP off his uniform could save the situation, then it should be done immediately. But he didn't think that it would. In disgust, the home minister asked, 'Then what will?' The response was, 'Prompt investigation and fast trial leading to conviction.' We, young IPS officers who were still learning our ropes, had such great leaders to show us the way.

He also called us to his office in Patna and told us how to tackle crisis situations. What he told us was a lesson that helped me defuse so many issues later in my career. 'The first step,' he said, 'is to ask yourself whether you are a cause of that crisis. You can proceed only if the answer is no. The process of law has to then be carried out at an exceedingly fast pace till its logical end.'

He once decided to inspect my office. Going by his style of functioning, I could make out that he was coming over mainly to drill the understanding of law into me. He came down to Sasaram and spent about five hours in my office. He kept grilling me with his incisive questions. My inquisitive nature and my constant thirst for finding answers to all questions that arose in my mind in my early years of policing helped me answer his navigatory questions. This entire exercise piqued my mind. It gave me clarity on the concept of policing and the application of law in finding solutions to impending problems.

I remember during his session, he made me plot undetected

crimes on the crime map and write down the modus operandi of those crimes to bring out the similarities. This discussion itself started throwing up many ideas. His interaction led me to believe strongly that policing, too, could be as much a cerebral activity as any other profession. Unfortunately, some people have made it more muscular than mental. No wonder Singh rose to become the Union minister of state in the Ministry of Defence during 1990-91.

D.N. Sahay had joined as the new DIG at Patna. He instructed me to attend his inspection of the office of SP Rohtas at Dehri-on-Sone. His inspection, which lasted two days, gave me a good peek into the functioning of an SP office in all its details. He, like a fatherly figure, taught me all the nuances. It was an enlightening experience for me, and I still cherish it.

I was promoted and posted as SP Madhepura, a newly created district on the eastern extreme of Bihar. I collected the inspection note of the DIG, who later became the governor of Chhattisgarh, and moved on to set up the new district from scratch.

BE A HERO IN THE STRIFE

> *In the world's broad field of battle,*
> *In the bivouac of Life,*
> *Be not like dumb, driven cattle!*
> *Be a hero in the strife!*
>
> —Henry Wadsworth Longfellow

SP Madhepura (7 May 1981 to 30 March 1982)

The train chugged to a halt at Saharsa railway station. Madhepura was still about 25 kilometres away. I saw an old man in uniform waiting to receive me. He formally introduced himself as K.N. Singh, DSP Madhepura, and then informed me that he was to retire in a couple of months. I immediately understood that my deputy would not have much interest in my mission of setting up the new district. He further told me point blank that the official vehicle he had brought with him for my journey was a rickety police jeep. However, he had arranged for an Ambassador car of a local businessman as an alternative. I, therefore, had a choice between the two. I lost no time in choosing the police jeep, which was really in a ramshackle condition.

We reached Madhepura around 10 in the morning. Bereft of an office, a Police Line, a vehicle, even a residence; there was nothing that the district SP could be recognized by. I was at sea, left to decide my own course. I told Singh to take me to his office. On reaching there, I gave him ₹10 to get a hardbound register. On the new register, I, in my own hand, wrote down three orders.

1. Notification of creation of Madhepura district from erstwhile Saharsa by the Government of Bihar
2. My posting to Madhepura as its first district SP
3. My joining as the SP of Madhepura

The original notifications, including my joining report, were attached to it.

History had been created, and I was feeling happy at being at the centre of this momentous event. In police jargon, this register is called a DO or a district order book, on which an SP rank officer never writes anything. And here I was, writing the first three orders as the chief architect of the district. An additional feeling of responsibility for the district dawned on me no sooner I had signed on the joining report.

I knew the geography of the place, as I had been there earlier with my father when he was the DIG of this range. I decided to shift into the district board dak bungalow and put up a board declaring it my residence-cum-office.

The SP's office started functioning on the same day in the smallest room of the bungalow, with three people cramped into it: the SP himself, a stenographer and a constable, who could do receipt and despatch work.

My real journey as an IPS officer had just begun, in a condition of complete deprivation. I resolved that the people of Madhepura would never feel that their SP is a 'deprived of resources person', and therefore, will not deliver.

The next day, I woke up early to the news that a new DM had arrived late in the night and was sleeping in one of the rooms of the dak bungalow. This was my first meeting with S.P. Seth. We had a long chat. He told me that he would shift to the Kosi guest house and make that the residence of the DM. Both of us had found residences for ourselves. I hired a private building for my office. The district had started functioning.

Your willpower is your biggest resource

I was just four years old in the police. I left Sasaram to take up my new role with two pieces of paper in my hand—one, a notification of the formation of the new district, and the second, the official letter of my promotion and posting as the SP of Madhepura. I was also handed over another paper that said that a by-election was to be held in the Singheshwar constituency of the district in the coming month.

I went to meet the head of the state's police force to thank him as a cover to actually ask for a vehicle from the police headquarters to go to Madhepura. I was instead told that if the British could come to India after crossing oceans, locate all places in the country and also rule over them, I should also be able to find my own way.

This shook my self-respect awake. I decided that I would not ask for help from anyone. I reached my new place and started preparing for the by-elections. The only empathy I got was from the DM, who himself was holding his first charge.

The CM, and his three Cabinet ministers, called upon me to lecture me on how I should make the preparations for the elections. Although I did not understand most of the sermon, I surely understood that for the elections to be fair, it was important to ensure that no voter faces any hurdle in casting their vote.

On the day of the election, I found a powerful Cabinet minister from that area moving around in his car with an escort from the neighbouring district. I politely requested him to not do so, as it violated the rules. He tried to argue with me. When the conversation was going nowhere, I had to exhibit my stern behaviour to ground him.

After the elections, many old people came to bless me, saying that they had not been able to cast their vote even once since the country's independence. This was the first time. I felt so satisfied on seeing the people's confidence in the administration.

༺༻

This election was an important milestone in the early days of my career. It aroused in my mind questions such as: what role did we as policemen play in protecting the fabric of democracy? And how could we build the confidence of the people in the system while remaining politically detached and impartial? It helped me identify the tenets of a fair and peaceful election, and understand many issues of administration and policing in one go.

༺༻

Impartial election is the only pillar of democracy

Before Madhepura, I had seen only one general election during my district training at Ranchi. I always thought that the basis of democracy lies in an impartial election. The responsibility of an impartial election can never rest on the shoulders of the contestants in the election. The officers who conduct the election need to play the role of impartial referees. If this does not happen, people will lose faith in the process.

The CM, along with the Cabinet ministers, came to Madhepura with a plan to go around the constituency in a fleet of vehicles for an entire day. According to the rules, the DM and the SP had to accompany them. We both moved with the convoy in my open jeep. Back in those days, SPs travelled in an open vehicle in full view of the public to ensure a visible connection with the people.

We had started at around 7 in the morning, and in a couple of hours, were in rural areas deep inside the district. At one remote village, we stopped at a small house that carried the board of the office of the ruling party. The CM and his colleagues came out of their cars, went into that house, sat on the ground in a row and were served breakfast. We stayed back in our vehicles.

I suddenly saw one of the chaprasis of the CM running towards us, calling out that the CM was inviting us to join his team for breakfast. I politely refused the offer by telling him that we had got our food packed from home and would have it in our vehicle. He turned and went back. The CM, too, did not insist.

By this time, I noticed a huge crowd that had assembled near our vehicles. They were looking at us with a lot of questions and curiosity. I realized how important it was for us to not only conduct an impartial election but also do it most visibly, for the general people to see.

∽

This seat had never been won by the ruling party in any of the earlier elections since Independence. This area was considered a bastion of the opposition. A particular caste had an overwhelming majority population that could flex its muscles so that no other caste would dare to cast their vote as per their will.

I did a data analysis of votes cast in every booth of that constituency in the past two elections and drew it on a map. In retrospect, I think that in the year 1981, when computers were not to be seen, 'big data analysis' in a back-of-beyond place like Madhepura was an amazing achievement. My analysis led me to exotic solutions to the problem of booth capturing, ranging from rational deployments of force to preventive measures in law against identified persons.

Even today, when I visit the Singheshwar temple, people there don't forget to tell me that they were able to cast their vote for the first time during the 1981 by-elections.

Like my previous posting, even in this district, house dacoities and robberies were a serious menace. People who lived in certain inaccessible areas of this district were completely at the mercy of criminal gangs. When I visited such areas to see the plight of people, I felt overwhelmed. It seemed as if they had resigned to their fate, with no hope of any help from any quarter.

Law as a tool of crime control

Madhepura district lies in the flood-prone area of Kosi, on the borders of Nepal. The CM inaugurated the district and called me up on the dais to introduce me to the people of Madhepura. After this, he flew off on a helicopter, leaving me marooned on an island with no help and many responsibilities.

On joining, I realized that the place was seething with crime. I had no resource at my command except the police station and its meagre force. In the absence of traditional resources, I knew the traditional ways of policing that I had learned in my district training would be of no help here.

I applied my mind to all the law that I had read and learnt so far. The first thing I did was to gather the names of bailors who had taken the job of providing surety to the criminals and signing on bail bonds. I got them verified through the SHOs of the corresponding places and found a majority of them to be fake. I went into details and put them up before the CJM of Madhepura, requesting him to cancel those bail bonds.

The CJM took a few days to decide on the matter and then called me over for a discussion. He did not seem to be keen on pursuing it, so I had to debate it out with him on the basis of the principles of law. At last, he was convinced and issued a notice to all the advocates who had signed on these bail bonds.

In just about 15 days, more than 30 advocates had been served notices. When they came to know that I was pursuing the matter quite diligently, they became wary of the consequences it could bring to their careers. The Bar

Association was extremely apologetic about the whole episode and the sordid situation it had thrown up. They gathered in a group one day and showed up in my office, requesting a reprieve with folded hands. I had my conditions. I said, 'There are some ordinary cases, like rioting and other similar offences. If you desist from certifying the sureties involved in professional crimes, I will slow down my pace of pursuing matters on this front.' The group immediately agreed. They could still earn their money, but this time, without helping the professional criminals.

This was unprecedented in Bihar Police. No police officer had ever heard of this process. The outcome was phenomenal. In the next three months, dacoities came down to zero in the district. The change in the figures was so drastic that it caught the attention of the DGP of the state, who thought that I was burking offences. He decided to send a team of Crime Investigation Department (CID) officers to my district in a clandestine operation to validate the numbers. The team went back and reported to him that the numbers were real. The DGP was so impressed that he issued an instruction to all the SPs of the state to replicate the same method in their respective districts.

On my transfer from the district, I was given a farewell by the Bar Association. This had not been done for any police officer ever before.

∞

A portion of the district bordering Bhagalpur district was severely hit by criminal gangs operating in the riverine belts. I had heard that the people of this area lived in constant fear. The richest man of that region had met me in Madhepura and requested me to visit him once and see the condition they lived in. During one of my night rounds in that area, I decided to look him up on my way back. I reached his house at around 2 in the night. He had locked himself inside in seven layers. Even when his man shouted to him that the SP of the district had come visiting, he refused to unlock the gates, saying that he didn't trust anyone during the night.

Such was the state of affairs in these areas of Bihar. I had to use MMP to conduct continuous raids here. I personally led these raids until things returned to normal.

A new dimension in policing issues surfaced during this posting. I was able to see the dynamics of the caste and class divisions in society and how they interfered with the functions of the police.

'*Vatican Pope ka, Madhepura Gope ka* (Vatican belongs to the Pope, Madhepura belongs to the Gopes,' was a popular saying in this district. This district is home to an overwhelming population of the Yadav community, who are also called Gope. I was alerted by senior police officers about what to expect from Gopes. The picture painted before me was quite dismal, to say the least, but I decided to start working with an open mind, without being prejudiced for or against anyone.

This worked well for me. I was able to handle multiple law and order, and crime situations without looking at them through coloured lenses. This approach of mine got validated when I saw its acceptance by all sections of society.

Late Shashi Babu, who was socially quite influential in the district, was a distant relative of mine. He used to come to spend time with me in the evenings and always had interesting anecdotes to share. On one of his visits, we were chatting in my room and completely lost track of time while listening to his stories. Suddenly, he told me that B.P. Mandal, ex-CM of Bihar, was waiting for me outside. I felt annoyed that he had not told me about it earlier. I immediately went out, respectfully folded my hands and apologized profusely for making him wait so long. I took him to my room and invited him to have dinner with us.

What was both surprising and heartening was that his visit did not have any agenda. This was the only time I had met him, and I found him to be a reasonable man with a sound understanding of social issues. He hardly had any animus against any section of society. Is it quite tragic that his name got associated with the backward-forward class conflict that has raged in Bihar for many decades now and affected all aspects of this state in multiple ways.

In those days, bandhs by the opposition parties as a mark of protest used to be a regularity. One such nationwide bandh was called, and the state government took it seriously. A Cabinet minister was sent to each district to oversee the arrangements made by the district administration for the bandh.

One minister was sent to Madhepura too. The DM was on leave, so the minister called me and discussed every little detail of the arrangements that I was making. In the end, he asked me to impose Section 144 CrPC on the entire district. I refused instantly, as I did not think it was practical. The minister was obviously annoyed by this, but I stood my ground.

On the day of the bandh, things went smoothly till the last hour. The minister was returning from his tour of the district when a crowd of students gheraoed him in the district headquarters. The armed force had to intervene to rescue him. He found an opportunity to express his grudge against me. He went back to Patna and submitted a big, long report condemning me squarely. The CM marked it to the chief of police force, who asked me to provide a justification for the same with a comment that the report of the minister had made a sorry reading.

By this time, the DM had returned from his leave. When he saw these papers, he stopped me from responding. He himself replied that before going on leave, he had discussed the strategy with me, and we had taken a joint decision against the enforcement of Section 144 CrPC. The matter was put to rest, and it signalled clearly that the district administration was one in all its decisions; no force could drive a wedge between them.

Attempts to influence our ways of working was not limited

to external sources. There were times when internally, too, such issues became apparent.

A fight was blazing between the students of the local college and the bus owners of Madhepura. Cases of rioting were registered. I supervised these cases and had ordered for the bus owners to be chargesheeted. I received a letter from my Range DIG asking me to wait for his orders before submitting the charge sheet. When I checked with the IO, I found that the papers were ready. I ordered him to file it immediately and reported this fact to the DIG. It was then that I learned that my DIG had had instructions from the chief of the police force to withhold the charge sheet.

Obviously, I was summoned by the chief to discuss the evidence with him. I pre-empted the arguments that the bus owners would raise and had even prepared a to-the-scale map of the place of occurrence along with the positions of the witnesses. I was well-prepared for the discussion, perhaps more than what he could have ordinarily imagined.

By the end of the meeting, he understood that I couldn't be pushed over. He asked if I would object to the government withdrawing the case. I promptly answered, 'No, if I am not asked to recommend it.' The matter was given up by the bus owners association. People could now see that there was an SP who couldn't be manipulated even by people at the highest level.

This image of mine had started gaining strength in the district, as could be seen clearly during a crime meeting held by the Range DIG of Saharsa with two district SPs—SP Saharsa and SP Madhepura. I had inherited Madhepura from SP Saharsa, who happened to be senior to me. While the meeting was on, the constable on duty brought in a slip with a request by a person waiting outside to meet the DIG. The person was summoned in; he sat on a chair beside me and started narrating his problems. The case belonged to Saharsa district. He unabashedly said that he did not trust the SP Saharsa who was supervising the case and wanted the case to be handed over to me. He further added that he would accept any verdict I gave. There was an awkward silence in the room, and the DIG had to ask him to leave.

Such events made me realize how important it was for both police and people to have confidence in each other.

Singheshwar temple used to host a big rural mela every year. This mela had a bearing on the functioning of the entire district. When Madhepura was a part of Saharsa district, not enough importance was given to this event, either politically or administratively. Given the implicit faith I had in this temple, I decided to do my best to elevate this mela.

I realized that quite a few visitors who came from interior villages were being waylaid during their journey. Some of these incidents were reported, some weren't. I got a big contingent of MMP posted at Singheshwar to patrol the sensitive areas effectively. I myself used to lead the horse contingent, which doubled up for me as physical exercise and a spectacle for the villagers. I discussed with the DM, and we decided to camp in the mela ground for a few days during the peak period of the event. We put up Swiss cottage tents and made it our camp office. These measures not only created a safe ambience in the mela that year but the simple gestures of being visibly involved and accessible on the ground became real hits with the common man, who started associating with the district administration like never before.

As a part of another experiment, I made the two notorious persons of that area known for creating mischief on such occasions responsible for mela management. This idea worked exceptionally well too. They perhaps felt a sense of responsibility and did their best to be in the good books of the district administration.

The troublemakers within the department, too, needed to be fixed. An old man named J.N. Mishra was the SHO of Kishanganj Police Station. He was rough-tongued, and people brought in a lot of complaints against him. In other aspects of police functioning, he was fairly fine. I confronted him and drove home the point that his behaviour needed to improve. Thenceforth I observed that he made a conscious effort towards this. I wrote about it in his annual confidential report (ACR) too.

On the other end of the spectrum were people like Ramchandra Prasad Singh. He had joined the police department as a constable and had risen to become a SI of Bihariganj Police Station when I first met him as SP Madhepura. I noticed many things in his persona in the first few months of our interaction, which can do many a strict and honest IPS officers proud.

Once, I was inspecting his police station. I found that he had given a personal bond to a local bank for sanctioning a loan to two professional burglars of his police station. I grew inquisitive and bombarded him with questions. He explained to me that he had tried to find out the reason why those criminals committed the crime. He discovered that although they were interested in earning their livelihood lawfully, they were compelled to resort to crime because society wouldn't let them do any work. He, as SHO, decided to get them loans from a bank so that they could start some work on their own. He even tied them up with a rice mill where they could work as suppliers. With his help, they were now able to earn their livelihood without committing any crime.

Later, when I joined the CBI, I recommended his induction, but it failed because of the punishments I had given him for not writing case diaries. No amount of explanation could convince the CBI head office (HO) about his integrity. There are such honest and efficient policemen who do not wear it on their sleeves. I regretted having hurt his career by punishing him unwittingly without understanding things in their entirety.

Honesty is a personal choice

Before I got a chance to meet him, I had gone through the case files in which Ramchandra Singh was the IO. He had cleanly detected most of the serious and heinous offences as per the notes of the sub-divisional police officer. He could do this mainly through his exceedingly strong human intelligence network. To my dismay, I found that he never submitted case diaries in any of these cases. I awarded him a censure in each of these individually.

Next month, during the regular crime review meeting, I met him for the first time in person. I questioned him in the presence of all officers of the district. The answer that he gave enlightened me thoroughly. He said, 'Your clerk, who allots case diaries to the investigating officers, charges ₹5 for each case diary. I cannot pay that amount from my pocket, and therefore, do not write case diaries.' I had never heard such confident and fearless replies from officers of the rank of SI in front of their SP. I was particularly impressed.

I immediately brought case diaries for the entire district and got them distributed in my presence. Thereafter, I posted him to the most important police station of the district. He did exceptionally good work there and earned the trust of the people of not only that police station but also of the entire district.

One of the police stations in the district had a famous Shiva temple. During a particular time of the year, offerings made across two months would go up to crores of rupees. The temple management wanted me to depute only him for managing the security during this period. Such was the confidence that people had in his integrity. In another situation, two warring families in the district requested me to appoint him as their arbitrator.

People like him are rarely found in the police but give credence to its respectability and functioning. My salute to such a police officer.

My Range DIG once invited me to his residence over lunch to teach me the importance of time management in my profession. While we were talking in his drawing room, I noticed a few files lying on his table. I wondered what were official files doing here. He perhaps sensed this, took some of them and called me to his side. One of these files had a monthly summary of my work and my tour diary. He pointed out that I was extremely mobile in my district, which I most certainly was. Then he advised that with age, this habit would tire me out when I get posted to larger districts. So I must develop a method to optimize my throughput vis-à-vis my input. I really liked this idea. Normally, seniors would write long letters to convey such a simple message, but the way my DIG handled this really inspired me.

My tenure at Madhepura was drawing to a close. It taught me quite a few lessons, both in policing and general administration. I had started understanding that it was supremely important to calmly listen to all conflicting views but base my own decisions on the laws of the land and rely on them. The ultimate paradigm that I derived was: law is your weapon as well as your shield; how you apply it is your ingenuity.

With the blessing of Lord Singheshwar, just before I left Madhepura, my first child Richa was born. I had become a father.

STICK TO THE FIGHT WHEN YOU'RE HARDEST HIT

*When things go wrong, as they sometimes will,
When the road you're trudging seems all uphill [...]
So stick to the fight when you're hardest hit,
It's when things seem worst that you must not quit.*

—John Greenleaf Whittier

SP Aurangabad (24 July 1982 to 23 November 1983)

A crisis brewing in the Madhepura district needed immediate attention. I was away for a training course, and the government had to send someone in my absence to handle the situation. My transfer order came. Towards the end of my course, I received my new posting as SP Giridih (a district now in Jharkhand). I reached Patna only to be told by the DGP that I needed to wait, as my posting orders might change.

I was slightly amazed at the logic behind the choice of this new posting. My father had joined Central Coalfields Limited (CCL) on deputation as chief security cum chief vigilance officer, and Giridih was an important coal-mining district. I was told that I would find it difficult to function there because Giridih was infamous for the illegal mining of coal. When I heard this from the DGP, I immediately retorted that I believe my father and I would never have any conflict in our tenets so far as illegal activities were concerned. After a week's wait, I got posted as SP Aurangabad.

In retrospect, I feel that the change in my transfer order, for whatever reason, did me the greatest favour. During those days, Aurangabad was one of the few districts of Bihar seething with the fire of Naxalism. Not that it did not boast of other problems. I knew that I would not have a dull moment right from the day I took my charge.

My abilities as an IPS officer began to show up steadily as I was faced with life-threatening situations. It was here that I learnt to take tough decisions without caring for consequences to my life. It was this part of my career that brought out the best in me.

I drove down to Aurangabad and went to the SP's residence. My predecessor seemed reluctant to hand over the charge to me and wanted a week's time. I, therefore, met the DM to inform him of this delay. Just five days before my joining, a particular community had burnt down a Harijan[1] village in the district. The DM wrote letters to all concerned, emphasizing the tense situation and the urgency of handing over the charge to the new incumbent immediately.

My first day in office at Aurangabad opened up a path of woes and controversies for me. A dacoity had taken place in the block headquarters at Obra. A local junior officer had promptly detected the case, and I started my supervision by late evening. On record, the SHO had mentioned specifically that it was he who detected the case and apprehended the criminals and not his junior officer. He wanted the glory for himself. When I could validate that his claim was false, I placed him under suspension and asked his deputy to take charge in the interim.

This raised a huge storm, which perplexed me. I wondered why? Someone told me that the same SHO had been the IO in the recent, highly sensitive Harijan atrocity case and was himself a Harijan. On the other hand, the accused in that case belonged to

---

[1]The literal meaning of Harijan is 'children of God'. Mahatma Gandhi used the term for the first time for the Dalit community, which is the lowest caste according to the Indian caste system, the untouchables.

my caste. The junior I had ordered to take charge, too, belonged to my caste. This combination of caste equations was indefensible in Bihar's context. I was naive enough to have landed myself into it.

This had too many fallouts. I became conscious of the caste I belonged to, which, till this incident, I was not. Before making decisions, I had to now factor in this aspect while simultaneously ensuring that merit was never compromised and law was not forsaken. I learnt to gather information about the caste of officers discreetly and be conscious about it, but continue to keep all decisions within the framework of law and based on other genuine considerations.

This district entailed a lot of ground travel, day and night alike. I would move around 200 kilometres on an average every day, both in the rural and the semi-urban areas. My nights would be spent sitting in my jeep with closed eyes, holding on to the rod in front of me. All my other senses would stay alert to the slightest movement around me. The wireless on my jeep would remain on so that I could also keep a tab on everything happening in various police stations.

I had started to understand that the two most glaring problems in this district were that of Naxals and dacoits. Another thing that came to my notice was that the southern part of the district bordering present-day Jharkhand was extremely poor. Agriculture was primitive, and the area was inhabited by marginal farmers who had little to look forward to in life. I realized I was barking up the wrong tree during my attempts at implementing law processes on them. Attaching property of poor people to make them surrender to the might of the State is not an impressive idea, by any standard.

These poor people would toil the whole day in the fields and yet not earn enough for one meal. On the haat days, they would carry only a little edible oil and some mahua[2] with them

---

[2]Indian tropical tree, commonly found in the forests of Jharkhand, whose flowers, seed and wood are consumed. The flowers are also used as medicines by the tribals.

to feed their families. On one occasion, I happened to conduct a raid in their houses. What I saw there changed the perception of Naxalism I had developed from reading the police files. The lowest cadres of the Naxals lived in abject penury. On the other hand, there were others who were reaping the benefits of the Naxal movement.

Thus emerged the concept of the invisible 'economic force' behind this movement.

When two bulls fight, the grass gets trampled

I had never encountered the Naxal problem in my policing life until my posting at Aurangabad. I needed to, therefore, understand it right from scratch.

I took out a couple of cases to supervise. When I went into their details, I found that almost all Naxal attacks on civilians were carried out in huge numbers. The numbers could go up to more than a thousand. The investigation indicated that such attacks were planned and executed mostly in the dead of night, in a way that Naxals from all directions would coordinate their arrival and converge on the target. They would also ensure that nobody from the village would be a part of the attack.

This number perplexed me quite a lot because I was not prepared to believe that the number of Naxals in a district could be as high as in thousands who could mobilize themselves for action as and when needed. I, therefore, planned a controlled experiment to test this hypothesis.

I discovered a few warrants and attachment processes that were pending with the Aurangabad Police for execution. I decided to execute these in my presence, although it's considered infra dig for any SP to supervise the execution of an attachment process. These are usually carried out by the local officers of that area.

I was doing this for a local panchayat-level Naxal leader whose name had figured in the investigation and who was absconding. I arranged for armed force and, in broad daylight, went to the village only to find that there was hardly any house in his name. He only owned a few pieces of land on which rice was being grown. The crop was ready for harvest.

I spread the word in the village that this land was going to be attached, and the rice was free for anyone who wanted it. Within no time, the poor people of that area, hundreds of them, started descending upon the field to harvest the rice and take it away. My hypothesis was tested. The people in this village were so poor that if they could forcibly harvest the crop of the rich farmers under the protection of the Naxal leaders, they could also take away the crop of the Naxal leaders under the protection of the police.

This experiment convinced me that the poor villagers of the district should not be confused with the Naxals. In fact, police should not conduct any operation on them. The armed gangs and their leaders needed to be pursued, and that too within the purview of the law. Any measure otherwise would only prove detrimental to the cause of Naxal policing.

Needless to say, financial motives continued to be the common denominator across all other crimes in this district too. On a particular night raid in the town, I caught hold of a man with a country-made pistol. Upon his physical examination, I found a piece of paper on which six case numbers were written. I grew inquisitive and asked him what his connection with them was. He told me that his friend had been remanded unnecessarily in all those cases, and the advocate was demanding the payment of his fee. He was planning to commit a road robbery to arrange for the money to pay the advocate.

This was an eye-opener for me. I called a meeting of all my deputies and narrated this experience to them. I instructed them to pray for remand of persons in professional crime only if they had convincing grounds. The practice of keeping criminals in jail for longer than required was essentially turning out to be counterproductive. It resulted in more crime.

I used to wonder where the Naxals got their funds from to run the organization. I set all my possible sources into motion, including the intelligence agencies and the villagers, to get this information. To my dismay, I found that even the country's best intelligence agency had information only about the organizational structure of the Naxals and some bit of information about its leaders, nothing more. The anatomy was known, but the physiology wasn't.

I kept looking for an answer. I could finally put my finger on one source, which unlocked a large chunk of this problem. The hills and the jungles on the borders of Chatra subdivision of Hazaribagh district were covered in kendu[3] leaves. The Naxals had spread terror in that region so that no government agency, including the police, would dare venture into that area. They had free run of the precious leaves, which they carried on trucks to the market. A major share of this illegal income would go to their leaders, similar to how corruption takes place in the government.

I went to Hazaribagh to discuss this with my counterpart, who was five years senior to me. To my disappointment, he outrightly dismissed it. Later in my career, I applied the same theory to organized gangsters in Bettiah and planned my operations accordingly. It paid off quite well. When I reached the top post in the state, I got the opportunity to highlight this theory in the

---

[3]Similar to an ebony tree, the leaves of this tree are used for rolling beedis or local Indian cigarettes.

highest fora. This idea drew an instant acceptance from the CM of Chhattisgarh, who could easily see the connection between the kendu leaves and the power of the Naxals.

In the mental image that I had developed, the Naxals appeared to be similar to a legitimate government structure with one major difference—the government used the fear of law, while the Naxals relied on terror through weapons as their manifestation of power.

Who makes who run?

Year 1983. I was going through my dak in the office when I saw a demi official (DO) letter from the police chief. A DO letter, especially coming from the chief, is a serious matter. He had written to me about certain reports from the intelligence that indicated a threat to my life. He advised me to be alert and not move anywhere in the district without a proper pilot and escort. Apparently, the Naxals had brought out pamphlets with an open threat to kill me and pasted them on the trees in my district as well as in neighbouring districts.

I read through the letter carefully but somehow was not convinced of the security mechanism indicated in it. Still in thought, I looked up to find the officer-in-charge of Deo Police Station, K.G. Verma, standing in front of me. I asked him to take a seat and enquired what had brought him to the district headquarters. He instead asked me hesitatingly what the matter was, as I looked disturbed. I handed over the DO letter to him as an answer to his question. After reading through it, he grimly asked me if he could give some advice on the matter. I said, 'I'll be happy if I get any advice from my juniors.' The advice that he gave me was so good and so practical that I followed it till the end of my tenure in the police.

He told me that the only way to handle such situations was to move around without any notification. In short, I should continue to conduct raids and ambushes without letting anyone, even my bodyguard and driver, know about my whereabouts. He said that no amount of escort or pilot could protect me from a planned and perfectly laid ambush. To prepare for an ambush, it takes about 10-12 hours. If I moved randomly, without giving the Naxals those hours, I should be safe. If they never get a whiff of where I am and what I would be doing next, they would never be able to understand and plan anything against me.

I practised this tactic throughout my career to the extent that even while inspecting a police station, I would never plan anything or inform anyone, not even the police station itself. I would enter through one door and exit through another.

I extended this to my operations against the Naxals. I would lay an ambush against them according to the intelligence information about their armed dasta[4] movements. I later came to know that the Naxals had become wary of this strategy.

The advice given by K.G. Verma not only saw me through my tenure as the SP of Aurangabad but the principle that it relied on gave me a lot of clues to plan deputation of forces during elections in Naxal areas. The deputations based on this simple logic worked so well that even planned IED (improvised explosive device) explosions could not hurt the central armed forces.

༄

By the end of my tenure in Aurangabad, I had begun to get a kaleidoscopic view of policing. Three years after my transfer, when I was holding the charge of SP CBI, Ranchi, the infamous massacre of Dalelchak-Bhagaura took place. It raised a huge storm in the country. The intensity of the storm was such that Union

---

[4]Gang

Home Minister had to visit the village. People of the entire district voiced their concerns about how things had deteriorated in the past three years after the DM, B.K. Sinha, and I had left that district. Not only this, they vehemently demanded that we both should be returned to the district.

The home minister ordered both the officers to appear before a Cabinet subcommittee. We appeared for the meeting and faced too many questions. One question raised to me was about how I managed my tenure on the Naxal front. I answered it in the most non-bureaucratic manner. I said, 'It is always a scene of who makes who run. Whichever party waits for the other to make the first move keeps running pointlessly. With or without intelligence, raids had to be carried out every day in various formats. It's a game of "Who blinks first?"'

I do not know the content of the report thereafter. At the end of the interview, one minister asked me about the reason behind my transfer. I immediately retorted, saying that since transfers of officers are done in Cabinet meetings, they would know better.

It takes a thief to catch a thief

'My source has confirmed information that in a particular village under the Deo Police Station, there will be movement of an armed dasta of the Naxals,' the officer-in-charge of Deo Police Station told me. His information was detailed with the precise timing and location of the movement.

I arranged for a team of brave policemen, right from constables to SIs. Private weapons like double-barrel guns and 0.315 rifles were given to them. Clothes similar to what Naxals wore when they carried weapons, with bullet studded across their chest, were arranged for them. All in all, this group was dressed to look like an armed dasta of the Naxals.

I borrowed a tractor and a trailer from a farmer nearby

and arranged enough food to last a day. The team started for the village where the armed groups of Naxals were to assemble the next day. As per my instructions, they entered that area from a side from where the entry of police would be least expected. They reached the village by late evening.

To the local population, they introduced themselves as a Naxal dasta from a neighbouring district. They talked to the villagers in the language used by the Naxals, and managed to spend the whole night quite comfortably in the village, masquerading as Naxals. The villagers took great care of them.

I was keeping a close watch from a far-off place. Late in the night, I lost contact and started getting really worried about my men who were spending the night in Naxal heartland. I couldn't sleep that night. The next morning, I rushed to the police station and enquired whether the officer-in-charge had returned from the raid. Nobody in the police station was aware of this secret mission and had no clue about their whereabouts. I got impatient and decided to drive down to the vicinity of that locality and look around for them.

Suddenly, I saw a huge crowd of Naxals charging towards me from a distance. I did not have my force with me, so I retreated to a safe distance. I heard a firing sound from the other end, and in about 10 to 15 minutes, I could see my team coming out victoriously on the other side of the crowd. The trap they had laid for the Naxals had worked, and an encounter had taken place. When they came and met me, they started recounting all their experiences but were disappointed that I had arrived too soon. They felt that had I come just an hour later, the impact of the encounter could have been more.

Nevertheless, I was thrilled, as this was perhaps the only raid in the Naxal belt of Bihar where the police could enter into their heartland, stay there for more than 14 hours, engage in an encounter and succeed.

Tasting one's own medicine

At around 10 p.m., I started my journey on horseback, with only five other mounted policemen, towards the village of a Naxal leader in my district. We followed the beaten track in the field that shone in the moonlight to show us the way. A pleasant cool summer breeze blew across our faces. We cantered for most of the distance and after about 45 minutes, reached that village.

I entered the premises of the house of that leader on horseback itself. I wanted to take him by surprise, just how the Naxals do with the police. On hearing the noise of my horse, the villagers came out of their homes. It was quite a spectacle for them to find their SP conducting a raid on horseback. They had seen many raids on foot by the police, but they had never imagined a raid on horseback.

When I asked them about the whereabouts of the leader, I got to know that he was not there in the village. After conducting the reconnaissance in the village, all six of us started trotting and galloping back to the national highway where our vehicle was waiting for us. We drove back while our horses followed us, marching behind.

The next morning, it became the talk of the town.

∞

I was on a late-night round on the national highway when I suddenly saw the tail light of two stationary trucks. I immediately drew to a halt and found that their tyres had been pierced by nails planted on the road. These trucks had just been waylaid. I started following the trail in the paddy field and saw a man running away from us. My suspicion grew stronger, and we chased him. After about half a kilometre of the chase, we caught him in a pump house on the farm. On a primary instinct, I was convinced that we had caught the right person. We took him to the highway, where the truck drivers confirmed his identity as one of the men in the group. I was satisfied that I had done my job well. The man was sent to jail.

A couple of days later, I came to know that the man I had arrested was not a criminal. He was watering his farm when we reached there. On hearing the brief exchange of fire, he got scared and started running towards his pump house. After a thorough investigation, I verified the facts again and cleared him of the charge. The incident ended quite tragically when I learnt that his mother died due to the shocking news of his arrest. I couldn't reverse this event in his life.

I sometimes think, in the job of a policeman, there are so many lives, including his own, that are put at stake every day. One wrong move can cost a human life. It is important to not just be alert and aware but also right.

On the banks of the Sone River was a small village in Obra Police Station. The district administration had received reports that an old bataidaari[5] dispute had erupted and taken a violent turn. I reached there with my armed force and camped in a government school on the outskirts. Through the village functionaries, I called upon both parties to assemble at the school to sort out the issue in my presence.

In the middle of the discussion, I suddenly saw billows of black smoke emerging at a distance. The talk was disrupted as we rushed to the place. In the tola[6] of the village labourers, one out of the two rows of huts was on fire. I was standing with my force at the entrance of the tola and thinking about what to do next when three bombs exploded in a series, hurled at us from inside the tola. I knew that I had a battle on hand.

I immediately decided to move towards the other end of the tola stealthily. Only one officer, ASI Nandjee Singh, dared

---

[5]Sharecropping practice in which a landowner allows a tenant to cultivate a piece of land in return of a portion of the yield
[6]Ghetto or colony

to join me. Both of us literally crawled and entered the village from its rear. The men had gone towards the front in a bid to tackle the police force, while the women were peeping out of their doors. Little did the men realize that the two of us had entered their village from behind and were walking up to the front. In the last lap of our run, I gave a war cry and rushed towards them.

They were taken completely by surprise and thought that they had been sandwiched by the police from both sides. They started running in all directions in panic. Many of them were caught and arrested with explosives and firearms. Some had even come from outside the village to foment the dispute. The arrested leaders were put through the process of law without any excesses.

Since my training days, a question kept coming to my mind repeatedly. Where is that one place in the district that has the highest density of criminals? I thought it was important to answer this in order for me to harvest criminal intelligence most effectively. In my training days itself, it was almost in a flash that I realized this place had to be the jail. In an area of a few acres, it had the highest concentration of criminals, thousands of them. Their topics of discussion would mostly be around crimes committed by them in the past. I thought that if I get to know about their conversations, I would have done well for myself.

I was learning the tricks of the trade gradually. I developed a novel process of creating police sources from inside the district jail and used this technique in each district I worked in thereafter. I would never pick a professional criminal for this exercise. I tried to study the administration of the jail and its inmates. It gave me good insights and helped me plan my moves.

Prisoners who were undergoing life imprisonment in cases of murder did not belong to the category of professional criminals. Such people were feared, enjoyed the respect of jail inmates and suffered from a deep sense of remorse. The literate ones of this lot were put on the writing jobs in the office of the jail superintendent.

These young men worried about their family's security, especially if they had children. I would locate such men and provide their families outside support in lieu of intelligence from inside the jail.

I talked to one such man in confidence and personally assured him of help on any front for his family. We made an arrangement where one of his relatives would contact me personally without ever getting routed through any other police officer. It was a straight deal between us. Such systems helped me in ways that I had not imagined.

Police sends seven dead people to jail

One morning, I got a message that seven bodies were lying in an orchard in a rural part of the district. A large crowd had gathered and was swelling in size. I reached the spot immediately. A little enquiry revealed that a road dacoity had taken place on the adjoining highway, and the dacoits had been distributing the booty amongst themselves in the orchard. There had been a dispute regarding the distribution, and they had ended up killing each other in a rage.

I left the dead bodies on the spot for the entire day in an attempt to get their identity, but it yielded no result. I had almost given up when an idea struck me.

I called for a big truck from the Police Lines, loaded the dead bodies and took them to the district jail. I requested the jail superintendent to allow the truck inside the premises. The inmates were asked to queue up and see the dead bodies one by one. After this exercise was over, the truck was driven away, and the bodies were cremated according to the rules.

After a few hours, I came back to the jail and contacted my source. The cat was out of the bag. He gave me the names of all seven deceased and told me that they belonged to the neighbouring district of Rohtas. I could now understand why

STICK TO THE FIGHT WHEN YOU'RE HARDEST HIT

I had been unable to get them identified.

I immediately raided their places and could unearth the booty from a large number of dacoity cases covering both Aurangabad and Rohtas districts.

∞

The report of a major road hold-up on the national highway came to me at around 8 a.m. At 10 a.m., I went to meet one of my sources in the jail. To my surprise, he already knew the details of the gang responsible for it. When I asked him how and from where he got this information so fast, he revealed a fact that changed my approach towards using my human sources from the jail. He told me that around 8 a.m., people gather at the jail gate to meet criminals. They are called mulaqatis[7]. These are usually members of various gangs, and they discuss crimes that have occurred in the recent past. Using all the information he shared with me, I verified the location of the villages and conducted raids without the help of the local police station. I could crack the case with proper arrest and recovery.

My technique had started showing results without spending anything from the secret service money. In future, when my subordinates tried to replicate the same technique, it didn't yield desirable results, as they missed the important condition of not using professional criminals for this purpose.

When senior officers would come to inspect the office of the SP, each would have his own unique style. I, too, was learning, trying to assimilate things and creating my own style. Arun Chaudhary, my Zonal IG, came down to Aurangabad to inspect my office. Normally, these officers start with the historical record of inspections done by their predecessors, but his inspection was unique.

He asked me to stand at the crime map and explain the flow of

---

[7]From the word 'mulaqat', meaning meeting

crime through the one year that I had been there. He listened to my methodologies and probed incisively. When I finished explaining everything I had done, he identified two undetected cases for discussion. He went into the details of my efforts and wanted to assess whether I had followed all leads till the end before giving up. He also inspected my efforts towards the Naxal issues in the district. He meticulously took down notes and sent them to me as part of his inspection note. He seemed to be quite impressed overall, specifically on the Naxal front.

A few officers have left an indelible mark in my life through their honesty and simplicity.

∞

Reminiscing late Shri B.K. Sinha, IAS

'I would like to use your jeep to go to a place just beyond our jurisdiction, towards Sherghati.' Came an unusual request from the DM Aurangabad. I couldn't understand the objective but immediately acted upon it.

On the way, I enquired about the purpose of this journey and got to know that he had taken leave to go to Ranchi for some personal work. He wanted me to drop him till the national highway beyond the jurisdiction of the district so that he could board a truck and reach up to Charhi, a place in the neighbouring Hazaribagh district. From there, he planned to take a public tempo and go to Ranchi. He said that he didn't want to do this within his jurisdiction because he thought it would look awkward. The highway was a better place, as nobody would identify him there.

I didn't question him, although there were many that were coming to my mind. After reaching the highway, my driver and bodyguard managed to signal a truck to stop. I told the truck driver that the DM would like to use his truck to go to Charhi. The driver and his khalasi were greatly amused.

STICK TO THE FIGHT WHEN YOU'RE HARDEST HIT   91

They immediately made some space near the khalasi's seat, cleaned it up and helped the DM climb onto the truck. When he was comfortably perched on the truck, I folded my hands in a pranam and off he went.

I had extreme respect for him, mainly because of his integrity and competence. Such simplicity could be found in some people in those days. There are many such memories of B.K. Sinha, IAS 1975 batch, Bihar cadre, who retired as the rural secretary in the Government of India and who has already left us for his heavenly journey. My salute to such rare officers who are even rarer these days.

∞

As if the policing problems were not enough, a Cabinet minister, for reasons known best to him, was thoroughly annoyed with me. Many told me that he kept making attempts to get me transferred in each weekly Cabinet meeting, every Tuesday. This went on for a few months. The minister had a list of grievances against me, the primary being his notion that I do not provide him enough security. When asked to comment on this issue, I assured the government that his security was my concern and that I would discharge my responsibility as appropriate, and requested the government to have faith in me.

One day, the DM arranged for a meeting between the minister, himself and me at his residence. At one point in time, the minister said that he felt I never called on him. I reminded him that there is a concept of collective responsibility under which he could call me to meet him about issues relating to the police and I would be legally bound to come.

While on the one hand, I was dealing with the egos of such ministers, I also happened to come across politicians who helped me in controlling crime.

∞

Intervention by politicians is not always interference

Back in those days, dacoity was considered a serious offence, especially if it also included murder. One such incident was reported to me early one morning when I had just woken up. I took no time to get ready and reach the village to supervise the case.

On reaching there, I saw that the entire village was up in arms and blaming a co-villager for the incident. I recorded the statements of all the villagers and received such strong oral evidence that I ordered the arrest of this individual. I gave the same in writing to the SHO of the police station.

The next day, a local MLA came to meet me in my office. He told me bluntly that I had passed a wrong arrest order. I felt slightly irritated. Should I believe what I heard and saw myself in the village or should I believe the MLA who had neither seen the incident nor had any reason to say these things to me? When he found me unmoved by his statement, he almost challenged that he could prove it.

He suggested that I send with him someone I trust, who would listen to all his conversations with the same villagers and come back and report to me all that had transpired. A trainee IAS officer, who later became the chief secretary of Jharkhand, was sitting in my office. I requested him to participate. He was quite forthcoming and was more than eager to play along. He immediately changed into clothes that would make him look like one of the villagers and went with the MLA to the place of occurrence.

When he came back in the evening after completing the bidding, he told me that the MLA was indeed right. I had made a wrongful arrest. All the villagers who had deposed before me had deliberately done so because nobody liked this person. They were sick of this man and wanted to teach him a lesson. This man was essentially a nuisance, but he had not committed this crime.

I had to make a decision. Convinced I was, but it was not in the legalistic form. Therefore, I asked my CID and intelligence teams to form groups and determine the details exactly. Since I had passed the written order, I adopted all the legal processes before reversing it. Gone are those days when the interference of politicians was not to create a hindrance but to positively contribute to the dispensation of justice.

Separation of powers

Just when the country gained independence, India had got its first two constitutional services, the IAS and the IPS. The national-level examination for these would produce officers every year to serve huge districts in the various states of the country. People respected these officers like gods.

My father, Shri Jagadanand, got into the IPS in the year 1951. During my school and college days, he would recount his experiences, which helped me navigate my way through 37 years in the police.

This particular incident dates back to his SP Saran days. Saran used to be a big district comprising three smaller districts of Chhapra, Siwan and present-day Gopalganj. He was sitting in his campus, having his morning cup of tea, when a Cabinet minister of that area came to call on him. My father, with utmost respect, offered him a seat and asked him what had brought him there. The minister motioned towards a man standing at a distance and told my father that he was somebody he knew. This person had certain grievances for which he needed the police's help.

Just when my father wanted to express his opinion on the matter, the minister jerkily stopped him. He told my father that, being a government servant, he expected him to be neutral and particular about following the law of the land.

My father was told that he should act as a neutral party and hear both sides in the matter before taking a legally correct stand. After saying this, the Cabinet minister left the place. His tea, in fact, came after he left.

This kind of maturity of a politician impressed my father immensely. He respected the minister for the rest of his life. I felt that this was the model of the relationship between a bureaucrat and a politician that could have done this country a great deal of good. Unfortunately, the roles of the two have been so intermixed that the concept of separation of powers that the Constitution enshrines, has gone for a toss. I wish it could be restored.

∞

By the end of about five years in the job, I had started to get a hang of things. I felt there were two prerequisites of justice that government officials should always follow—transparency in administration and probity in public life.

Four clerks for the SP's office at Aurangabad were to be appointed. The DIG of Magadh range was made the chairman of the appointment committee, and the four SPs became its members. At 9 a.m., just before the process started, I requested the DIG to announce that the results would be declared by 9 p.m. on the same day, and the answer sheets of all candidates would be made available for scrutiny in case someone wished to do so. The DIG seemed hesitant, but I managed to convince him.

The examination was conducted in right earnest. Everyone was at the job throughout the day and, as planned, we were ready with the results by 9 p.m. There was excitement among the candidates. The results were announced and no one came to scrutinize the answer sheets. The crowd melted in silence.

∞

Implementation of law needs a creative mind

'Law will take its own course,' is a common adage I had heard since my childhood, although I never understood its meaning in entirety. It appeared as if law is an invisible force that runs this society from the background.

In the National Police Academy, I read the lessons in law in great detail, but only when I started functioning in the field, could I understand that IPS was created to find intelligent solutions to ever-emerging problems. Law is akin to Newton's laws of motion, which many can repeat ad nauseam but only a few can understand and apply to practical situations.

When I had started handling the responsibility of a district as an SP, I could see the mistrust between people and police. I saw many cases of complaints against officers being biased in family disputes. In one such dispute, one side had articulated against an officer to such an extent that I had almost decided to transfer him. Before taking any action, I gave the entire problem a deeper thought. I was trying to reason if transferring the officer would solve the root cause of the problem. I was not convinced. Suddenly, it occurred to me that I could pass an order to the effect that when any family dispute came up to the police station, the present SHO shall not take any action on it beyond recording that matter as placed before him. He should transfer the matter to the neighbouring police station for further action.

The entire district was debating this order for its propriety because none had seen anything of this kind earlier. This idea worked well and I thought law had taken its course quite creatively.

Today I even see superior courts transferring cases for investigation and trial to places other than the police station or court of jurisdiction on the grounds of bias. IPS was created and given a place in the Constitution so that the officers could use law innovatively and intelligently to deliver justice to the common man.

⁕

On 28 May 1983, I got the news that my wife had been admitted to the Ranchi Medical College Hospital, waiting to deliver our second child. I immediately took leave and, within five hours, was in the hospital. The next morning, our son Shwetank came into our family. Assured that everything was fine and taken care of, I drove down to Aurangabad the same day, back to work.

In a few months, time had come for me to hand over my charge at Aurangabad. Practically, it was just a piece of paper where I had to append my signature. It is such an intriguing feeling that when you sign on a paper while taking charge, you take up the responsibility for everything that happens in the district, and the next moment, when you again sign on a piece of paper to hand over that charge, you are expected to forget everything as if it never existed. I started taking my transfers in the spirit of 'all and then nothing'.

It reminded me of Ramakrishna Paramahamsa, who tells the tale of a servant working for a bhadralok. The servant takes care of everything as his own as long as the master-servant relationship exists, but the moment he quits his job, he forgets everything and moves on. Paramahamsa talks of detachment. I, too, was learning and practising detachment with each transfer.

ROUND PEGS IN SQUARE HOLES

Here's to the crazy ones. The misfits. The rebels. The troublemakers. The round pegs in the square holes [...] You can quote them, disagree with them, glorify or vilify them. About the only thing you can't do is ignore them. Because they change things. They push the human race forward.

—Steve Jobs

SP Sahibganj (28 November 1983 to 21 April 1984)

On a cold November morning, at around 7, with a map in my hand, I started my journey from Aurangabad to Sahibganj. After a long drive, I reached my destination at 3 p.m. and went straight to the official residence of the SP. Little did I know that the long road journey will terminate at the beginning of a brief career journey of just five months.

I held my first meeting with my officers at 4 p.m. on the same day. I learnt from them that the crimes in the district were hardly related to incidents of violence. I felt mentally relaxed after a tiresome experience at both Madhepura and Aurangabad. Typical violence and nocturnal raids would be pleasantly missing in this posting. Had I decided to just stay put, I could have carried on for a few years without any concern. The most that would happen in this district was house theft of utensils and chickens. The rural population was tribal and lived across forests and hills. Those residing in the forests were called Adivasis, and those in the hills were called Pahadiya. Both lagged behind in the race of development. This new component in the district invoked my curiosity. I thought I would get a chance to see the economics of social life for the first time.

I was almost sure that the government was spending a reasonable amount of money in the name of development on these tribes. But development, even in the ordinary sense, was not discernible. So, where was this money going?

By 6 p.m., I was again on the move, without knowing exactly where to. After an hour's drive, I reached a police station named Barhait, around 40 kilometres from the district headquarters. As expected, the SHO told me that there was hardly any significant issue brewing in his area. I aimlessly entered, sat on the chair of the SHO and started flipping through the general diary of the police station. This diary serves as a running record of events at the police station, updated every two hours. I couldn't find anything interesting; every entry seemed quite routine and mundane. Suddenly, I found an entry from a month ago, waking me up from the slumber I was slipping into.

Mukhiya robs the government

The entry was about an incident related to a fight between the headmaster of a school in a rural area of that district with his panchayat mukhiya. A simple case of rioting and hurt had been registered. I got interested in the incident and wanted to know the reason behind the fight.

The SHO told me that new teachers had been appointed in the entire district. The mukhiya had given instructions to the headmaster to antedate their appointment by three months, draw their salary and distribute the money amongst the stakeholders. The salary of those three months was a fraud on the government exchequer. Even the district-level officers, including the district treasury, were involved in this activity. The proportion of the share to each one was the bone of contention between the two.

I uttered to myself, 'This is the case to be registered.'

I asked him, 'Don't you think that is a more serious issue than the fight itself?' The SHO looked at me and didn't know how to answer. I asked him to get all the details by the following day so that I could order for a case of fraud to be registered against both parties and the teachers. Since the teachers were drawing a salary for a period they didn't work for, they were accused as well, though not to the same degree of severity.

I moved on to another police station in the district called Borrio. To my surprise, I found that the same issue existed here too. When I looked further, I realized that this had happened in the entire district. I pursued this matter, and within about five days, there was a case registered in each police station of the district. A problem that had been dormant until then had now started showing up in a virile form.

A hornet's nest had been stirred in the district. Everyone in the education department, including the deputy commissioner of the district, was shaken to the core. Every officer of the department was seen running to the district court for anticipatory bail.

Officers were upset and apprehensive, but the common man found the situation amusing.

∞

I had hit the nail on its head, but this was just one of the problems that I had created; there were many more to come. My mind challenged the status quo in the district, as I thought there must be problems ready to erupt, and the silence was only the calm before the storm.

I realized that mining was being done on a large scale in this district and was a significant part of the lives of the people here. I tried to study the legal and financial aspects of this activity. Soon, I could see that the state was losing revenue on an unimaginable scale in this sector. I pursued this and unearthed big scams on tax embezzlement. I got cases registered against big people who had mining leases in their names but hardly paid any sort of taxes. They were looting the mine labourers as well by not paying them their legal and rightful dues. Unfortunately, not every issue could be brought under police jurisdiction. I had to think of creative ways to end these unfair practices to whatever extent possible.

Lessees cannot become owners

I moved around the district for a few days and realized many economic crimes were being committed. The government's money was being looted in almost every department. In the mining sector, even the mine labourers were not spared. These labourers had no job security and remained at the mercy of the so-called mine owners for their daily wages and salaries.

I summoned a meeting of the labour union in my office with an intent to extract as much information possible from them. I discovered that too many issues needed to be addressed, some of which fell outside my jurisdiction. They told me that on the next day, the deputy commissioner of the district had summoned a meeting of the mine owners and the labourers to discuss all their internal disputes as well as those with the government.

I advised the labour union leaders that henceforth they should refuse to address the mine owners as khaan[1] maalik[2] and start addressing them as khaan pattedaar[3] instead. They seemed to be quite confused with this suggestion, as they

---

[1] Mine
[2] Owner/Master
[3] Lessee

thought that the people who owned the mines and paid them salaries were indeed maaliks.

I showed them the facts. I told them that the property, which is called mines, belongs to the State. The State gives the right of mining to certain people in lieu of a paid lease. Therefore, if at all there is an owner of the minerals beneath the earth's surface, it is the State and not the lessees. Khaan pattedaar is, hence, the right word for them.

The next day, just at the start of the meeting in the office of the deputy commissioner of Sahibganj, the leader of the mazdoor union put up a paper announcing that they have resolved to address the so-called owners of the mines as khaan pattedaar and not as khaan maalik.

This pricked the ears of the entire propertied class of Sahibganj. The powerful lobby, including the politicians, thought that this was a perilous trend and that I should be sent out of the district as soon as possible.

∞

The stakeholders in the mines and crushers were scurrying for cover in only a few weeks. My approach towards policing had sent a whiff of fresh air across the district, and a huge number of like-minded people in the district began sending me letters containing details of unlawful activities going on in various walks, which were causing wrongful loss of revenue to the government exchequer.

In most of these cases, I would request the deputy commissioner to get the matter enquired into by a magistrate. Since the details were open and verifiable, he could not reject my request but remained hesitant to take action. The magistrates were further instructed to show me the draft report before submission. Once I received these reports, I would order the registration of criminal cases under the appropriate sections of law.

Contrary to what the police department thought, I always considered white-collar crimes as cognizable offences. People were feeling satisfied, but the corrupt government servants were seeking shelter. Within a few months of my joining, there was hardly any department whose activity was not brought under police scrutiny.

∞

What asset does a labourer have?

'Dumka-Sahibganj road has been blocked by agitating labourers of a contracting firm.' I was a little puzzled to receive this message, as matters like these are usually handled by the SHO of the concerned police station. But I felt that I should personally go and see what the matter was. The SHO, in the meanwhile, had asked for a contingent of lathi and armed force to tackle the situation because the jam was quite severe, and the agitating labourers were protesting vociferously.

I immediately left Sahibganj to reach the spot. By my ways of functioning, the people in the district had built a pro-poor image of me. This helped me defuse the situation just by speaking to the leaders of the agitation after reaching there. I could convince them for a dialogue, and they helped me understand the problem in its minutest detail. The agitation was called off, the road was cleared and traffic normalized.

I got to know that these labourers had been hired by a road construction company under a contract. They were supposed to get paid at the end of each month. The total amount comprised a monthly salary, over and above a daily wage. For the last three months, they received their wage, which covered their day-to-day needs, but had been denied their monthly salary.

I personally thought that this was unjust. It was another issue that the labourers had blocked the road and technically committed an offence of illegal restraint under Section 341 IPC. I asked the leader of the agitators to accompany me to the police station. At the police station, I asked the SHO of Barhait to register a case against the contractor for not having paid the agreed-upon salary to the labourers for three months.

The SHO was quite aghast at my orders. He argued, saying that such matters are of civil dispute and should not attract criminal law. On the face of it, he seemed to be correct. He questioned me forthrightly as to which section of law should be used to file this case. I promptly asked him to register it under sections of misappropriation and breach of trust, but he just couldn't understand my logic behind this and questioned me again. In my typical style, I asked him a question, 'What do you think is the property of a labourer given in trust to the contractor? His only asset is his labour, which he delivered under this contract. This labour gets converted into an equivalent amount of money deposited with the contractor at the end of every month. In a way, this money, which rightfully belongs to the labourers, lies in trust with the contractor and should be returned to them according to the agreement.' The SHO felt that I made sense and went ahead and registered a case. I left the police station.

The contractors filed applications for anticipatory bail in the local CJM's and district judge's court. These were rejected as I had already briefed the public prosecutor about the issue. The contractors then went and filed a petition under Section 482 CrPC in the high court at Ranchi, arguing that this case was not a criminal case but a civil one. This logic did not render any relief to them either.

My interpretation of breach of trust in such matters was a precedent of some sort that has now been accepted in many forms of law, where contributory provident fund matters have been declared as criminal offences based on similar logic.

There was heavy railway traffic carrying granite boulders from a place called Pakur to West Bengal for industrial use. My sources told me that the weight of the boulders that was being recorded by the railways was lesser compared to what was actually being carried. I decided to get one rake stopped en route in my jurisdiction by submitting a delay memo and got it reweighed in the presence of railway authorities. Even the senior railway authorities came down to witness this event, as this had never been done before. Fines were levied and paid by the party promptly. It was quite shocking for me that, back in 1984, the size of this fine crossed a lakh.

I got to know that the railway authorities became quite alert, and honesty was being restored, but there was an undercurrent feeling that the SP was overstepping his jurisdiction. This didn't bother me because I was confident that I was doing everything acceptable under the relevant sections of CrPC. I had experienced the strength of local public support in all my unconventional actions at my earlier places of posting. All information that I would get verified would invariably turn out to be factually accurate. There was no malice in my action in any case.

Here, I was detecting house thefts amounting to a few hundred on one hand, and cognizable offences leading to unlawful loss to the State to the tune of crores on the other hand, in just a small district of Bihar.

The local media, by now, was literally singing odes in favour of the police. Every action of the police was being discussed at the city's chowks in great detail.

My sources provided me with a wealth of information. I remember once I got information about a big contractor who was supplying boulders for an NTPC project in West Bengal. I collected all data from railways on the actual supply at the project site and tallied it with the payment being made to him by NTPC. The difference between the two numbers was staggering. As a young policeman, I was trying to find my feet in this dirty world.

I would definitely initiate the legal process, but the magnitude of the filth around shook me up no end.

The question popped up again: were we in police uniform meant to protect the property of white-collared criminals against dacoities and thefts while closing our eyes to massive offences of embezzlement and cheating that was being committed with impunity all around?

My quest for answers kept growing more intense. Right from the district administration to the Union government agencies in my vicinity—all could feel the heat.

It was a routine day in my office. I suddenly got the news of a fight that had started between the cinema staff of the local theatre and some students. The theatre was selling tickets in black, which angered the students. It was taking a violent turn—many people were landing up in the district hospital with injuries.

I rushed to the place of occurrence with the other subordinate police formations. The show was forced to stop, and things had become topsy-turvy. The dispute had arisen due to black marketing of tickets for a new popular movie. I was trying to ease the tension between the students and the owner of the theatre when someone whispered into my ears about counterfoils of the black-marketed tickets that had been kept concealed under a heap of sand in the theatre premises. I got the place located, and out came the counterfoils that had been concealed from the Sales Tax department. I had unearthed the documentary evidence of the reason behind the issue.

Two cases were registered. One was the typical case of the rioting that had taken place, and the other, more important one, was against the theatre owner and his sales staff. The moment the student group heard about the second case, the entire tension eased out.

I was summoned to depose at the local court. My cross-examination started with the question: 'Who gave you the information about the hidden tickets?' I objected to this question because it was privileged communication. The judge understood the legality, but the defence lawyer kept insisting on an answer. I jokingly said that a bird flying past dropped a piece of paper with this information. There was laughter in the court, but the lawyer again insisted on the name of the source. I then requested the court to kindly record my answer this time before moving further. A sudden silence descended in the courtroom. I said, 'Aap hi hamare source the (You only were my source).' The judge smiled and the lawyer decided to move ahead.

The background of the riot is more important than the riot itself. Unfortunately, the subordinate policemen get overwhelmed by the grotesque presentation of the riots. It is akin to losing the feel of a forest for a tree. A superior police officer is not superior because of the stars on his shoulders but because of superior skills that get sharpened through rigorous training in policing.

Interestingly, for the first time, I happened to handle a case connected to one of the most respected professions in society, the medical practice. In fact, it was a case to which I got formally invited. 'Sir, I want to retire peacefully,' this was a request made by a surgeon of the referral hospital of Rajmahal town situated in my jurisdiction. He told me that he was the store in-charge of the hospital from where a lot of things were wrongfully being taken away by the hospital employees. He, therefore, wanted a case to be registered against this. I asked him to keep his written information ready and hand it over to me when I came to the Rajmahal Police Station on the day of his retirement.

The farewell ceremony was on when I got his written petition. I ordered for a case to be registered and immediate searches to be conducted to recover the embezzled items. The order was executed without any delay. The farewell party turned into a scary chaos. When the employees found that all this was happening because of a petition filed by the surgeon himself, they complained that most of the surgical equipment was indeed taken by him for his private clinic. I told the SHO to search the premises of the informant too. A huge number of surgical equipment belonging to the hospital were recovered.

The informant was arrested, while the other employees quietly slipped away. Unfortunately, the surgeon had to put up in jail for a week. He couldn't obviously retire in peace!

In only five months of my stay in Sahibganj, I had become a pariah for the so-called powerful people of that area. I observed that such people would avoid me in social gatherings and not even meet me in my office. I had a pleasant dispensation in interpersonal communication but perhaps my unconventional policing made them uncomfortable.

On one occasion, in a way-off place in the district, I was lying down for an afternoon nap in a room of a government rest house that had only two rooms. The caretaker came in to tell me that the local MP had come and was looking for a room too. When he was allotted the other room, he wanted to know who was the other guest in the rest house. As soon as he learnt it was me, he lost no time getting into his car and leaving the place. The caretaker narrated this story to me with a smile on his face. I never got the privilege of meeting the MP before or after this.

The 'less important' people though, like the poor, the labourers and similar groups, would throng my residence and office. I realized how important even my small gestures were, right from my initial days in the district, which went a long way in earning their trust and confidence.

∞

Morning shows the day

Sahibganj is located on the bank of the Ganges. On the opposite bank runs a huge ravine, a diyara[4], which is a haven

---

[4] A basin that gets created between two or more rivers or in the middle of the same river due to deposition of sand over a long period of time.

for criminals. These criminals would occasionally descend on the town and cause mayhem.

Immediately after my joining, on a chilly winter evening, I decided to raid their den. I requested the owner of a private steamer service that ferried people to the other side of the river to ferry us later in the night at around 10. I led the team as their SP, and it took us about 45 minutes to cross the river. When we got there, we saw a huge area full of sand dunes. Chilly winds were blowing across the open field, making it colder. We started walking to warm ourselves up, but it wasn't enough.

We continued till around 2 a.m., and by this time, we were shivering. We had seen a few uninhabited small huts sporadically strewn all over on the way. We decided to light a few huts for the much-needed warmth. But alas, the fire would extinguish too soon since the huts were made out of straw.

Acknowledging that discretion is the better part of valour, we decided to return empty-handed. On our way back, the constables found a few horses, perhaps belonging to the criminals. They caught hold of these horses to be taken along with us. By the time we reached the spot from where we could board the ferry, it was around 6 a.m.

When we reached Sahibganj, we saw that the morning passengers for the ferry were waiting for the steamer. They were amazed to see us coming from the diyara after a night raid. Word had spread. People of Sahibganj assembled on the bank to witness the sight. Such raids, I believe, raised the confidence of the people in the police.

※

General mass recruitment of constables was being held in the Dumka range. All the SPs were members of the board, while the Range DIG was its chairman. The process was conducted impeccably on the ground over three days. It was a pleasant experience for me to be a part of it through the long jump component of the gamut.

Each evening, all papers of the day would be collected and kept with the chairman. At the end of the activity, the chairman announced that he would summon us for a meeting in which candidates would be selected on the basis of their performance. He casually asked us if we had our candidates too. I found that out of the four of us, three already had a list of names in their minds. When my turn came, I requested the DIG to declare the result in a fair manner. However, the DIG told me that he had already received a list from the police headquarters. I chose to keep quiet at that time.

The next evening, when I was working in my residential office, a constable came from the DIG office and handed me a big envelope. It contained the final list of the selected candidates who had to be appointed by me in the Sahibganj district police force. There and then, I sent my reply through the constable, saying that no meeting had been held to decide on this list, and I had not participated in the paperwork either. I, therefore, would not be able to appoint these so-called selected persons. I even marked a copy to the Zonal IG.

The next day, the Zonal IG shot off an order and put the process on hold. It continued to be on hold for a few months till it was finally cancelled. When it comes to probity in public life, hierarchy begins to lose its importance. Commands are acceptable only as long as they are within their Lakshman rekha[5].

The biggest weapons to earn trust are being honest, having the right intentions and being transparent in your dealings. This applies to all interactions we have.

---

[5] Figuratively refers to a boundary drawn to define certain limits or rules which are never to be broken

Trust and respect need to be earned

'Constable. Halt. Salute.' These were the words of sergeant major of Sahibganj. As a part of my regular routine, I was inspecting the Police Lines, which I would do twice a week, to look after the logistical issues involving human resources, vehicles, arms and the like. During these inspections, the sergeant major would raise all matters to the SP for his addressal.

When this command was given, I was in the orderly room where all matters of discipline relating to constables are raised. This constable who was brought before me was an absconder for the past three years. He chose to reappear in the Police Lines on this very day. He was an Adivasi and belonged to a neighbouring district of Santhal Pargana. I could see that he was terrified and was almost trembling with fear.

When I saw his condition, I asked him to 'stand at ease', quite against the norms of an orderly room. I wanted to make him comfortable and calm his fears so that I could get to the truth. He told me that his wife was ill, and therefore, he had gone home to look after her. He had sought approval from the authorities for this but never got one. So, he was left with no option but to disappear without informing. I then enquired about his wife's illness and whether it had been taken care of. He assured me that everything was fine now, and that is why he was back here to rejoin.

'What about the salary for the last three years?' I asked. Without thinking for even a moment, he replied, 'Since I have not functioned in that period, I cannot claim salary for it.'

I took my decision and wrote my order saying that he didn't need to be punished because he told me the truth and had been fair. Most of the constables, in such situations, cook up all sorts of excuses and fight it out in a departmental proceeding, maybe even in a court.

When I look back now, I know that there could be many technical faults in that order, but its spirit was the relationship between an SP and his men who look up to him as the head of the family. I, as the SP, should take care of them both in times of crisis as well as happiness. I still feel that today, this order will be thrown out of the window by a senior inspecting officer, but in those days, I thought I had earned the respect of the constabulary by doling out natural justice to them.

All the departments in the district, whether state or central, were feeling the heat of the way they were being policed. On the borders of Sahibganj lay the Malda district of West Bengal. An MP from this place was a powerful minister in the central Cabinet. My actions were hurting his financial interests, so I was told just a few days before my transfer.

Perhaps some people decided that it was time for me to receive my transfer order. I got my central deputation to the Intelligence Bureau (IB) as its joint assistant director. This was quite surprising, as I had put in less than six years in IPS and had not applied for or tried to get this deputation. As soon as this news spread, the common people of the district rose in a movement against it. Dharna, procession, roadblock, rail roko[6], trainloads of people going to Patna to protest and whatnot. All of this went on for three days.

Rewards of honesty

A district that was considered to be too placid for policing remained in turmoil during my short tenure as its SP. I had undoubtedly created problems for the police.

---

[6]Stopping of trains

It did not take time for the state government to transfer me out of the district because neither the politicians nor the civil administration liked my style of working. It did not matter to me in any case. When I received my transfer order, there was a huge uproar. The labourers who worked on the crusher machines in the mines organized themselves and started creating so-called law and order problems. They blocked all roads, including the heavy rail traffic at Sahibganj and Taljhaari in the district. This obviously meant huge problems for the state administration.

Looking at the severity of the issue, the state government ordered the SP from a neighbouring district, Dumka, to temporarily take over charge from me. My transfer was done in such a hurry that even though my successor hadn't been identified, I was ordered to leave the district immediately. The divisional commissioner of Dumka, an illustrious IAS officer, J.M. Lyngdoh, was asked to supervise the handing over, ensuring that it was done peacefully.

He came down on the appointed day to Sahibganj, camped at the Circuit House and sent word for me. I went there during lunchtime and paid my respects to him. He asked me politely, 'Have you eaten?' I said, 'No.' He immediately ordered for his homemade lunch that he had carried with him from Dumka. While we had our food, he discussed the whole issue with me, and I, too, explained everything to him forthrightly. He listened to every word of mine quietly and intently. In the end, he said, 'Look, I have been following your activities all through these five months, and I must tell you that I endorse every action of yours, mainly on two counts. One, they are all legally correct; and two, they help the people who have been hurt by law and who do not have the means to defend themselves.'

Coming from a person who I respected immensely, these words were a treasure for me. I respected him not for his post but for his impeccable integrity. Salute to such officers, the likes of whom come on to the stage rarely.

⸺

On the day I was to hand over my charge, I got information that a subedar in the Police Lines had committed suicide by hanging himself from the ceiling fan. I rushed to his room where this had happened. I had known him as an honest, professional and competent policeman. I started to look for a suicide note. I instead found a petition written by him, which was addressed to me. He wanted me to get an enquiry conducted.

He was in charge of government cash, which he kept in a locked box in the armoury of the Police Lines. While he was away for a few days, some other officer had been given this charge. Upon his return, when he checked the armoury, he was quite disturbed to see that the total cash was less than what he had left. He suspected that the other officer had done something wrong. I asked the SHO to search the house of this officer. The SHO was able to recover large investment papers and cash. I couldn't follow up on the case, but what I heard as rumours made for a sordid tale.

The subedar had also written a suicide note that read: 'Sir, nobody will believe that I am not a thief. Only you could have found out the truth. I have heard that you are going away today. I have no option left.' I handed over my charge and saluted the departed soul. The only consolation I had was that at least I could redeem his integrity.

Sahibganj was a brief stay, yet it taught me many lessons. The foremost was that money is the most powerful force in the world. Anyone who tries to ignore it or go against it will do so at his peril. People who had accumulated tons of money through looting the government exchequer and the rights of poor labourers quietly organized my central deputation. I realized that stepping on the toes of gangsters was not a big deal but hurting the money bags of rich people, the white-collared clan, is many times more potent.

My deputation to the IB finally got changed to the CBI. The CBI director posted me to the Patna branch. Bihar government intervened quite strongly, saying that I could be posted anywhere but Patna. Someone close to the powers that be told me that my style of functioning, as seen in Sahibganj, had alerted everyone in the Bihar government. I finally got posted as SP CBI, Ranchi, in August 1984.

THE WORLD WILL NOT BE DESTROYED BY THOSE WHO DO EVIL

The world will not be destroyed by those who do evil, but by those who watch them without doing anything.

—Albert Einstein

SP CBI, Ranchi
(14 August 1984 to 14 August 1988)

My tenure in the Ranchi branch of the CBI lasted precisely for four years. It began with nostalgia. 2 Booty Road, Ranchi, was an address I had heard and written numerous times as a young schoolboy. My father was the first SP of this branch. I was back in the same house as an SP this time, but a part of me would always see this place with childhood fondness.

This building used to be the summer residence of a Cabinet minister in yesteryears when the state capital of Bihar would shift to Ranchi in the summer months. My father had procured it for the CBI through his own efforts. It was a double-storeyed massive building facing the Morabadi ground, surrounded by the Tagore Hill, just opposite the residence of the deputy commissioner. The first floor was the residence of the SP, while the ground floor served as the office. In its sprawling campus, it had quarters for the staff as well. There couldn't be a better location for a CBI branch.

The joint director (JD), who once came visiting for an inspection during my tenure, commented that it was the best building and the best location that a CBI office had in the whole country.

Memories kept pleasantly visiting me throughout my stay here. A few people who had worked in my father's office were still there, making me feel at home once again.

Innocence that did not get lost with time

A foot constable of the SP CBI, Ranchi office was looted by the wayside while returning from his village. He came back to the office and filed a petition saying that his CBI identity card was also taken away by the miscreants in the loot and he would need a new one.

During my previous stay in this office as a child, I had become friends with a clerk named Kariya Munda, who worked in my father's office. I would quietly get into his room and try my hand at his archaic typewriter. He would happily teach me too.

Today, he was the head clerk. I marked that petition to him for the issuance of a new identity card. This petition was promptly put up in a file to me with a note from Kariya Munda quoting a rule from the CBI Manual. According to this rule, the constable would need to pay a fine of ₹10 for having lost his identity card and only then a new one could be issued. When I read that note, I was alone in my office room. I had a hearty laugh to myself. I wrote a reply and sent back the file to him, 'I have still to come across a rule which envisages a fine for having been robbed.' He came to me with a grim face, questioning me about what I had written on the file. I tried to explain that these fines are collected from people who lose their identity cards due to negligence. But this case is different, and therefore, the new card should be issued without any fine.

I got to know that when he went back to his room, he was mumbling to his colleagues, 'This SP used to learn typewriting from me when he was a child, and now he writes such orders to me.' His innocence brought a smile to my face.

⁂

I had joined on the eve of the Independence Day. I picked a case file from the office to read at home at leisure the next day, with the intent of understanding how investigations are carried out in the CBI. Before joining, I had approached my father to initiate me into the legal aspects of the functioning of this organization but was shown the door with a suggestion to ask this question to some prosecutor who would have served in the CBI in the past.

I knew I was on my own. I started reading the history of the organization and read the Delhi Special Police Establishment (DSPE) Act to brace myself for the challenges ahead. On my first day in office, I called three prosecutors for a discussion on the case file that I had carried home to read. The issue was regarding a fake leave travel concession (LTC) claim made by a Coal India officer for his children, who were attending school while he was on his tour without them. I thought this was an open-and-shut case with straightforward evidence. When I expressed this view, the prosecutors started arguing as defence lawyers. This came as a shock to me because I was trained in a system wherein arguing in favour of the accused was considered no less than blasphemy. It took me a lot of effort to appreciate that investigation should always be done with all possible defence in mind. The requirement of law for conviction in a trial is 'beyond all reasonable doubts'. They rightly pointed out that till I have doubts in my mind, evidence cannot measure up to the standard of 'beyond doubt'. I got two volumes of C.D. Field's *Commentary on Law of Evidence* and kept them with me. Those books were my companions all through my tenure in the CBI.

I was being prepared for a steep learning curve that I had to traverse in the coming four years.

Within a week of joining, I got orders from the CBI HO to report for a week-long formal induction programme. As a part of it, I attended a talk by the CBI director, in his office. His name was J.S. Bawa, and he belonged to the Punjab cadre. His talk was one of the most enlightening talks, one which I can never forget for its simplicity and maturity. After welcoming us, he told us that he did not intend to teach investigation since that was our core business. He instead was there to tell us how we should conduct ourselves in the CBI and to familiarize us with its culture.

He laid down some golden rules. He said, 'As a district SP, if I drive in my official vehicle with my wife to go to a party, I will not be held at fault by the people of the district, but I cannot do the same in the CBI. Here, I should use the official vehicle only for official purposes and never with a family member. As a district SP, it is acceptable to the people around me if my official staff helps me in my household chores, but not in the CBI.'

'A district SP could come to office at a chosen time and work at irregular hours, but CBI has fixed working hours, which should be adhered to. A district SP tends to double up official visits with personal obligations; no one raises an eyebrow. This should never be done in the CBI.' Finally, he said that we should avoid regular visitors to either our office or residence. He wrapped up the talk, wished us well while reminding us that officers will come and go, but the essence of the CBI must remain intact.

What great thoughts! There was nothing big or fancy about his talk, but the strength in his simple statements was phenomenal. It is perhaps the failure of this organization in following these simple rules that has landed it into the controversies that we see today. It takes time to absorb and inherit a culture. Unfortunately, many officers get injected at the top of the hierarchy in this organization and end up bringing with them all the ills of the state police.

I had started to see the differences between working with the state police and with the CBI. There were occasions where I could see these differences starkly, and there were incidents that naturally made me cognizant of the decorum of the CBI.

Perception matters

The telephone bell rang. The deputy commissioner of Ranchi was on the other side. He told me that the Bihar CM was camping in the guest house of Metallurgical & Engineering Consultants Limited (MECON) and wanted to meet me as early as possible. It was 7 a.m., and I told him that I could make it to the guest house in about an hour's time. He expressed urgency as the CM was waiting to meet me before taking the Bihar government aircraft back to Patna. I got ready as fast as I could and reached the guest house. I was ushered into his room immediately. This was my first meeting with Bhagwat Jha Azad.

He offered me a seat and came straight to the point. Quite crisply, he said that there was a lot of corruption in the agencies of the Bihar government, which included forest, mines and developmental activities in the Adivasi areas. He was quite upset about it and asked me if, for the Chota Nagpur area of Bihar, I was prepared to register cases of corruption, which he wanted to refer to me as SP CBI, Ranchi.

I could understand that he was not aware of the process through which matters could be sent to the CBI. I told him that it'd be better if he referred the whole thing to the central government, which would, in turn, send it to the CBI HO. If the CBI director wanted the case to be investigated by the Ranchi unit, I would begin it in right earnest and carry out the investigation thoroughly.

Looking at his grim face, I put up a proposal: 'Sir, why

don't you move your best SPs to the vigilance department and get these cases investigated under their leadership? The laws that govern the functioning of the CBI do not empower it to have more powers than the state police.' He promptly asked me to suggest the names of such SPs. As soon as I made a recommendation, he retorted, '*Ye sabhi bahut hi imaandar aur achche padadhikaari hain. Inki samasya hai ki ye ek achchi neeyat se kisi kaam ko shuru karte hain par us kaam ko anjaam nahi de paate hain. Kuchh anya samasyaayen bhi khadi kar dete hain* (These are honest officers. Their problem is that they begin their work with good intentions but are not able to complete it. They end up creating a few new problems instead).'

I did not have anything more to offer, so I paid my respects to him and left the room. His last statement kept ringing in my ears and made me understand how mature politicians viewed well-meaning and well-intentioned honest police officers.

I learned a few technical nuances in the first few months at the CBI. One of them was FIRs based on source information report (SIR). In most corruption cases, nobody comes forward to lodge an FIR. The CBI had devised a method of developing source information through a discreet enquiry done in complete secrecy within the organization. In fact, it is so secret that the IO would not disclose or discuss anything even with his colleagues, but only with the SP, and that too in complete exclusivity.

From this information, a regular case (RC), which is essentially an FIR, can be registered. This is where I noticed ingenuity. Unlike an FIR, there is no informant for an RC. The informant gets mentioned as 'sourced through' some named inspector. This makes the inspector a channel through which the information is being passed without disclosing the name of the source itself. The CBI had devised a brilliant legal subterfuge in law using provisions of the Indian Evidence Act, 1872, and the CrPC. This methodology was absolutely new for me.

My stay at Ranchi was mentally quite invigorating. I was able to see and feel many new dimensions of policing. My mind kept throwing ideas in spurts, ideas the department would have never imagined.

Marketing the police

Early in the morning one day, an ad in the daily newspaper caught my attention. It was about admission to a part-time course in management at the renowned college BIT Mesra. The eligibility criterion was simple: undergraduate who has been employed or is under self-employment. The admission process involved a written test followed by an interview. I suddenly felt the drive to apply for it. I had always felt dissatisfied that my journey in academics had stopped at graduation. This was a great chance to fulfil that incomplete desire.

I obtained the required permission from the CBI HO and appeared for the written test following Sunday. Soon I got a letter saying that I had qualified for the interview.

The chairman of the interview board was the chairman of CCL, with whom I had had various interactions professionally. When he saw me entering the board room, he was perplexed and asked me what I was doing there. I told him that I was a candidate appearing for this interview. He shot his first question in a serious tone, 'In this three-year course, what would you choose as your specialization?' I was prepared for this question. I answered, 'Marketing.' He perhaps did not expect this answer at all. He said, 'Being in the police, what will you do with Marketing? You should go for personnel management.' I said, 'I have been intrigued by the word "service" in "IPS". I have read many books on marketing, especially those written by Philip Kotler, who is supposed to be a leader in this field. The essence of his writings suggests that the principles of marketing are the same whether applied to goods or services. I would like to study and find out whether these principles can be applied equally to police as a service.'

That was the end of my interview. He did not ask any further questions. I was selected for that course.

∽∞∽

I always wanted to see how CBI raids are conducted. The first opportunity I got was in a case relating to a place called Ghatshila. I observed that the legal formalities before the raid were carried out strictly, to the letter, as laid out in CrPC. I compared this to the raids we conducted in the state police and felt that the way we worked there, it appeared as if CrPC did not exist at all.

I got really interested in witnessing the operation myself and went along with the raiding team. It started early in the morning when the inmates of the house were just about to wake up. A cordon was laid to observe anything unusual. When the main gate was opened, no one rushed in like in the state police operations. The IO briefed the house owner about the purpose of the visit and presented a copy of the FIR and the search warrant. It took a few minutes for the house owner to realize the gravity of the situation, whereafter he succumbed to it and allowed the process to proceed. The CBI team was extremely calm and natural during the entire search operation. This appeared to be similar to the way doctors in big hospitals brief patients before any major intervention.

The entire process was carried out so professionally and with such poise; the team had even carried extra food packets for the inmates of the house, considerate of the fact that during the search, they would not be able to fix any food for themselves.

∽∞∽

Knowledge and integrity make an invincible team

I had developed a long association with three very smart and inquisitive officers in the Income Tax Department who were of similar seniority. I learnt a lot from them about how their department conducted searches and verified information. I found that their systems of enquiry were also instructive, and I could apply my learnings in the CBI, even after that.

I recall one such case about a particular public-sector bank in a place called Ramgarh in the Hazaribagh district of Bihar. We received information that black money, belonging to people who did business in coal, was being stacked in this bank. The Income Tax Department drove down to conduct a search of the bank premises. I decided to unofficially be a part of it.

During the search, one of the officers was going through the bank locker register. I was observing him, and I saw his finger stop at a particular locker number. This locker had not been allotted to anyone. He asked the branch manager to produce both the keys of the locker. The branch manager started trembling and weeping, as he did not have the keys. Enquiry began. It finally transpired that this locker was unofficially allotted to a particular businessman of Ramgarh, and both the keys were in his custody. The branch manager was ordered to call the businessman to the bank with the keys. This person came, and the locker was opened. I was really surprised to see that the only thing in the locker was about 100 passbooks of the same bank in various fake names. The Income Tax Department had unearthed huge black money in the bank itself. They went ahead to conduct a search in his house, post which they were able to register a serious case against him.

After the searches were over, I asked that officer how could he sense that he should be questioning that particular locker? His answer was, 'My gut feeling and a lot of intuition.' I felt that such feelings can only come to people with honest intentions and who are sincere towards their work. Sincerity and integrity are essential catalysts that can lead to much better results than just logic and knowledge.

⚜

The CBI used to be quite particular about delays in the investigation of cases. It was not tolerated and was questioned severely. A particular case was getting delayed, and the CBI HO started cracking down on the branch. I started pursuing the IO, who happened to be an old warhorse, thoroughly demotivated and indifferent. I warned him that if he didn't complete the investigation, I would take over. He seemed unmoved, so I ended up writing case diaries as the IO and, in the process, learnt the smallest nuances of the process. I completed the investigation and filed the charge sheet too.

When the HO came to know of this, they didn't seem to be happy about what I had done. However, I felt satisfied that I had earned tremendous respect in the eyes of the IOs of the branch.

Secrecy is another prime work ethic in the CBI. Usually, a vigilance officer is appointed to liaise between the CBI and the organization where the CBI is investigating. When I used to develop information against the top functionaries of such organizations, I would use my own very unconventional methods. As a result, even the chief vigilance officer (CVO) would not know anything before the searches were conducted. Once a very senior IPS officer was working as the CVO of a very big organization where I was supposed to check corruption. I applied my own style, and the chairman cum managing director (MD) of the organization was not happy that his CVO was not even made aware of anything, especially considering that the SP was so much junior to him.

The JD, who happened to be the batchmate of the CVO, came in for inspection. The CVO had invited him over lunch.

The JD asked me to join him for an evening stroll later that day. During our stroll, he asked me whether I take the CVO into confidence while developing information in a case. I could sense that my behaviour had been discussed over lunch. I answered, 'No, sir, such things are only between the concerned IO and me.' He did not probe further. The management of the organization kept wondering as to how I could gather official details of their officers without any such correspondences.

The Bokaro Steel Plant came under the jurisdiction of CBI Ranchi. I used to frequent the campus with my team for multiple corruption-related issues.

A good leader never deserts his team

Once I had visited Bokaro for a lengthy meeting with the MD of the steel plant. At the end of this meeting, the MD graciously asked me how I was returning to Ranchi. I told him that my usual mode of transport was the train, which took about two hours to travel and I found it quite convenient. On hearing this, he said that an aircraft of the Bokaro Steel Plant would be ferrying him to Ranchi for a meeting the next day. He offered me a ride.

I politely refused by saying that I had travelled to Bokaro with my inspector and the foot constable. I would not like to go with him alone and would much prefer to be with my team. The MD quipped back, saying that there was enough room for all of us, and therefore, I must accept his offer. I couldn't say no to this. The next day, all three of us enjoyed a free ride from Bokaro to Ranchi in his aircraft.

In the huge campus of Bokaro Steel Plant was a mountain of slag, dumped after the operation of steelmaking, which was treated as waste. New technology was emerging for the production of cement from slag. The management of the steel plant used to tender and award a contract for clearing the slag dump but was not getting any notable amount for it.

This caught my attention. To get to the root of the problem, I camped in Bokaro for a week. I would go through the thick tender file at night and then visit the site for an entire day to observe the process. I saw that in some of the ladles brought from the blast furnace after separating molten metal, the lower portion looked bright red. This didn't seem right because the temperature of slag is much lower than molten metal. I immediately understood what was happening. A few people in the blast furnace were informing the contractor once certain ladles got dumped. The contractor would leave the slag and pick the metal from the dump. The size of the slag dump kept increasing while the contractor kept getting richer by selling metal. I calculated the value of this metal that was getting dumped with slag. This amount, in those times, went up to ₹10 crore, a direct loss to the Bokaro Steel Plant.

I discussed this with the MD of the plant as an issue of corruption. To my shock, the top men felt that the amount was too small in their scheme of things. Out of irritation, I asked the MD, 'What is the amount you would earn in your job?' He immediately conceded. The minimum amount to be paid by the contractor was raised ten times.

This was not the only division of the plant where corruption was happening in broad daylight.

English words help in corruption

Year 1986. A source told me that there was a bungling of almost ₹50 lakh in a particular project in the oxygen plant of the Bokaro Steel Plant. I requisitioned the file of that project for study to understand where the bungling had happened.

It was such a voluminous file that even after reading through it completely, I, unfortunately, could not understand much. So I decided to have a look at the plant itself in the hope that it would help me understand the content of the file.

I went around the huge plant. There were eight cylindrical containers that were as high as six-storeyed buildings, webbed with all types of pipes and connections, making the entire set-up look really complicated. I drew a schematic diagram of the plant so that I could filter the grain from the chaff and gain some insight into the issue. After doing this, I read through the whole file again, made my notes and observed that two words were used throughout the file, which seemed important from the vigilance point of view of the case. The two words were 'dismantling' and 're-erection'. The eight cylinders had to be dismantled and then a new set of eight cylinders brought from the USSR had to be re-erected at their place.

This contract was given to a firm with free logistical support by the Bokaro Steel Plant management. The job had been completed, but my source kept insisting that it cost less than ₹5 lakh as against the ₹50 lakh payment that was made. I was still at a loss to find the source of the corruption he was talking about.

I sought help from a few senior officers of a PSU called MECON in Ranchi, gave them the file and requested them to help me understand the whole issue. They came back saying that they could not identify anything wrong in this project. The tenders were properly floated, the job was properly allotted and the rates were correctly set.

I was almost convinced that I was chasing the wrong horse. I drew up the schematic diagram and tried to apply my mind to it afresh, maybe for the last time. I suddenly had my eureka moment. In a flash, it came to me that the words 'dismantling' and 're-erection' were not the exact words to be used in this project. The work that had actually been done was that of 'removal' and 'replacement'. The huge steel cylinders had started malfunctioning, and therefore, had to be removed from their places and thrown as waste. In place of these, the new ones from the USSR had to be put up with the help of huge cranes that Bokaro Steel Plant was providing free of cost.

I could then also connect how my source, who, although could not lay his finger on where the corruption had taken place, knew that the firm that was allotted the contract had been heavily favoured. I got the case registered in the CBI Ranchi branch. The use of two English words had created such a huge loss to the Bokaro Steel Plant. The case proved to be even costlier when the MD was transferred to another steel plant of the Steel Authority of India Limited (SAIL). The departmental enquiry initiated by the CBI ended in his nemesis, as he could not reach the highest post in the organization. Had it not been for those two English words, he would have been the head of SAIL.

∞

Similar cases appeared in the other PSUs of the state as well. One major focus area, which was also given to me as a mandate, was related to the corruption activities in the CCL.

∞

Arresting money in place of criminals

While investigating cases in CCL, I could gather that right from production to storage to the sale of coal, which was and is even today nationalized, all stages were riddled with corruption. I would register straightforward cases to the extent of 10 tonnes, maybe 15 tonnes of industrial coal that was being used by the consumers on a 'bought by them' basis from the CCL. I thought that I was heading in the right direction, but soon, I realized that these were fringe cases; the major activity was happening somewhere else, the malaise I had not identified as yet.

I realized that a huge amount of black money was being invested from the marketing division of the CCL in the purchase of coal. There were cartels functioning, who bribed the CCL officers, and the amount of the bribe used to be enormous. I had to bust this racket.

CCL used to release regular notifications every two months for the sale of coal produced at hundreds of its pitheads. This coal would be dumped at the pithead after production, and the marketing division would put it up for sale. People would apply for purchase, deposit money and lift the coal. I patiently waited for the next sale notification.

As soon as it came, I contacted my three friends from the Income Tax Department. I requested them to freeze, under the Income Tax Act, the money that had been deposited by the cartels for coal purchase. I had to take their help, as I had the power to arrest criminals but not their black money.

They obliged and issued a notice to that effect to the marketing division of the CCL. This, therefore, implied that no coal should be released against that money from that pithead. This created a huge upheaval. It was a sight to behold when the people who had deposited money to purchase coal from the other pitheads started applying for withdrawal of their money in panic. They were scared that their money, too, would be brought under the ambit of the Income Tax Department. This run for money went on for a couple of days. The enquiry of the department started.

We found that the address of the people who were depositing the money was so vague that nobody could locate them. It became quite easy for the Income Tax Department to conclude that this money was not traceable, and therefore, was unclaimed. Formal processes after the enquiry were carried out, and finally, without a single house search, back in 1987, an amount of ₹3 crore could be seized by the Income Tax Department to be deposited with the central government exchequer.

I felt this was such a simple yet effective way to mop up as much black money as there is, that too without conducting any house search or arrest. No wonder this activity was chosen as one of the 10 best operations of the Income Tax Department for that year.

꼬꼬

'Asset disproportionate to known sources of income,'—a phrase I had been taught at the National Police Academy but never understood its import till I faced one such case after coming to the CBI. I was convinced that if there is one allegation on corruption that is most objective, it is this. Even in cases that are caught red-handed, there are chances of subjectivity or bias, but in disproportionate assets (DA) cases, there is absolutely no shades of grey.

I tried to develop my skills in such cases, almost to the same level as the brilliant IOs, mainly due to two reasons—it was the most straightforward evidence of corruption, and the top echelons could be pinned down only in DA matters. I was fortunate that early in my sojourn in the CBI, I met a DIG who had worked under my father as a DSP. He was known for his prowess in investigative skills. I happened to meet him in the induction course. When he came to know that I was his senior's son, he took special care of me and gave me extremely precious tips. I admit that most of what I did in police life had a stamp of those tips. He had prepared a booklet that he had kept for himself exclusively. I was overwhelmed with gratitude when he gave it to me as a special gift.

The CBI had a team of auditors who used to help in analysing the seized bank accounts during these searches. One such team came to visit my branch to help me in a DA case. When I came to know of this, I knew this was a learning opportunity. I spent three days continuously with them, following their every step inquisitively to understand exactly how they went about things. By the end of the three-day-long session, I had learned the art of reading a bank account statement to the extent that by merely reading one of a government servant, I could accurately tell his personality characteristics.

On one such occasion, my team had just entered the house of a senior CCL officer to begin a search operation. I was parked in my vehicle outside. It appeared as though only the officer's wife was present at the house. As per the drill, the team had to get the keys to the locker first and foremost. The lady kept denying the presence of any locker. Collection of documents from the various rooms had started, but the locker key was still elusive. An officer from the raiding team came out to meet me in my car outside and told me about the situation. I asked him to scan through the bank passbook and look for entries under 'deduction for locker rent'. It would guide them to the locker and the bank from where they could seal it.

He went back inside and told the lady how he could easily find out the location of every locker and get them sealed. She broke down and brought out the key from the safest place in the female anatomy. I was well aware of this practice, thanks to the man who taught me so many skills that even the skilled and experienced IOs in the CBI didn't know of. This skill even helped a batchmate of mine in the State Vigilance who was facing an issue of unearthing too many keys during his search operations.

In another episode, I was leading a house search of a senior Bharat Coking Coal Limited (BCCL) officer. My team started collecting documents. I took all the cheque books, both used and unused, and started studying them. I made a list of Life Insurance Corporation (LIC) of India policy numbers from the counterfoils of the used cheque books. I could find eight of them. At the end of the search, when I asked for all the LIC documents, he could only produce three. After a bit of haggling, he conceded that the rest were with his chartered accountant (CA), who was preparing his income tax return (ITR). We went to his CA and managed to get many of his asset documents, which we would have surely missed otherwise.

Midway through my tenure in the CBI, I was taking care of about six DA cases against very senior officers, mostly belonging to the CCL. It suddenly struck me that these officers were getting a salary from their company and fighting out their cases against the State. This did not seem right to me. Article 311 of the Constitution could not protect them, as they were only public servants and not government servants. I fixed up a meeting with the chairman of Coal India at Calcutta to discuss this.

୰ଉଚ

Would you pay someone to cheat you?

Investigation of DA cases is a lengthy process and takes a long time. I spoke to the CCL chairman cum MD and convinced him that such officers who had serious DA cases against them should first be terminated from service and then fight their case in court. Legal provisions were examined for this proposal, and it was finally implemented. The chairman gave them a three-month severance salary and asked them to quit the service. These officers, ultimately, fought it out till the Supreme Court but couldn't succeed.

This sent serious shock waves amongst officers, not only in CCL but almost every other organization that I was looking into.

I applied this concept again in the Bihar government, but this time, the flavour of the law was slightly different. The officers of the government are expected to file their property returns every year. I prepared a chart of the properties that were recovered after house searches in DA cases and compared it with the property return shown by the officers. I was not surprised to find huge discrepancies in the two sets of data. This was reason enough for me to start departmental proceedings for concealing information from the government. Every department was asked to complete the proceeding against their officers promptly and punish them suitably. With the kind of charges, most of the disciplinary authorities considered it fit to dismiss them. Even before the officers got convicted, they were departmentally dismissed so that the delinquents had to fight out their cases on their own.

∞

The offence of possessing disproportionate assets doesn't find a mention of expenditure and likely savings. Yet, the CBI uses these additional constructs to prove the charge. I have posed this question to many CBI officers, right from my days at Ranchi till today, right from competent IOs to the very senior supervisory officers, but could not elicit a proper reply.

I tried to figure out my own answer. In my opinion, all items that we called expenditure are essentially evidence of intangible assets like receipts, etc., which cannot not be recovered physically. So instead of calling them expenditure, we should call them intangible assets. This will plug all holes in the process.

Similarly, there is another construct called 'check period' that the CBI uses in investigating DA cases. This refers to the time period starting from the date of entry into a job to the date of search. Obviously, this period is too long and makes the investigation cumbersome. I could relate this to the concept of average velocity vs instantaneous velocity in physics. I started shortening the check period in those cases where IOs would recommend a case closure in the absence of a reasonable disproportion. A table of asset growth with time was the best way to decide the length of the check period.

In one case, I had investigated just one big asset, which was more momentary than over a time period. I used the Indian Evidence Act, where the onus of proving a charge against an accused lies with the prosecution, and was able to pin down the accused squarely. I feel that instead of just blindly following the traditional ways of investigation, senior officers should create innovative ways that will show the way to the future generation of CBI officers.

DA cases were only a manifestation of the widespread corruption among the upper rungs of society. The extent to which this infection had spread across both public and government servants was horrendous. It was an easy play for any coloured-collar criminal to bribe his way through crime. This was such an open secret that one did not hesitate in using it as and when needed. I was caught unawares when I faced this situation myself.

How many zeroes are there in 1 crore?

It was like any other day at the office when a slip arrived at my desk. It had the name of an important accused who held a top position in a PSU and was about to be promoted as the head of another PSU in the Ministry of Commerce and Industry of the Government of India. Before his promotion, CBI Ranchi had filed a charge sheet against him in a corruption matter in the court of the special judge (CBI, Ranchi), thus jeopardizing his promotion. The accused had tried his best at the CBI HO through the government but couldn't escape.

He filed a case before the special judge at Ranchi, saying that the sanction was not proper, and therefore, cognisance should not be taken against him. He got top Supreme Court lawyers to argue for him, but his contention was not upheld by the special judge. Therefore, he had filed another case on the same ground as an appeal before the high court at

Ranchi. A couple of hearings had already been made, which I attended personally along with the public prosecutor of the CBI.

When I saw his name on the slip, I summoned him into my chamber and politely asked him to sit down. I waited for him to start the conversation. After a few moments of silence, he began explaining his position to me. I listened to him patiently and told him that I was aware of it all, as he had mentioned the same in his petition. I suggested that it would be worthwhile to wait for the final outcome of the matter in the high court.

He then made a proposal to me, which I had never imagined in my wildest of dreams. He said that his only request to me was that I do not come to the high court for the hearings. I did not know why he wanted this from me, but he carried on by saying that he was willing to pay me ₹1 crore in any form in return for this favour.

Throughout my career, I had never been offered anything like this, so my impulsive feeling was to get up from my chair and throw him out of the office. Sanity prevailed, and I cooled myself down. I held my breath for a while and dragged a writing pad lying on my table towards myself. I then pushed it across to him with a pencil. He looked up at me, confused. I said, 'Can you write this figure of ₹1 crore on this pad?' He promptly did so and counted the zeroes to be doubly sure.

I took the pad back, looked at him and said, 'Do you know that I see only zeroes in this figure and nothing more. You can keep adding zeroes; it will still remain a bunch of zeroes for me.' I spoke in a calm tone so that he could understand my ethos and the pain that I had undergone while doing all this. I carried on, saying that God had given him a lot of money, so he should get the best of the country's lawyers to fight out his case. If he won on firm legal grounds, I'll be the gainer because I would have learnt the niceties of law and the nuances of the issue. I advised him that there was no point in trying to waste his money like this.

He quietly got up and left the room. In the end, he lost his case in the Ranchi Bench of the Patna High Court and then lost it again in the Supreme Court. He was tried for the case and finally lost his placement as the chief of the PSU in the commerce ministry.

By now, I had started getting on the wrong side of the HO in a growing number of cases. I recalled that my father, too, had faced similar situations during his tenure as the Zone DIG. Earlier, senior officers would never try to influence an investigation. They were so experienced that they could spot gaps in both the investigation and the conclusions by the SP but would never try to manipulate them under any pressure. This was the real CBI culture. This was the essential difference between the CBI and the state police.

I was now summoned by the HO to be put through a sermonizing session by the additional director after a small session with the JD. I was advised to fall in line.

A wise man can read the sign of things to come

The CBI is a great place for officers in the rank of SP to learn proper investigation techniques. It helps young IPS officers to get trials conducted under their supervision. This is a crucial element in understanding nuances of trials, an opportunity that is missing completely in the state police. I, therefore, am extremely thankful to CBI for all this. But towards the last six months of my tenure, there were too many cases in which I had differences of opinion with the CBI HO.

A case had been registered under the Prevention of Corruption Act against a top official of a PSU headquartered at Calcutta. By the time the case was finalized, the concerned accused had been selected to head a powerful PSU in the Government of India. The CBI HO had passed the orders for submitting a charge sheet after obtaining a sanction. The officer filed an application saying that the sanction was not with the approval of the competent authority, which, according to him in his present case, should have been the president of India.

Since this was a legal debate, my contention was that it should be brought before the courts for a decision. I could sense that this differed from the opinion of the CBI HO. The matter was finally taken up by the Ranchi bench of the high court and got decided in favour of the CBI. It was further appealed in the Supreme Court, and again, the decision was the same.

There were many more cases where simple to complex differences of opinion existed between my branch and the CBI HO. I still had about three months of my tenure left when I was summoned by the CBI HO. I took a train to reach Delhi and reported to the then JD of CBI. He tried to cajole me at times, nudge me to see reason and accept certain things. I did not hesitate to put my points of view across.

On my way back to Ranchi, I gave it some serious thought and concluded that perhaps, administratively, I had reached the peak in the CBI, and further controversies may not be good for both me and the CBI. I should, therefore, call it a day, irrespective of how eager I was to continue.

Upon return, the first thing I did was to write a request to the CBI HO to relieve me on 14 August 1988, which would also mark the completion of my tenure specified in the written notification at the time of my joining. That was the end of my journey in the CBI, never to be relived. I am forever thankful to it for having taught me skills in using various aspects of law that I successfully applied to handle state police when entrusted with the mandate of taking charge of crime control in Bihar from 2005 to mid-2014. I could experiment with the law, thanks to the basics I had learnt in the CBI.

∞

I felt honoured when, even after years of leaving the CBI, my trainee officers, Mishra, Singh, Prasad and Panigrahi, would want to stay in contact with me and at times discuss technical issues too. During my tenure, I had conducted a DA operation against one top government official and had registered a case against him. I was transferred before a decision could be taken on that case. The deputy legal advisor to the CBI DIG recommended that the case be closed. The DIG felt this was faulty, called me and asked me to read the RC file and identify the fault. I was then serving as an SP in a district. I went to his office on his request, carried the RC file and read through it the whole night. The branch recommendation and that of the legal advisor were so faulty that I started wondering whether it could be intentional. A case that was extremely good for prosecution would have been closed wrongly.

While quitting the CBI, I felt that its image was not exactly what it used to be when I had joined it. When I read this RC file, my opinions slipped further. Instead of the good practices of the CBI curing the ills of state police, the bad practices of the state police had polluted the CBI.

A COG IN A GIANT MACHINE

I am only a cog in a giant machine, but a vital link in the chain; [...]
Cog on cog in the gun-machine, link on link in the chain!

—Gilbert Frankau

SRP Dhanbad
(16 August 1988 to 14 January 1989)

I joined back in my cadre and got posted as superintendent of Rail Police (SRP) Dhanbad in August 1988.

The work of the Rail Police was mostly confined to various types of property crimes—thefts or robberies or dacoities in railway stations or running trains. Once in a while, there would be cognizable crimes that could get registered at the police stations for investigation. My journey as SRP Dhanbad took off at a point that was a complete departure from my traditional ways of working.

After working in the CBI for four years and handling organized crimes and problems of Naxal-affected districts in the past, this charge felt too light to keep me mentally engaged. True to my nature, I started creating problems for myself. I thought if my jurisdiction has more length than breadth, I should be able to register all cognizable offences, from the white-collar crimes to the brown ones. People should realize that law sees each man equally. They say charity begins at home, so I started cleaning my own department first.

Corruption kills at any level

It is very well known that the ticket checking staff of the railways is prone to corruption at the lowest level. I was particularly worried because the policemen of the Rail Police had also become a part of the process. This really pained me.

One day, I decided to personally witness this at the railway stations. I took my bodyguard along with me; neither of us was dressed in our uniforms. We stood in a dark area of the platform from where we could see the activities around. We glanced upon a ticket checking staff at a distance, standing with a constable of the Rail Police, merrily collecting ₹2 from passengers who perhaps were crossing the platform without a ticket. On an impulse, I went to catch them red-handed. After apprehending them, I took them to the police station, where the ticket checking staff was handed over to the railway authorities, while I decided to departmentally proceed against my Rail Police constable.

When the departmental proceedings got underway, I decided to offer myself as a witness as I was indeed one. The accused constable cross-examined me. The proceedings were over, and the matter came to me for passing final orders. At this stage, I felt that it would not be legally right for me to pass orders for a case in which I was a witness. I would be violating the principle of 'no one can be a judge in his own case.'

I wrote to the DIG to transfer this matter to another SP. The punishment that the other SP gave to the constable was only impounding his annual increments for a few years. Considering the type of charge, I thought this was not enough. Yet, I did not escalate the matter because it would then still amount to me indirectly being a judge in my own case.

The telephone bell rang. I heard the voice of the IG (Rail Police) from the other side. He sounded very grave. Rajdhani Express from New Delhi to Howrah had just been saved from derailment due to sabotage of tracks on the Bihar side of the borders with West Bengal.

This, by all standards, was a very worrisome situation for the Rail Police. I sprung up from my chair and headed straight to the wayside railway station where this had happened. Rajdhani Express is a train that is constantly monitored by the Rail Bhawan, and any such incident stirs up every single railway official of whichever department, of whatever seniority. All of them converged to the place of the incident.

To reach this place, I had to travel the last mile on foot because it had no road connectivity. The SHO of the local Rail Police station had arrived before me and was struggling with the volley of questions of the railway officials. The poor SI was completely clueless. The railway track had been damaged, the detached fish plates along with a couple of screws were missing, and two of the screws were bent, with their screw threads mutilated.

I collected myself and tried to calm down in the midst of the noise. I was trying to make sense of what would have happened there. The gangman had noticed the condition of the tracks when he was on his routine patrol, just about 10 minutes before the train was to cross over. He panicked and ran to the nearest manual signal, shouting at the man there to light the signal red to stop the train. The derailment was averted. It was just a matter of chance that this got noticed in time, else the consequences would have been disastrous. The magnitude and the dimension of the situation the Rail Police faced had started uncovering before me.

I got into my typical investigative mode while my surrounding was still in crisis management mode. My scientific thinking had taken control. The track was damaged, but why were the fish plates and the screws missing?

I called the SHO and asked him to send a few chowkidars

to the location. I gathered them at a place away from the rail officials and briefed them to search for the missing fish plates and screws in that area. The place was filthy, and it was getting really difficult to stand there, but the gravity of the situation demanded my presence.

The chowkidars spread out to search. The chaos amongst the railway officials settled down a little when they noticed and got curious about my moves. In about 20 minutes, one chowkidar came running with a damaged fish plate in his hand. Soon another came back with a damaged screw. Both had been collected at a distance of about 200 yards from the track. I could hear the silence descending around me. I asked the SHO to properly and legally seal the fish plate and the screw and present them before the local judicial magistrate with an order to get them scientifically examined by the Bokaro Steel Plant. All of this was done very rapidly, and I reached the office of the MD of the Bokaro Steel Plant just when he was leaving for the day.

The MD knew me from my CBI days. When he saw me in an unkempt condition, he first made me comfortable. I told him about the incident and requested him to direct his metallurgical laboratory to test the exhibits so that we could get to the reason behind their damage. He opened the seal and saw the exhibits. It took him hardly 15 seconds to tell me that their condition could be explained through a gradual process of wear and tear. It was not a case of sabotage. He himself had worked in the railway part of steel plants of SAIL, so he had enough experience to make such assessments at first glance. However, at my request, he summoned the chief of the metallurgical laboratory and directed him to carry out the lab tests and submit a formal report.

The report took about a month to arrive, but it was totally worth the wait. It was a beautiful piece of scientific work that proved that the stress in these metals was over a long period of time and not impulsive, as in the case of sabotage. The case had been solved. It was gross negligence of the track maintenance division of the railways, who conveniently wanted to trade this off as a sabotage case so that the blame is shifted to the police.

If I had chosen to be swept away by the din created by the rail officials, this incident would have been reported for posterity as sabotage, and we would have ended up blaming one or the other group of terrorists.

During this period, two brief rendezvous need a mention. In the initial years of policing, I tended to get passionately involved in my work to the extent that I would become attached to the result. Some experiences awakened me to an ethos in police life and taught me that I not only needed to be professional in my job but also be conscious about not getting emotionally attached to it at a personal level. The philosophy of the Gita really applies.

Be a man before being a policeman

'Sir, please sit on my seat. I will arrange a berth for you in the meanwhile.' A stranger offered his seat to me on the North East Express when I was travelling from Delhi to Patna in 1988. I had not been able to reserve a seat, as I had to urgently travel for an important reason.

I quietly sat on his seat. This gentleman came back after 15 minutes to tell me that a berth had been arranged for me from Aligarh. I thanked him immediately but got really curious to know who he was. I asked him directly, 'You helped me so much in this hour of need, but I am really sorry I could not recognize you. Could you please introduce yourself?'

He told me that he was a businessman from Varanasi, and I had raided his house a year ago as the SP CBI, Ranchi. I suddenly remembered in a flash that this was for a case related to NTPC, where he was a contractor in one of their jobs. The raid had gone on for two consecutive days, and I had got a charge sheet submitted against him in the CBI

Court at Ranchi. This baffled me even more. I asked him, 'Why did you help me?' I was deeply touched by the reply.

He told me that he had developed a lot of respect for me because of my humane behaviour towards him and his family during the raid. What I did was my duty as a police officer, but what impressed him was that I never treated him like an accused during the entire process. Even the fact that I submitted charge sheet against him did not take away his good feeling towards me.

This incident shook me. A man's behaviour towards another man should always be humane and respectful, irrespective of their position in society. I followed this principle in all circumstances, all through my police career.

Duties should be performed without expectations

I was driving my Maruti 800 car in a forlorn colony of Bharat Coking Coal Limited (BCCL) Dhanbad, trying to locate an address. It was late in the evening, and the dim street lights were the only visible cover of safety that I could feel. On my way, in the verandah of a house, I vaguely saw a silhouette of a man. I stopped my car and shouted from the road itself, asking for his help with directions. Instead of answering, he got up from his chair and walked towards me. He mentioned a specific name and asked if I was looking for that person. I nodded my head in affirmation. He offered that if I could give him a lift in my car, he would guide me to that flat.

I was a little surprised at this gesture and curious to understand the reason behind his generosity. I beckoned to him to come and take a seat. I switched on the light inside the car, and I was even more perplexed when I saw his face no sooner than he sat by my side.

He was a senior CCL officer whose house I had raided a year ago as SP CBI, Ranchi in a DA case. This person had filed numerous petitions against me in the CBI HO. I was scared for a moment. I had no idea what this man was planning to do. There was an eerie silence in the car, with darkness all around.

He perhaps read my mind and broke the silence by introducing himself. 'Sir,' he said, 'I hold no grudge against you. What you did was your job, and you did it in the most professional and humane way. I had no defence but to keep writing against you, alleging frivolously.' He kept on justifying his side, and I could not speak a word in reply. We reached our destination. The car halted, and he got down. I thanked him profusely before he disappeared into the darkness.

∞

I kept questioning myself on the utility of my presence in my role as an SRP but failed to get a satisfactory answer. Railways is essentially a revenue-generating agency of the Government of India and a very big one at that. A realization dawned on me that if I do not contribute to this objective of the Indian Railways, perhaps I will not be able to justify my existence here.

To this end, I talked to the senior divisional commercial superintendent (Sr. DCS) of Dhanbad and offered my active involvement in the ticket-checking drive. I planned my night round of checking of police patrols along with it. He was elated at this proposal, as one of the biggest pain points for the railway officials used to be the manhandling by commoners during such drives. Getting police help always and regularly was a godsend for them. Thereafter, it became a daily affair for both the Sr. DCS and me. In the first month, the revenue through ticket purchase rose manifold. It was a matter of joy at the level of the divisional railway manager (DRM). No wonder when he learnt about my inspection trip to Daltonganj, he offered his saloon to me, which was a first such experience for me.

During one of our joint checking operations, we came

across a three-tier sleeper with all 75 seats occupied and no ticket booked. I could imagine the level of financial losses that the railways were going through. The Sr. DCS asked the coach superintendent to pay for all the 75 berths and fined him according to his rule book. This news spread like wildfire. He told me that my association with him had given teeth to his operations. Sadly, after my transfer from the post of SRP, he was shot dead during one of his rail travels.

Crimes like dacoities and robberies in running trains were taken very seriously by the state police headquarters, as it brought a bad name to the state government. I found that detecting these offences was very difficult because the place of occurrence was not stationary, and the victims of the crime were scattered all over the country, who themselves lost interest in the detection of the crime. These crimes did not hog the limelight but still created a huge impact on the overall picture.

The devil is in the details

One of the major issues that concerned the Rail Police was the baggage theft of passengers in running trains. This may not sound like a very big issue, but it was a cause of great pain to the passengers. The overall proportion of detection of such cases was very low, and the problem continued for ages.

I hit upon an idea. My assessment was that most of the time, this crime was being committed during the night by professional criminals who would sit in the coach as a co-passenger and quietly walk out with stolen baggage while the victim was sleeping.

I instructed all railway stations in my jurisdiction to start performing random checks of all passengers who got down from the trains. The Rail Police would request passengers to unlock their baggage using the keys. If the person was carrying his own baggage, he would have the right key and would be able to unlock it. If he did not have the keys, it was a clear case of theft. For baggage that did not have a lock, the person carrying was to be questioned on its contents and then asked to open it. If the contents did not match, it would again mean that it did not belong to him.

I tried this technique during night hours on all railway stations within my jurisdiction and found that some cases were detected, some people were caught. In just about a month, word of this went around. The impact of this exercise on running train thefts was surprisingly quite high.

※

Detecting the crime was not enough. I wanted to figure out ways of prevention. The trains used to be escorted by armed policemen. Despite their presence, train dacoities would take place. The only reaction of senior officers would be to suspend and initiate a charge against the patrol party. This didn't seem fair. Senior officers are meant to get to the root of the problem and help their juniors perform better instead of only punishing them in a knee-jerk reaction. I decided to accompany the patrol party on a couple of nights to see things on the ground.

I realized that in a long train, the team could occupy only a couple of coaches. When dacoity occurred in other coaches, the criminals would pull the chain or disconnect the clapper valve to slow down the train and get off just after finishing their act. The idea, therefore, was to be able to alert the patrol party before the train came to an unscheduled halt.

In search of a solution to this problem, I spent a whole day and a night in the control room of DRM Dhanbad to understand the mechanism of train traffic. I found a couple of very useful inputs that worked really well.

※

Only a genius can be ingenious

The dacoities in running trains were mostly committed during night hours. First thing in the morning, I would wake up to a dacoity report of the last night. What made me really uneasy was the time lag between the actual event and its information. I felt that as a police agency, I was losing valuable time in investigating a crime.

I decided to visit the control room of DRM Dhanbad. The system inside looked very big and complicated. I learnt that the control room had a system whereby they could find out the time taken for a train to travel from one station to another. As a routine process, when the actual time of travel exceeded the expected duration, even by half a minute, an alert would be sounded in the control room.

I got a brilliant idea. I decided to put a policeman on that counter—his job was to alert the SHO of the police station of that jurisdiction as soon as he got an alert. This method helped me in tracking such dacoities, and I could gain on the time taken for the flow of information. I could address the problem more promptly and more effectively.

The second clue that I discovered in the control room was that of a slip called 'caution slip', which used to be given to all train drivers. These slips are indicators for the drivers to slow down the train in areas where repair work of the track was going on. I could immediately sense that the caution slip could be of great value to the escort party.

I instructed that one copy of the slip should be given to the escort party so that if the speed of the train slowed down in an area where there was no caution mentioned in the slip, they should become alert. They could come to the door of the coach and beam a torchlight to see if criminals were coming out of compartments. Unexpected slowing down of the train was a possible indication that the dacoits would have pulled the chain to deboard at some intermediate place after committing their crime. This was a training that I imparted to them.

Both methods worked really well for the Rail Police in the state, and helped me in detecting and preventing some of the rail dacoities. The senior officers who were supervising my work were very appreciative of this.

Next, I turned my attention to the revenue generated from freight. Freight is a much bigger source of revenue for the railways, many times more than passenger traffic. In fact, I feel that the railways carry the passengers at a loss as a goodwill gesture to the people of India. Their real earnings come from carrying material for industries.

Coal transportation was being done through passengers trains. This was a racket that went on with the connivance of the rail and police officials. I initiated an operation to check this for about a month, and it annoyed almost everyone.

In the meanwhile, I got information that another huge racket was causing a great loss to the railways in carrying freight from the region of Kutch to Garhwa in Palamu district. I verified the facts in every detail and finally registered a case. I formed a team of officers to visit Kutch and start the investigation. When people came to know of this, I started receiving even better information about scams of higher magnitude in the railways.

The price of a pinch of salt

A source of mine told me that a big private firm was producing chemicals in the Palamu district. The railway line that passed through this district fell in my jurisdiction. This firm would get materials by rake from a city in Gujarat, but the railways were getting paid a very nominal amount for this transportation. I devoted some time and energy to get to the details of this.

What I found was that, according to the rules, only if common salt is transported by the railways, the charges are exempted. The suppliers in Gujarat belonged to a big business house in which the local and even state politicians had financial interests. The private firm in Palamu was getting chemicals from them in the name of common salt but used it to manufacture chemicals for sale in the market. In all, this huge fraud of revenue worth two rakes every month was being committed.

I got a case registered against the employees of the railways, the supplier from Gujarat and the factory authorities in Palamu. My officer and his team left for Gujarat to start investigating. Not surprisingly, even before the team could return, I was transferred.

∞

I was gearing up to transform the Rail Police, Dhanbad, from a theft-investigating agency into a scam-investigating agency. My acceleration was jolted by a sudden break when one fine morning, I saw news of my transfer in a meagre five months of stay, without any ostensible reason.

I had realized that if you tread on the toes of corrupt people, powers that get shaken can displace you in no time, much faster than you can believe. As long as you just continue chasing thieves, robbers and dacoits, systems don't get rattled as much.

CRIMINAL JUSTICE SYSTEM

The fate of a relay race depends on the performance of each runner in the race.

The CJS is a perfect example of a four-runner relay, where every participant has to run an equal distance in their best capacities in order to win. The legislature (the Parliament and the State Assemblies), which makes the laws, starts this run. The baton is handed over to the enforcement, which is the police, to identify the subjects for implementation of these laws. The police then needs to hand over the baton to the judiciary, the courts which implement the laws on these subjects. Finally, the baton is handed over to the last runner, the reformatory so that it can correct these subjects and bring them back to society. Society, funnily, is both the subject as well as the audience of this race.

The point to note is that it is crucial for each runner to run his share of the race. Unfortunately, not just the audience but even the other runners expect the second runner to run the entire race.

What amuses me further is that the nature of this runner is entirely different from the others. Our system has designed the police to be very 'military-like', while the other three are structurally very 'civil' in nature with very high esteem, so much so that they are even addressed as honourables. It is quite disheartening to realize that the power of police is perceived to be in its brute force, the LATHI, while the other dignitaries are seen as the preservers of LAW. This is such a sorry misconstruction.

The psyche of the people of this country is replete with the thought that all wrongs are 'criminal' in nature. Anyone who is wronged has been intentionally harmed; therefore, his redress should begin with an FIR in the local police station. Since childhood, we are fed with stories of a superhero who descends to exterminate all evil in society. He demonstrates the 'victory of good over evil.' Unfortunately, the police is expected to fulfil this image. Even civil wrongs are given a criminal colour, creating a massive clutter in our CJS. No wonder, The Law of Torts, did not show the desired growth in this country.

I recall, during my ADG (HQ) tenure, one evening, the CM, in a casual conversation with some principal secretaries, gave us an insight into the functioning of the state at the highest level. The CM plays two roles—one as the head of the legislature and the other as the head of the executive. In both, the principle of collective responsibility is paramount.

This was a revelation for me. I realized that the CM invariably works under the safety cover of this 'collective responsibility'. He can hardly be hauled up for faults unless he foolishly chooses to stick his neck out. The necks of the officers who execute the policies remain constantly exposed. I carefully understood this aspect and chose law as my protective cover.

In my student days, my mind was ignited by Raphael Lemkin's discourse on genocide, followed by United Nations (UN) debates on mass exodus incidents in world history, like Nazi offences against Jews, the sordid tale of Bosnian Serb aggression, and so on. When I joined the IPS, I was first faced with commonplace crimes like murder, and then, with extermination of entire families.

Later in my career, I witnessed two distinct phenomena, which, conceptually, I thought, had similarities with the picture Lemkin's discourse created—Naxalism and the scourge of kidnapping/rangdaari[1] that Bihar witnessed in the 1990s. Both caused mass exodus of specific classes of persons, and this specificity was not limited to sociology but extended to economy as well.

Genocide has not even been defined in Indian law, though

---

[1]Extortion

India is a signatory to the UN Genocide Convention. Refusal of the Indian criminal jurisprudential ethos to respond to changing milieu of the crime of murder showed how obstinate our law-framing bodies can become.

I was knee-jerked at times by the state policies on crime control that were totally 'unauthorized'. The top political executives, in ugly collaboration with top policemen and bureaucrats, would create such unholy policies that never exposed them to prosecution in law but blatantly exposed the rank juniors instead.

Nazi leaders had created and executed a horrendous policy, which the international community held as crimes against humanity. A parallel needs to be drawn such that law is created to give 'genocide' a wide definition.

Our criminal jurisprudence lacks a legal system to not only define a whole slew of substantive offences committed by unscrupulous policymakers who get away with it with impunity but also to lay out a separate procedural law for handling them.

Presently, such people feel that they can be judged only at the people's court, while the bureaucrats hang on to the tail coat of politicians and try to sail through after committing the genocidal crimes, which ideally require 'Nuremberg' trials.

Today, as I reminiscence from the comfort of my home, trying to clear the fog from my memory, serious questions emerge. Why has police earned the image it has today? Have we in the IPS, who were purposed to lead the police and shape the destiny of the department through the meandering path of society's development, lived up to the expectations of the framers of our Constitution?

Even the most developed nations do not have such highly educated people in the police. The IPS owes the nation a police force that is the best in the world.

With few exceptions, which are mostly short-lived, stories of police brutality, incompetence, insensitivity and other similar adjectives are galore. Police has been given raw brute force, but no faith has been reposed to date. Again and again, there have been efforts to change the face of the police, but none have stood the test of time. This change has never been as discernible as desired. The IPS officers who could actually make it happen always spent their time and energy in finding faults in their surroundings and externalizing the problems. The fault, on the contrary, has always been within, and fixing it should have been the most important task of the police leaders. The aam aadmi[2] sees the police as its adversary. The IPS could have reversed this unwanted development, but it never happened. Instead of winning the hearts of the aam aadmi, most policemen take the easier route of pleasing the 'khaas aadmi'[3].

What they fail to understand is that no system can provide as much armour to the police as the implicit support of the aam aadmi. I had felt the power of this support quite tangibly through simple experiences, when even the so-called most powerful people in both politics and administration would need to think many times before treating me callously.

Law books are replete with articles, sections and judicial pronouncements, which can be intelligently used by IPS officers to handle crime, and law and order issues. It is their responsibility to use their ingenuity to find legal solutions to new and unforeseen problems that crop up every now and then. However, they choose to close their eyes to these problems, leaving them to the subordinate ranks, who end up doing a crude job. Such practices contribute significantly to the erosion of the credibility of the police.

The police does not have the luxury of shelving issues to a date of its choice. It also does not have the advantage of listening to both sides before making decisions. It's almost akin to playing 'blind'. This makes it all the more necessary for the IPS leadership

---

[2]Common man
[3]Special man

to lead the force with their thinking cap always on, keeping in mind the boundaries they cannot cross.

The first trigger which sets the CJS into motion is usually called the FIR, the beginning of the road to justice. Begin it does, but ends, it never. Arrest and bail. Jump bail and then arrest again. The game goes on. The periphery of the event occupies more time and energy of the CJS than its core, which is the trial and the concomitant appeal, leading finally to the reformatory process. The CJS starts diverging from the point an FIR is registered and continues to do so in a never-ending process. Blessed are those who can get justice from this system.

The thing that struck me most about this system was the steep gradient between its lowest and highest rungs. This gradient is equally steep, both in the police as well as in the judiciary.

Laws are created in the legislature by the top intellectuals of the country with utmost deft, complexity and precision. Bills are drafted by IAS officers with the help of legal luminaries. The task of putting these laws into action has to obviously be handed over to equally qualified people with sharp minds. IPS officers, along with the higher judiciary, are expected to fulfil this role and implement these laws in the best way possible to make the system work in the way it was meant to.

It is a grave misfortune that the police department is designed in a way that a huge chunk comprises the investigating officers in the rank of sub, assistant and inspectors. This class of policemen does not even understand the technicalities of law, yet has been given all the basic legal powers and authority. This is usually seen as obtrusive by society at large. The group doesn't have administrative powers to orchestrate the legal process to a conclusive end. The result is a dirty battle between the police and the people.

Something very similar happens in the judiciary too. The basic judiciary is numerically very big and comprises men who are intellectually mere shadows of their superiors in the two courts above them. The basic work done both by the lowest rung of the police and the judiciary is, in many cases, overruled by their superiors. This leads to a lack of faith in society towards the concepts of justice.

The police is responsible for initiating the CJS by registering the FIR and quickly following it up with the arrest or its denial. Beyond that, the path of the CJS is full of 'watchdogs' both within and outside the police to counter the problem of excessive brutal legal powers of the police over citizens. The number and types of agencies, who very sincerely perform this function of keeping a close and critical eye, continue to burgeon. The whole hierarchy of senior police officers, the IAS who form a part of the government, the hierarchy of ministers, the Assembly, the entire lineage of courts, various commissions, and the list goes on and on.

The system tends to get stalled more than it moves. Police has to wrap up investigation super fast, but trial can go on at leisure.

The system provides for so many legal processes that it proliferates like a fibrous root. No case ever converges completely. Police becomes the easiest scapegoat for this failure. People feel that the duty of delivering justice needs to be carried out single-handedly by the police. Such undue importance dumped on the shoulders of the department, clubbed with its 'physical might', makes it an object of fear more than anything else. Phrases like *'police ka rutba'* have become a cliché, in vogue with the media and politicians equally.

This invariably results in a situation where the CJS can pat its back if it ensures that the police is checked from committing atrocities. The main issue, of detecting the criminal incident and bringing it to a logical end, gets entirely lost. The watchdogs feel they have done a good job if they are able to prevent a miscarriage of justice.

The fact that carriage of justice is way more than just prevention of miscarriage of justice, gets completely overlooked.

In an evolved society, fear transforms into respect. In our

society, this fear is placed wrongly with the police and not law, while all solutions lie in fear of law.

In my experiments of 'speedy trial' and 'speedy appeal', I wanted to be the bridge that could bring all the participants of the CJS on one platform, to work together. In the process, a buzzword had emerged, and I could hear it sounding and resounding from all parts of Bihar. A common man who wouldn't even understand English would say, '*Speedy trial kara dijiye* (Please get speedy trial done),' without even understanding the meaning of the phrase. He perhaps wanted to convey that he wanted justice instantly, and most importantly, through the process of law. He could understand that there was a process, and a very legal one, that could be sped up and through which he could get justice.

As a senior IPS officer, I put all efforts towards establishing such guard rails that the system need not focus on preventing miscarriage of justice; it could instead focus on delivering justice as was needed.

We, in the police, are very privileged to be an exclusive part of society that is supposed to deliver criminal justice to the people. But, we will always have to remember that we are being judged by the people we serve. They want justice, and we have to deliver it.

The legislature, the executive, the judiciary and the reformatory, all four gears of the machinery named the CJS, need to work together to serve the people who approach it for justice.

THE MAN MUST FURNISH THE WILL TO WIN

God has equipped you for life, but He
Lets you decide what you want to be.
Courage must come from the soul within,
The man must furnish the will to win.

—Edgar A. Guest

SP Nalanda
(16 January 1989 to 24 December 1989)

The newspapers reported that I had been posted as SP Jamshedpur. The wireless from the police headquarters sounded my new posting as SP Nalanda. For me, it made little difference whether it was Jamshedpur or Nalanda, but I was really worried about the education of my two children who had just been admitted to good institutions in Dhanbad, which had demanded a fairly large sum of money. This was the first time I felt the pang of a transfer, which hitherto I had brushed aside as inconsequential.

Nevertheless, I followed orders and came to Bihar Sharif, the headquarters town of Nalanda district and joined my charge. I got both children admitted to a local school, which was way below standard.

After a couple of days, I made a visit to the police headquarters to call on the DGP, J.M. Qureshi, who was from the Madhya Pradesh cadre but had been handpicked by the CM, Bhagwat

Jha Azad, as the DGP of Bihar. He was considered to be a tough and no-nonsense cop. Even the CM never turned down his recommendations. I got to know that my posting was the only exception. He had proposed me for Jamshedpur, while the CM changed it to Nalanda. I had met the CM earlier at Ranchi but had never got a chance to meet the DGP. Why was I the only exception made in the tenure of J.M. Qureshi still remains a mystery to me.

When I went to meet him in his office, I could feel an aura around him. The uncertainty of the outcome of our first meeting just added to the tension. The beginning was quite solemn, to the extent that I felt unwelcome. After a formal salute, I took off my beret, placed it on his table, pulled a chair and sat down in front of him. He looked sternly at me. If I had not been confident, I would have started shivering.

'What brings you to Patna?' I heard a very gruff voice. 'I have come to tell you that I have suffered financially because of my untimely transfer from Dhanbad.' With no response to my statement, he dismissed me from his presence. I at once picked up my beret, put it on, saluted and told him that he perhaps didn't know my way of functioning; I would not come back to him again unless summoned officially. I left the room.

My father, by this time, had retired and was practising in the Patna High Court. When he questioned me about the school education of my children, I told him that the frequency with which I was getting transferred, I had lost hope of getting decent schooling for them. He suggested that I leave my wife and children in Patna, while I keep my luggage always rolled for any transfer. This suggestion was like a revelation for me. Without losing time, I made efforts to get my children admitted to two of the most reputed schools in Patna, Notre Dame Academy and St Michaels High School. My wife, a gynaecologist, joined a private hospital, and they started living in our ancestral house in Patna. I returned to Nalanda confident that I could start functioning in my characteristic style without the lurking fear of frequent transfers.

Only a few days after I joined, a murder took place in Bihar Sharif town in broad daylight. A shopkeeper who had refused to pay rangdaari had been shot dead. I took this case as a challenge. The accused was known. I sped up the legal process, completed the investigation as well as the attendant legal formalities, got the charge sheet filed within two days of the incident, and a request was laid before the CJM to initiate the trial. The trial got conducted expeditiously, and the accused was awarded a life sentence within a month of the incident.

This was perhaps the first instance of 'speedy trial' in the state of Bihar. The entire district was stunned at the speed with which the judicial process was completed. Rangdaari and rangdaars very soon became a thing of the past in Nalanda.

Early on in my career, I had started thinking on the lines of innovations in policing. However, only after I became the DGP could I put concepts like speedy trials or even bail cancellations into practical application. The seeds that were sown long back took years to bear fruit.

Crime is a profession

A raid on a mini-gun factory had just got over. The team that I had led personally had completed the seizure list and the arrest of the accused. I started interrogating this person, who was manufacturing country-made weapons in a locality of the district. I suddenly remembered that only about five–six months ago, I had arrested the same person for the same crime in a different locality in my district. When I confronted him with this fact, he very sheepishly accepted it. I demanded an explanation.

He said that he had got his bail in just about two months after being jailed in the previous case. Initially, his bail petition was rejected by the CJM and the district judge, but when he approached the Patna High Court, it was granted to him. He argued that his offence had a maximum punishment of a few years, while the trial might take a long time to conclude, so he should be granted bail in the interim. What he said after that was where my entire concept of crime almost took a U-turn.

He told me that what he did was his profession and his livelihood. A gap of two months or maybe even three to four months when he is in jail, does not damage his profession severely. This hit me hard. Two things became very clear. One, cancellation of bail was a must for such characters, and two, an alternate profession needs to be found for them. The latter was not in my domain, but I felt that the government could solve this problem if it wanted to. In fact, I had seen one of my SIs do it for a particular case in the district of Madhepura. Ramchandra Singh had successfully converted a professional thief into a farm labourer. If only the government was sensitive about such issues, any effort in this direction could bring a new paradigm to policing and crime prevention.

In the year 1989, Lok Sabha general elections had been announced. My experience in this election gave birth to new understandings and methodologies that I developed for handling an electoral process. The practices that I adopted in this election were applied with more finesse in the year 2005, which saw the biggest change in the thought processes of elections in Bihar.

What is a fair election?

In every general election, there is a huge dispute regarding which and how many booths should be treated as sensitive and hyper-sensitive. Throughout my career in the police, I would wonder who could decide this and on what basis. I saw that most of the time, this classification was done on the basis of the number of violent incidents at a booth during the past elections. The entire logic appeared to be police-oriented, thereby implying that the entire onus of conducting fair elections rested on the shoulders of the police, and absolutely none on the managers and other participants of the process. The question that stayed in my mind since my probation days was: is a violence-free election synonymous with fair election? I was not quite convinced.

During the parliamentary elections in Bihar that year, I applied the principles I had primitively used for the by-election to the Singheshwar Assembly elections in 1981, when I was posted there as SP Madhepura.

I pulled out a map and located on it all booths on which either more than 90 per cent or less than 20 per cent of the votes were polled historically. In both cases, I identified the parties that polled these votes. I assigned a colour to each of these political parties and plotted them on the map. When the exercise was complete, the visual impression of the whole constituency became so evident that I could almost guess what forces were working against a fair election in the constituency. For the regions where a pattern was not very clear, I sat down with the prominent people in that area and held discussions along with my subordinates, including even chowkidars.

When I tried to connect these findings to violence, I found that it had the least impact on the fairness of the elections. In a mere four years of getting into the IPS, back in 1981, I was thoroughly convinced that free and fair have only a small overlap; that fair is more important than free. If there is violence at a booth, the elections can be reconducted for that booth, but if there is silent rigging, it will pass off as 'polls held well', and the damage will never be repaired.

I applied this principle after discussing my approach with the DM, who agreed with my views. We planned our moves together in the constituency elections of both Nalanda and Barh.

The people of that area, including the subordinates in the district administration, could not fathom our process. Since it was not possible for us to monitor each booth individually, we bundled a group of booths that were rigged by a particular party in one region, thereby breaking down the problem into smaller parts. Reasons were identified, and efforts were made towards solving them. The process was implemented in such a way that no overt police action was visible, and yet, everything got done. In fact, the general perception that developed amongst the subordinates and the people of the constituency was that the entire election was conducted without any police force.

The election of 1989 was a really good lesson for both the DM and me on how fair elections could be conducted.

Fair election is whose responsibility?

In those days, the might of the Election Commission was unheard of. At the district level, ensuring fair elections was the responsibility of the DM and the SP. At the state level, it was the chief secretary and the DGP.

I had planned to initiate sections 107/113/116 CrPC proceedings quite extensively under my direct supervision in the entire district. This had created huge upheavals in the district. In a conference held in the office of the chief secretary with all the DMs and SPs of the entire state, the CM addressed everyone for about a couple of minutes. The only point raised in his speech was about a particular DM and SP who were using sections 107 and 113 CrPC to disturb the supporters of his party. He expressed great disappointment with this activity.

After the meeting was over, the chief secretary and the DGP announced for the DM and the SP of Nalanda to stay back and meet them in the office of the chief secretary. It became very clear to all officials present in the room that we had been the 'mischief-makers'.

When we went into his office, the chief secretary politely offered us a seat and a cup of tea before asking us what exactly had we done to irk the CM. We explained the whole procedure to him. The chief secretary looked at us very benignly and then asked us, 'Are you sure the process that you have followed is completely legal?' Both of us sounded a 'Yes' in unison.

He then gave a very apt piece of advice. He said, 'Look, the CM himself is a party to the election, and therefore, you should not be worried about what he said. Just ensure that whatever you do is backed by law. In any case, since he, as the CM, has brought this out in an open conference, it is advisable that you submit a joint report mentioning facts of the whole matter. It will help you answer questions later.' We quietly left the room and did exactly as advised. I wish we had more such people today who could guide young officers in the right direction.

The story of my night raids continued. I don't know whether I could say that I missed them during the four years in the CBI, but I could surely say that it was one of the most important ways to gauge and manage crime in a district. With experience, I started to understand that not all raids are guided by brawn and surprise; they could also be used as a strategic means towards controlling crime.

Be alert, plan your moves

I finished my dinner and got ready for my daily night raid. I climbed onto my jeep, with the driver and the only available havildar who had a Sten gun. The road was devoid of any traffic. I was swaying in and out of sleep, when I suddenly noticed in the light of the jeep's headlight that the road ahead had been blocked by huge boulders. I instantly knew that a gang had prepared for a long hold up. We were about 100 yards from the roadblock when I asked the driver to stop the vehicle urgently. The driver applied full brakes and we stopped at about 75 yards from the roadblock.

I asked my havildar to fire just one round in the air. Within no time, there was a spurt of fire from somewhere near the roadblock. I could make out from the sound of the shots that these were from a regular gun and not a rifle. I could also make out that there must be at least 10 people hiding near the roadblock. I assessed my position. With one Sten machine carbine, which is a close-quarter combat weapon, I could not take on the criminals. This weapon, although semi-automatic, cannot strike effectively more than about 25 yards. In my entire police career, I never carried my weapon with me, even during raids, so I decided to keep quiet and stay put.

On the wireless fitted in my vehicle, I made a call to the control room and requested them to send reinforcement. I knew the location of the nearest support place and was aware that it would take about 20 minutes for any help to arrive. I decided to wait at the location, as I thought that in case some vehicle gets trapped in the roadblock and gets looted, I should be there to help them.

When the reinforcement arrived, we moved towards the roadblock only to find that the criminal gang had already left. Nevertheless, I followed the legal procedure of getting an FIR registered. We employed sources in that area for investigation and finally succeeded in detecting the gang.

Bhagalpur communal riots aftermath was at its peak. Since Bihar Sharif was a communally sensitive place, we had to be extremely alert. Even a small incident in the night could flare up into an uncontrolled situation by the morning. Both the DM, N.K. Sinha, and I would move around in the district town for at least an hour during unearthly hours in the night.

It was about the fall of the evening. Offices had just closed. There was news of panic in the town of Bihar Sharif due to a stabbing incident in a communal clash. This was a sure recipe for a communal riot. The typical knee-jerk reaction of heavy deployment of forces, patrolling in sensitive pockets, deployment of magistrates and a few similar things got done almost mechanically. The DM, the SDO and I reached the place of occurrence, which was in a densely populated locality. Tension was palpable all around us. It felt as if we were sitting atop a communal volcano.

I knew in my heart of hearts that if something visible and tangible was not done immediately, the situation would deteriorate faster than I could have imagined. In fact, according to the local intelligence inputs, every house had gathered brickbats and firearms, ready to be used at the slightest provocation. I was clueless and getting unnerved. With every passing moment, I knew I was losing precious time. The accused were known, but their arrest was becoming impossible, as they had gone underground and out of our reach.

Suddenly an idea struck me—I could use Section 107 CrPC to handle this situation. This section allows the executive magistrate to issue a show-cause notice to any person who he thinks is likely to disturb public peace, to execute a bond with or without sureties. I hastily talked to the DM and explained its mechanism. He ordered the SDO to conduct a camp court at the place of occurrence itself. Since the accused was absconding, warrants under Section 113 CrPC were issued and followed up by attachment processes. The processes were ruthlessly executed in the presence of the DM and the SP in the night itself. This worked almost instantly. The accused surrendered, peace was restored, and we heaved a sigh of relief. If we had not experimented with this process and returned without any tangible result, no amount of force could have saved the consequent situation.

Situations in life do not operate on a pre-determined formula. Only when we think on our feet can we emerge successfully from the surprises thrown at us. In the kind of profession I was in, these stakes were really high.

Your attitude can change a person's life

'Sir, please supervise this case personally at the place of occurrence. This is my request to you.'

District Nalanda, Telhara Police Station. The case was of possession of illegal firearms, and the accused was a poor, small-time shopkeeper.

The SHO had received secret information that an illegal countrymade weapon was kept in an almirah in the house of the accused. He collected his armed force and raided the house. The weapon was recovered and an FIR was registered. The houseowner was arrested and sent to judicial custody. The DSP had supervised this case in a routine manner, and the supervision note had come to me for my approval. The DM, too, granted his sanction for proceeding with prosecution according to the Arms Act, 1959.

This incident was too insignificant to find a mention in the annals of the history of Nalanda or even make waves in the contemporaneous times of the place. It was 50 days later that the accused approached me after he had gotten bail from the Patna High Court.

When he made the request for supervision, I was in a hurry, and in a fit, asked him, 'Why?'

He couldn't answer but looked at me expectantly. I could sense that injustice had been done somewhere. I conceded to his request and fixed a date for the supervision. I also sent a notice to the DSP, along with the SHO, to be ready with the witnesses on the appointed date. Suddenly, a thought flashed through my mind that if I followed the typical process of supervision, I might not be able to get to the truth. I told the accused that I would not ask any question to any witness. He would have to cross-examine as is done in a court, and I would only record it. There was a smile on his face; he bowed in a pranam and left my office.

The day arrived. I reached the house of the accused. The first witness was the SHO himself. The accused confronted him with a document of the sale deed of a piece of land in Telhara bazaar. I could see the SHO break into a nervous sweat. This land was a bone of contention; the accused was being falsely implicated. My assessment was confirmed when the SHO could not reproduce the seized firearm on being asked to do so.

This incident shook my belief in the process that we, as policemen, followed for supervisions. I returned to my office in a state of shock and cancelled the earlier orders against the poor man who had been identified as an accused.

Why is the police expected to investigate without the support of cross-examination, which is the only way to find the truth? Why is the system designed in a way that the police first does injustice and then the victims have to go to the courts for justice? Perhaps that is why the courts have been named nyaayalay.

Recently, somebody from Telhara paid me a visit. He told me that this person had put up a picture of mine in his house in gratitude for the justice I got delivered to him. I felt very humbled.

On another day, I left in my jeep for a visit to some rural police station in my district. I would have travelled around 20 kilometres from my district headquarters when I heard my very high frequency (VHF) control beaming a message for me saying that communal tension had erupted in a locality. Several vehicles had been torched, and the situation was getting out of control. I reversed my jeep immediately, and in about half an hour, was back at my base, driving straight to the place of occurrence. The crowd was behaving belligerently, and I didn't even have any police force with me. Being short in height, I decided to climb onto a heap of bricks kept by the roadside to make myself visible to the crowd. I started addressing them without any microphone.

What happened next was phenomenal. The mob turned its attention towards me, and soon I was able to initiate a dialogue with the people. In about 10 minutes, I saw the mob transforming into an intent audience towards their SP. No lathi or weapon could have done this. I felt what had really worked was my continuous accessibility to the aam aadmi. Perhaps they wanted to reciprocate.

There are two large groups of people belonging to two mutually exclusive categories that senior police officers have to contend with. One is called the aam aadmi, and the other is the group of subordinate police officers. These two groups are not only large in number but also antagonistic to each other. The irony is that the two 'warring' groups do not trust each other but would love and wish to trust a system of a small pool of senior police officers, called the IPS officers. As if the situation wasn't complex enough, herein came a third group of people, the people's representatives commonly known as politicians. According to the administrative structure in our country, this group has become the most powerful. It invariably tries to dominate over every other group or its subgroup by driving wedges through wherever it finds a possibility.

From my personal experience, I had observed that the IPS officers who could handle the conflicting demands of the first two groups separately, without letting them clash, were able to thwart the moves of the third group. Those who lean towards either side, give ample opportunity to the politicians to create intractable problems. Problems that invariably lead to endless woes for IPS officers, leaving them with only two options: withdraw and get depressed or, as the saying goes, join the bandwagon.

My days used to begin with meeting the aam aadmi, continue with it and never end. I had realized that these people had two serious limitations. Firstly, they came from remote parts of the district, from where there weren't ample means to commute to the headquarters. If a person who had travelled from a remote area was not able to meet the SP during the day, he would spend the night by the wayside. Secondly, most of them were illiterate and could not give their grievances in writing.

The private section of my official residence had become more of a public place than a portion meant for the family. People would wait for hours to meet me, on my return from my tours. There was a battery of literate constables on duty whose job was to write out the petitions of the aam aadmi to save their money and effort. I closely monitored these and would solve these issues then and there. My subordinates had little option but to listen to them at the police station level itself. They knew that I was keeping a tab on the accessibility of my police station-level officers.

Police Lines is the place from where the SP manages the grievances of the second group of people, his subordinate policemen. I made it a point to devote a complete day every week, without exception, at the Police Lines to tackle every little issue. If my visit was scheduled at seven in the morning, it would start sharp at 7 a.m., even if I had returned at 6 a.m. from a night raid.

These efforts that I put towards the two groups got me their support in crisis situations, even when politicians tried to create a split.

Bihar Board exams were on. We, in the district administration, took it upon ourselves to successfully conduct fair examinations.

However, the unfortunate outcome of this was that the pass percentage of students dropped sharply in the district. Most colleges in the rural parts had to be shut down because they didn't get students for admission. Only a couple in the district headquarters survived.

I was with the DM one day, when a delegation of college students came to meet us. They placed a very logical and fair demand: if examinations were to be conducted fairly, then classes should also be held regularly. We decided to do something about it.

We landed in a local college at around 7 a.m., during morning classes, and felt pleased to see that there were hardly any absentees. The physics teacher, who was to conduct the laboratory class, could not be seen. When the principal got to know that the DM and the SP were in the college, he rushed to the laboratory and admitted that the faculty was not on leave. The SHO was asked to go to the house of the missing teacher to get him to the class. In the meanwhile, we started conducting a laboratory lesson on Vernier Caliper for the students.

The SHO went in his official jeep to bring the teacher. Embarrassed as he was, the teacher was even more surprised at our presence in his place when he came to the laboratory. We politely told him that we were only deputizing for him and now that he was here, we would take leave. Hereafter, classes were held regularly with no complaints from the students. The matter was handled very subtly and smoothly without raising any dust.

In an unfortunate situation, a constable had to be arrested from the SP's residence on the charge of rape and murder. I had supervised that case and ordered his arrest. The Reserve sergeant major, who looks after the Police Lines, mischievously posted him to my residential office. I was sitting on my lawn early in the morning when the SHO came to seek my permission for his arrest. I unhesitatingly permitted him, and the arrest was made.

All hell broke loose. The police association went up in arms. They met the CM at Patna. My seniors called me up to almost warn me that I would have to face the music of the issue I had created. I asked them not to worry about it.

The police association sought time from me and requested my permission to call a general body meeting of the constabulary to discuss the issue. I sent a reply on their petition, 'Granted. After your address, inform me. I will also address my constables.' They looked quite surprised and asked me whether I was planning to come to the Police Lines to address the agitated police constables. I said, 'Yes, I will.'

In my address, I felt what finally worked was the efforts that I had sincerely made hitherto in solving the issues of the constables and the empathetic attitude I had for them. I was able to ride over this issue.

These two incidents are simple examples that prove that if an IPS officer applies constant effort in tackling the problems of people, it helps him in any type of crisis situation. If this doesn't happen, the use of force becomes inevitable.

Apart from policing the district and experimenting with administrative skills, I was discovering a newfound love for interacting with my children, who had just started going to school. I was watching them grow and learn new things every day. I wanted to be a part of their growth in as organic and natural way as I could. They would be very keen on running around and soiling themselves in the tilled soil of the residential garden while it would be readied for plantation; I would give them full liberty to do so. The people outside found it unusual, but I knew how vital it was for them to experience nature and create these memories. I am not a teacher by profession, still I would spend whatever time I could snatch, talking to them, asking them absurd questions. I knew that learning is not about storing or gathering knowledge but processing these to create better knowledge.

My wife, who had completed her MBBS from Ranchi, was technically ready to practice as a doctor. She had attended a few medical camps as a volunteer surgeon in the rural parts of the district. She liked the place and the people, and expressed her desire to practice as a gynaecologist in the district town. I promptly turned this proposal down, as I knew it would be misread by people. She followed my advice of setting up her practice in Patna instead. The family stayed in Patna for the weekdays and would come to Bihar Sharif for the weekend. Our family union would last for those two days of the week before they were shipped off to Patna on Monday morning again.

Life was slowly settling down and taking shape.

Many attempts were made by acquaintances and distant relatives to invite me to their house on some pretext or the other. The list of such people was quite large, and the opportunity of finding such excuses was too many. I had consciously decided to not accept any such invitation, as the consequences were fraught with danger, and would politely turn down these requests. An unintended consequence of this was that I was beginning to get labelled as an asocial being in society. This label grew stronger as I moved on in the job. In retrospect, I feel this had done me more good than harm.

I was returning early morning from a night raid when I noticed the SHO of a rural police station standing on the roadside. I stopped my vehicle to find out the reason. He told me that a lady was reporting a case of dacoity with murder under Section 396 IPC wherein her husband had been killed. The SHO was on his way back from the place of occurrence after recording her fard bayaan[1], but he felt that the incident was made up. He suspected that the wife, a young lady, had murdered her old husband with the help of her paramour to get ownership of his property. He expressed that he wanted to lodge a case against the lady on his own statement. I advised him against it.

The investigation proved that the dacoity case was false, but the murder was true. A charge sheet against the informant was laid as a conspirator for murder with unknown persons. The

---

[1]Written statement

lady was convicted. Had we started the case of murder on our statement, we would have had to prove the details of the murder, which would have been an uphill task. We instead just proved that the dacoity was fake, so the onus shifted on the informant to explain the death of her husband. This was an experiment in law that got appreciation by the police and the judiciary.

Another case came to light where the CJM was releasing bail bonds for accused persons based on fake bail orders of the district judge. When I got the details of the case from the district judge, I could clearly see a racket. I ordered the registration of a case in the local police station but instructed the SHO to not make any arrests in a hurry.

Since the district judge was the informant, and the CJM was the accused, the entire judiciary was in a state of panic. They went up in arms against the police. The district judge started asking me why, instead of inquiring into the whole matter, had I got a case registered? I told him that inquiries are conducted by magistrates; the police can only investigate. The matter came to the notice of the high court, and I got summoned unofficially. I could answer every question that was shot at me by the judges. When they could not find any fallacies, they advised me to complete the investigation. This reinforced my belief that law can help you survive any difficult situation. Unfortunately, I could not see the end of this matter, as I was transferred before its closure.

Almost every important section of people in the district was unhappy with me. A powerful Cabinet minister was aggrieved that I had not acceded to his requests during the election process. Finally, when he lost in the election, transfer orders of both the DM and the SP came the very next day. This did not come as a surprise to either of us; in fact, we were ready for it with packed baggage. We left Bihar Sharif in no time. The only section of people who felt pained by this was the aam aadmi and the constabulary. I do not know what the minister would have felt, but at least I felt relieved at the transfer.

Honest officers must not fear transfers

I was sitting in the office room of my residence, applying my mind to the issues of the general election that was to be held all over the state of Bihar. The windows of my room were open, overlooking the gate. I noticed a fleet of cars entering my campus. From a distance, I could see a Cabinet minister along with a relative of mine, who was a member of the ruling party, getting down from the car. I could immediately sense that their visit had something to do with some request in the bandobast of the upcoming election.

I came out of my room to receive both the visitors. I motioned my relative to take a seat in the drawing room, while I asked my constable to make the minister comfortable in my confidential office. I knew that if I did not separate them, it would be difficult for me to handle the situation. After exchanging pleasantries with my relative, I came to my office room.

The minister lost no time in taking out a piece of paper that had names of about 20 subordinate officers, with one booth name written alongside each one of them. He had essentially prepared a booth allocation list of officers as per his whims and wanted me to execute it. When I read it, I said, 'Minister sahab, this time all deputations will be done by computers through a randomization process. No individual will have any role to play.' The minister looked at me, amazed. He said, 'Do you think the SP will not make the deputation; only computer sahab will do it?' I said, 'Yes, that is true.' He persisted, 'So you are not going to accept this small request of mine?' I politely replied, 'Sorry, the process has already been deployed.' He got up and left.

I went to the room where my relative was waiting and informed him about the departure of the minister. He got up to leave as well, and I accompanied him to see them off. I bowed in a pranam to the minister, and the fleet of cars drove out of the campus. I came back to my room and resumed my work.

When the results of the election came, the minister had lost. A young man from the opposition had won. This man later enjoyed long tenures of successful political life both at the Centre and the state.

THE MAN IN THE ARENA

It is not the critic who counts; not the man who points out how the strong man stumbles, or where the doer of deeds could have done them better. The credit belongs to the man who is actually in the arena, whose face is marred by dust and sweat and blood; who strives valiantly; who errs, who comes short again and again...

—Theodore Roosevelt

SP (Special Branch)
(25 December 1989 to 22 April 1992)

For the first time in my career, I got posted in the police headquarters as the SP (Security). Security of VIPs, including that of the CM, was my charge. A non-Congress government had just been formed, and the election of the leader of the legislature was in progress. We in the intelligence were alert and following all developments very closely. News came in that Ram Sunder Das had been elected. We immediately created a group of security men of an agreeable social combination. I signed the order, and the group was ready to leave. Just then, we got the news that the decision had been changed, and Lalu Prasad Yadav was the newly elected leader. The earlier order had to be revoked and a new group of a different social composition was selected and despatched.

For the first time, I saw blatant use of social dynamics overriding merit in professional work. I was shaken to see this in such a raw form.

After about a month of my joining, a SI of the Special Branch came to my room and handed me an envelope with '500' written on it. I felt clueless and asked him to educate me. To my shock, he explained that every SP rank officer in the police headquarters was given ₹500 from the Secret Service Fund (SS Fund) for using human sources. The way this money was being given appeared as a bribe. I immediately asked him to take it back. This got reported to the DG (Special Branch), who then summoned me. He gave me an illuminating talk on the utility of the SS Fund and how not taking it would be tantamount to being an unprofessional intelligence officer. I told him that the sources would get paid directly if they performed well and that I did not need any funds from him.

The department in the headquarters that handled the SS Fund told me that I was the first SP who had refused this money, even after being cajoled by the chief. I was dead against the concept of the SS money being doled out to senior officers every month and stuck to my stand all through my career.

Up until this point in time, I had led the life of a field police officer who took independent decisions based on law and merit. I was now witnessing that caste was not only unavoidable in decision-making but was also central to any administrative process in Bihar. This aspect, I never realized, was so important. It became ridiculous one day when I was asked to find out the caste of the victims of a serious road accident. This upset me no end that day. I didn't know where this was heading or if it was a bottomless pit.

My work in the Special Branch, otherwise, was mentally quite invigorating. The real challenge in this branch was to elicit information without having legal coercive police powers. This area of policing requires complete anonymity, unlike the men in uniform who can easily be identified even from a distance. The latter need to prove all conclusions of an investigation in a court of law, but the intelligence reports are meant only for the eyes of political leaders in power, almost always for the CM of the state.

I was coming in close proximity to the politicians. In the initial days, when I had the first occasion to talk to the CM on an issue relating to his personal security during his three-day election visit to UP, the discussion would in no time veer round to the caste politics of Bihar. I felt very uncomfortable talking about caste politics with the head of the state when I was there to brief him about a professional topic like security. The CM soon realized that I could not be drawn into such discussions and maintained a safe silence with me on these issues, thereafter.

Providing security for him was a challenge for any intelligence agency. He would hardly follow any security norms. He had his own instincts and would do only what appealed to him at any instant. I had a tough time handling this.

On a particular visit in an election campaign in UP, we were travelling in the evening, in a taxi, somewhere in the rural part of Benares without any local police support. There were three of us—the CM, my deputy and me. All of a sudden, the CM felt like having lassi. He asked the taxi driver to stop at a wayside dhaba, got out of the taxi and made himself comfortable on a bench there. Lassi was ordered for all three of us. I was becoming nervous and was keeping my fingers crossed. I was responsible for the security of the CM, and here I was, exposing my subject completely without any logistic support.

The problem became compounded when the people around started recognizing the CM of Bihar in a matter of a few minutes. A crowd started gathering around him, and he now wanted to address them! At this point, he sought my advice on something. He asked me if he could climb on the taxi's bonnet and address the people. All theories I had learnt of VVIP security had gone for a toss. I told him that he could stand on the bumper but not the bonnet. If he fell from the bonnet, he would be badly hurt. He thought I made sense and addressed from the elevation of the bumper. Fortunately, it wasn't long, and we pushed out of the crowd before it swelled.

The story of caste massacres in central Bihar had just begun. What was perceived as a Naxal issue in the eighties had started to transform into a violent and despicable caste battle in the nineties.

Early in the morning, news of a massacre of a caste, called Bhumihars, trickled in from a village in the Gaya district. The casualty was huge, almost countless, including old, women and infants alike. I got a message from the CM house that he had decided to visit that village. Thankfully, the SP had got all the bodies lifted from the village before we could reach there.

I knew it would be a Herculean task for me to manage the CM's security this time because the local population believed that the incident was caused by him. He was being addressed as the hatyara[1]. I arranged for a very robust ring around the CM, but I knew nothing would be good enough. I was just praying that this situation would get over without any harm to him, as that would mean a slur on my professional capability.

In addition to the ring for providing proximity security, I carried cane shields with us to handle the aerial route of projectiles in case brickbatting happened. My apprehensions proved right. The villagers guided him to a body that was still lying in a field. It was an open field, an ideal place for him to be attacked from a distance. In no time, a brickbatting took place. I could somehow manage to save him and bring him out unscathed. Professionally, I was satisfied, but the gory scenes I witnessed left me saddened and pensive.

My next challenge came when a politician called Hemant Sahi was murdered somewhere in the Vaishali district of Bihar. A lot of dust and noise got generated instantly. A huge violent mob came menacingly towards Patna. I still remember the panic that hit the CM. There was an apprehension that the mob would

---

[1]Murderer

surround the house and try to vandalize it. I urgently got light machine guns (LMGs) mounted all around the perimeter. The mob came and vandalized the Assembly building instead.

This incident perhaps shook the confidence of the CM in me, not because of my professional competence but because of my caste. As a natural consequence, I was eagerly sent off for my next assignment to West Champaran as SP.

ECONOMICS OF CRIME

Crime is essentially an economic activity.
Have you ever wondered why criminals who loot tonnes of wealth remain poor, while there are people in society who have successfully accumulated enormous amounts of wealth and property with no ostensible source of income?

Let me explain this through one of my earliest experiences of nearly four decades of my policing career. A heinous dacoity gets committed in a small town of Bihar. Wanton violence and loss of a lot of property occur. Police is swift in detecting the crime, nabbing the criminals and recovering an insignificantly small part of the looted property. This becomes a success story for my seniors as well as my subordinates. I am unhappy. I am unsettled because I can't stop thinking about the rest of the property that we could not recover.

Why didn't the criminals have the entire loot? Where did the balance go? Who are the beneficiaries of the major part of the loot?

As a young police officer, I would often wonder why dacoits committed dacoities. The life that they led was far from cosy. Their activity was fraught with danger, including death in a police encounter. For what was it worth?

When any crime gets committed, be it a petty theft, kidnapping, gruesome murder or even a riot, the media is immediately ablaze. The focus is entirely on the details of the incident, how it can be politicized and which administrative machinery should be blamed. This script runs unexceptionally for every such case. In the end, they might even find out the 'reasons' behind the crime. What we don't understand is that these reasons are just the symptoms of a plague that engulfs the roots.

I kept looking in the hope to find answers to these nagging questions. As years rolled by and as I gained more experience, I was able to observe some connection between this missing share of the loot and the ill-gotten wealth in the society. The shape and form would change, but the source essentially remained the same. The blue-collared criminals would graduate into white-collared ones.

I could see clearly that crime generates black money, and concomitantly black money fuels crime in society. The preponderance of black money in the economy of a State is a sure recipe for a journey towards a black alley. It is unfortunate that the police department is neither designed nor trained to track the trail of black money created in the wake of the series of crimes. We are traditionally trained to investigate, detect crimes, and bring offenders to justice. I, too, grew up in this school of thought and passed it on to my juniors.

We, as policemen, are tasked to protect this wealth against predators and are not supposed to question how it gets access into the big palatial houses. The police functions as nothing more than a 'valve'. This society is littered with smart and corrupt people who make money on the sly. They do not contribute to the wealth-creating activity permitted by economics, namely goods and services, yet produce wealth. I would regret my role as a police officer who is assigned to the job of protecting the same illegally gotten wealth, which was some time ago a subject of another crime.

I am convinced that the power of criminals and the potential to commit crimes does not lie in his 'person'; instead, it lies in his 'assets' and his properties. This desire to shift the focus of policing from person to property burned within me for a long time. I got a mere three years to put my ideas into practice when I became the police chief.

The concept behind what I wanted to do can be illustrated through a very simple schematic diagram.

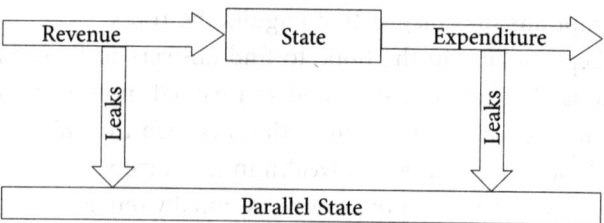

The leaks in the channels of revenue collection on one end and in the development expenditure on the other end, due to rampant corruption, create a huge torrent of black money. A monstrous Parallel State is born. In fact, this Parallel State is bigger than the State itself and grows at the cost of the State.

Is the police protecting the Parallel State in the name of the State?

With its evolution over the years, we now have given a creative name to the output of this cycle—'money laundering'. We as a society are creating white-laundered assets of criminals. The consequence of this is very evidently visible, yet we choose to behave like ostriches. This money laundering has created another by-product, which I call 'social laundering'—forming a class of people who are economically, and hence, socially powerful. These people have so much power that even the most honest policeman is not able to take them on.

My only silver lining was the Prevention of Money Laundering Act (PMLA), 2002. Unfortunately, this Act does not provide police with any power whatsoever. I felt so handicapped. As the ADG (HQ), I tried to convince the CM that the State Assembly could also pass its own equivalent of PMLA. I had examined this issue and was convinced that the only vires that had to be kept in mind was: 'no conflict with the Parliamentary legislation.' I stuck to my point but was thwarted on the grounds of legislative competence.

The CM, however, agreed to request the Government of India to delegate some power to a designated officer in the state government as is the home secretary in the Unlawful Activities (Prevention) Act (UAPA). The request was made, but it never saw the light of day.

In my tenure as the DGP, I saw another CM for a few months only. I again discussed the issue of legislation, but there was no visible interest shown.

The fight against crime begins with the legislature. This is the organ of the State that creates the weapon with which the police fights crime. There was no weapon that I could use against black money. In my tenure of six to seven years as ADG (HQ) and DGP, I got a more positive response from the judiciary than the legislature in my efforts at creating such weapons at the state level.

The only role I could play was that of a catalyst for the Enforcement Directorate (ED), the agency created under the PMLA for the execution of the Act.

The process that began was tortuous.

Bihar Police gathered relevant data and documents and made a formal proposal to the ED to initiate action against all hues and colours of gangs operating across Bihar. These included gangs of kidnappers, bootleggers, the ones who indulged in hooch tragedies, flesh trade, and the list went on. The police and the ED worked in tandem and in complete unison. Soon, ED had what it needed to pass confiscation orders of properties of illegal wealth and laundered white assets of gangsters.

Results were visible, and the impact on the psyche of the criminals was palpable. They were stunned because they had never expected this response from any police force. Bihar was perhaps the first state to have experimented with this idea in this form. The media got curious, as they also had never seen anything like this before. The intellectuals in the society sang praises, as they felt this process was attacking the root of the disease.

Unfortunately, the police still hasn't been given any power under the PMLA, but nothing stops them from being the driving force, making it worthwhile. It is high time that the mission statement of the police gets modified from 'prevention and detection of crime' to 'detection of black money and prevention of laundering thereof.'

The idea that every crime is essentially an economic activity was cemented in my mind from the early days of my career. In my 37-year-long journey, I never hesitated in taking uncharted paths, trying to uncover new horizons of policing. My successful experiments on this journey reassured me and gave me some sense of satisfaction that I was making some difference in the landscape of crime and policing.

Fake sureties: [Madhepura, 1981–82] Dacoities in Madhepura dropped to nil when I started getting bail bonds that were based on fake sureties cancelled. These fake sureties were a source of income for the advocates who were certifying these for professional criminals. The real beneficiaries were the criminals, who could get out on bail and resume their business.

Naxal operations: [Aurangabad, 1982–83] The economic force behind the Naxal operations came through illegal activities. The crimes that they committed were not their source of income, surely not enough to support their organization. Illegal activities, like the smuggling of kendu leaves to farming on benaami land, funded their operations. A quick check on these illegal activities was more than enough to weaken their terror in the area.

I realized that the government benignly vacated areas of the state, surrendering those to the extremist organizations. These organizations unhesitatingly collected taxes in place of the government. My plan revolved around slowly moving into the so-called 'liberated' areas and then permanently occupying them bit by bit. The extremists lost their 'tax' base, while the government could collect its legitimate taxes. It was a double whammy for the extremists.

Disproportionate assets: [CBI, 1984–88] This is more than self-explanatory. Assets accumulated more than what one can earn, clearly point to illegal activity. During my CBI tenure and even later in the Bihar government, my attack on top officials against DA cases helped curb corruption.

Kidnappings: [Bettiah, 1992–93] The ransom money the gangsters received was peanuts, not even sufficient to sustain the establishment cost of the gang. These gangs were covertly running the business of forest felling, international smuggling, illegal mining and illegal selling of sugarcane challans. These were their major sources of money. The kidnappings were done to produce terror, which would make their money-spinning illegal activities easy. I started hitting at these illegal activities directly, which put the plans of these gangsters in disarray, making it easy for me to tackle the kidnapping menace.

Mining mafia: [ADG (HQ), 2006–08] White-collared illegal sand and rock mining in the Magadh and Rohtas belt was rampant. Swift action against these illegal activities saw an immediate drastic decline in Naxal activities in this area.

Economic Offences Unit: [DGP, 2011–14] This unit was created, directly reporting to the DGP to check black money to mitigate crime. It became the driving agency for the ED to implement PMLA. Needless to say, it completely justified the purpose for which it was created.

Hooch tragedies: [DGP, 2011–14] During this period, three successive hooch tragedy incidents occurred in the state. Since there was no alcohol ban at that time, there could be no direct criminal action against the presence of alcohol itself. I converted these incidents into economic crimes, projecting them as loss of revenue to the State. Their properties got attached under PMLA, snatching away their funding source.

Bail cancellations: [DGP, 2011–14] The main idea behind cancelling bail was not to put the criminal behind bars again. This action put these criminals out of their 'jobs', their sources of livelihood. During my Nalanda tenure in 1989, I had learnt that criminals treated crimes as their profession, which had convinced me about the impact that bail cancellations could have.

Communal riots: It might appear very non-intuitive if I tell you that even riots have a financial agenda, especially considering that the word 'riot' has been given an inseparable prefix 'communal' over time. The truth is that every riot, whether communal, ethnic, caste or like, attacks a minority and creates enough terror to chase them out from riot-affected areas. The people who flee sell off their properties.

Bhagalpur riots of 1989: After almost 17 years of the incident, which changed the political course of this country in many ways, Retd Justice N.N. Singh issued the inquiry commission report. My contribution to this report were two terms of reference (III and IV), which had never been mentioned in any such report in the past. They spoke about (III) inquiring and finding whether distress/duress sale of properties in the riot-affected areas had taken place, and (IV) suggesting and supervising ways for rehabilitation and relief to victims, particularly in the light of restoring their possession over the land and houses from where they had been uprooted forcibly.

These changed the way communal riots were perceived in the country. The impact was more far-reaching than one can imagine.

Bradford ethnic riots of 2001: I was in the UK to study the handling of riots and investigation thereof. I could see that the police force had carried out an exceptionally professional process. I asked the chief constable if any study had been made on the transfer of property under distress/duress. His eye lit up as he suddenly remembered that an aggrieved individual had sold off his BMW garage to a riot aggressor immediately after the riot. He could very quickly understand the point I was trying to make.

Nawada riots of 2013: Another communal riot had erupted. I instructed the SP to keep an eye on the most propertied people of both the concerned communities. The violence faded sooner than we had expected.

The list is endless, and the possibilities are infinite.

We are a country with a peculiar social trait rarely found anywhere else. Those who are 'educated' do not do any physical work, and those who do the physical work are not called educated. In a sense, these two groups are mutually exclusive. The educated group essentially behaves as clerks. Bereft of all contact with reality, they just write erudite essays in files, the majority of which are not even their original ideas. This class is the most highly paid.

Review the definition of gross domestic product (GDP), and you will be convinced that the output of this highest-paid class contributes the least to the GDP of the nation. Over and above all this lies the burden of corrupt practices. The end result is the creation of wealth without going through the mandatory dynamics of goods and services.

What an interesting challenge for economists around the world!

A PROBLEM WELL-STATED IS A PROBLEM HALF-SOLVED

A problem well-stated is a problem half-solved.
—Charles F. Kettering

SP Bettiah (23 April 1992 to 13 June 1993)

My promotion to the post of DIG was just a few months away. In such crucial times, getting posted to difficult field assignments is a dicey proposition. Any mishandling of a situation and the officer can land in a soup, risking his promotion. Well aware of what I was signing up for, I not only joined at Bettiah but also decided to go about my charge in my characteristic style.

SP sahab sleeps on thana bench

After a long tiring drive on the bad roads from Patna, I reached dead tired at Bettiah to take my new charge. My predecessor had left even before I could arrive. I went to the circuit house, dumped my bag in a room and came out to sit in my official vehicle.

My driver asked, 'Where do we go, sir?'
'Let's go to the interior areas.'
'Should we go to Bagaha, Valmiki Nagar?'
When I said yes to this, he suggested that we must take

armed force along, as that terrain was troubled. I brushed his suggestion aside, and we drove off. Like a true guide, he kept talking to me about the places we passed on our way.

After traversing the non-existent roads and forlorn forest regions, we reached Bagaha Police Station late in the night. I was talking to the SHO when a group of villagers came to the police station in a state of panic, asking for urgent police help. Criminals had entered their village. The SHO suggested that I rest in the rest house of the private sugar mill of Bagaha, while he proceeds to the village with the armed force. I did not find it appropriate to go to a guest house of a private mill owner. I told the SHO to move ahead, while I made my arrangements.

I came out and saw a line of chowkis of constables neatly laid out in the verandah of the police station. The constables had all left with the SHO. Tired as I was, I felt terribly sleepy. The wooden cots in front of my eyes were calling me. I quietly got inside the mosquito net that hung over one of them, took off my shoes, and immediately slipped into a deep slumber.

When I opened my eyes the next morning, the sun was up and bright. I saw the constables busy in their morning rituals. I asked them why had they not woken me up earlier? They said that I looked too tired and was in such deep sleep that they did not have the heart to disturb me.

My very first night in the district sent the right message to the private mill owners as well as the constables. It also made me aware of the regular state of affairs in the district.

∞

A new DM, who I had never met before, arrived the very next day. This was his first charge as a DM. I was perhaps in my last assignment as an SP.

I had returned from night raids late in the night when the caretaker informed me that the new DM was sleeping in one of the rooms of the circuit house but had instructed that he should be woken up whenever I returned. The DM came to my room in a sleepy state, and we ended up having a long chat.

We decided that for the next five days, we would move separately in the district to assess the situation and the problems. At the end of this exercise, we would meet in a secluded forest inspection bungalow in an interior part of the district to discuss our observations and draw up a common plan of action. The crux of our discussion brought out that black money being generated through a few illegal activities created most of the issues, including the menace of kidnapping. We planned a crackdown on these.

In my view, kidnapping, though in police parlance was called kidnapping for ransom, was not exactly being done for money. Police investigations convinced me that the ransom was not even a small fraction of the cost needed to run these gangs. It was obviously not being done for fun. These crimes actually intended to create so much terror amongst the common man that none raises his voice against the illegal activities rampant in the district. The distribution of the black money amongst the gangs and the few big families lay at the root.

Champaran is a historically important place in Bihar. Gandhi's freedom movement witnessed great strides in this region. Unfortunately, in the early nineties, kidnapping had assumed the proportion of an industry here. The frequency would be almost one per day. It would be a school teacher today, a small-time shopkeeper the next day and a village-level farmer on the third. One can imagine the mental state of the SP who is faced with a problem of this dimension.

I needed to do something immediately about this. My answer was raids and more raids. The number of raids had to outnumber the kidnappings. I had to overwhelm them with the sheer number of raids to shake their confidence while being cautious of my boundaries, as I knew that any overstepping could put a lot of things at stake.

Respect begets respect

The rural terrain of Bettiah was mountainous, with dense natural forest on the north and a huge riverine belt on the west. This added to my woes.

One of my sources informed me that the biggest gangster of the district, who had acquired a godfather status for all the other gangs, had been approached for a meeting by the gangs. A big gathering took place. The main agenda of the meeting was a list of complaints against the new SP. 'This man is raiding and following us almost incessantly. No hideout is safe. We are not able to sleep.' The list went on and on. Their demand was to organize a massive encounter with the police so that they could execute their plan of eliminating the SP.

Their godfather listened to them patiently and then asked, 'Does the SP misbehave with the inmates of the house, especially women, during the raids?' 'No,' was the prompt and unanimous reply. 'In fact,' they said, 'he has issued strict instructions to his men that the other members of the family should be treated with care.'

'Does the SP book cases in which you are not wanted?' They again said in a chorus that this was not being done.

Their leader's final words were: 'The SP is doing his duty professionally, without stepping out of his Lakshman rekha. You should also behave within your boundaries.' He rejected their plea for an encounter, saying that maryada[1] should not be violated, especially if the SP is not doing so.

---

[1] Decorum

New Year celebrations with the music of mosquitoes and faecal perfume

31 December 1992. I was sitting in a sugarcane field in Bagaha subdivision of Bettiah. At around five in the evening, I got a call from an informer that a kidnapper gang was going to cross a particular place in the interior of the subdivision. We rushed towards this location.

It had become dark by the time we reached this place after travelling around 150 kilometres through the jungle area of the district. The informer guided me to the location and advised me to lie in an ambush in a sugarcane field. December is the month when the sugarcane is in full growth and the mill season is already on. At around 10 in the night, with very limited visibility, we were lying in ambush in a sugarcane field littered with mosquitoes and human defecation. Yet, the passion in me, that I should not allow any crime in my jurisdiction, was too fervent to dissuade me to leave that place and go back to the comfort of the SP's bungalow.

The officer who was with me told me very shyly at 11 p.m. that in an hour, a New Year was to begin. I motioned to him to focus on the task at hand. The ambush went on. My source came at around one in the night and informed me that the gang was too heavily drunk in their New Year celebrations and had decided to not get out of their shelter. It was a dampener for us, but it remained a lesson for everyone in my team that business means business, irrespective of what day of the year it is.

⁂

A few families in the district possessed extraordinarily large amounts of land and literally controlled the economic activities of the district in all its paradigms. The land ceiling laws had been tried by previous DMs, but each of them got stuck at various levels in the proceedings of high courts and the Supreme Court. In such a backdrop, applying legal provisions appeared difficult. The list of these so-called powerful people included government officials, politicians and criminals alike.

Power rests with the law, not with the police

I had heard a lot of stories, some true, some imaginary, about the biggest gangster in the district who had an aura around himself. That aura was not completely misplaced, although I felt that the district police, too, had not applied themselves to the problem wholeheartedly.

The image that this gangster had was as if he was law unto himself. He would settle cases and would even go to the extent of deciding who should be arrested. He himself happened to be an absconder in around 60 cases. The problem was that nobody ever made a serious effort to catch him and put him before the court for trial. I tried at my level, but no individual came forward to give any information about him.

People showed me a huge house in the town of Bettiah, which belonged to him. It was a challenge to get his moveable and immovable properties attached. Even in the judiciary, it was difficult to get warrants against him. I pursued it at my level, complying with all the requirements of the law. The judicial officers could not reject my request for the warrants and the processes under Section 82/83 CrPC. I obtained these in absolute confidentiality, not even the court employees got to know about it. Therefore, its execution was done without much noise. I monitored the operation as the SP.

It became the talk of the town. The next day, the newspapers from Patna, as well as the local ones, covered this unique attachment that was done as a police operation. I was verbally questioned by the powers to be, on the newspapers reports that said that the house of this gangster was going to be demolished. I responded by saying that since I did not make the laws, I would look for the existing ones, and if they permit, demolition would be carried out, not otherwise. This statement spread like wildfire, and the message was sent loud and clear that no gangster, however powerful, would be allowed to ride over law. This helped me clear the clouds that covered the police department of that district.

I got an idea. I argued that instead of using the land ceiling law, we should presume that the land these few families owned was legally justified. The administration should then undertake a measurement drive to check that possession of land was in consonance with the title on paper. I knew for a fact that even government land was being claimed by these powerful people as their own property. At least this could be identified.

This exercise started the next day. Massive land measurement exercises were carried out. Land in excess of that shown on record was taken over and distributed to the landless. The powerful people, who never got kidnapped but would always keep the district administration on their toes, had been put on the back foot for once.

Who funds the kidnappings?

Early one morning, all ameens[2] of the anchal[3] were summoned, and measurement of land was done extensively in the district. The DM and I started recording the differences between the actual size and that mentioned on the records. This stirred up the entire district. Common people were feeling happy, while

---

[2]People who maintain records of precious properties and deposits.
[3]Zone

those who enjoyed undue powers felt very uneasy, so much so that their feelings got conveyed to the highest political functionaries. But, the DM stuck to his guns.

The economic backbone of the kidnapper gangs in the district had been broken for good.

I was promoted and transferred before my due date. The DM was also transferred to a neighbouring district only to be killed by a mob. I got posted to a so-called shunting assignment, where I used my time to teach my children. Here is where I discovered the teacher in me.

∞

The next issue was of sugarcane challans that were being issued by the mills in the name of registered farmers. Sugarcane fields were pervasive in the entire district. In fact, the economy of Bettiah was largely dependent on sugarcane farming and the six to seven sugar mills in the district and its neighbourhood. Out of the five mills, one was government-owned, while the other four were private. During the crushing season, all the ills would surface spontaneously. The whole process is ideally controlled by an Act of the state government. However, this process had become depraved and gone into the hands of unscrupulous people, thus creating all types of problems for the administration. Both the DM and I had about a month after our joining before the start of the crushing season. This gave us adequate time to understand and plan our moves.

I started getting information about government land where the criminal gangs were cultivating sugarcane. They would sell the harvest to the sugar mills thereafter. I identified these plots and employed the provision of attaching unclaimed property under the Police Act, 1861, in a big way. The DM would issue orders to the mills to issue challans in the name of anchal adhikari[4],

---

[4] Zonal officer

while the payment was made to the government treasury. Such measures had started weakening the economic strength of the kidnapper gangs. In one stroke, we conveyed to the powerful families that they couldn't protect these gang leaders.

༄

Economics of crime

The government-owned Lauriya Sugar Mill was in the poorest shape. The powerful people, including the criminal gangs, the government servants and people who were socially and politically powerful, had control over the sugarcane challans, which were their prized possessions during the crushing season.

I devised a system whereby all these players could be neutralized without any direct action against them, which, anyway, would not have been easy for me. I tried to understand the law behind sugarcane production and the management of the mills. What struck me the most was the concept of 'sugarcane controller', who, under the Sugar-Cane Act, 1934, is essentially the DM. I requested the DM, G. Krishnaiah, to pass one simple order saying that all sugarcane payments by the sugar mills would be on an account payee cheque directly to the agriculturists in whose name the land was registered. No cash payment was to be made. He agreed instantly, as he could see the logic in my request. We set upon implementing this order.

The gramin bank[5] threw up their hands, saying that they did not have enough wherewithal for opening accounts of so many cultivators. I offered help by loaning them my literate constables. The output was fabulous. The local politicians were dead against this proposal, and so were the powerful people who had formed coteries. In fact, the subordinate staff

---

[5] Rural Bank

on both the police and civil administration side also did not accept this order. It only confirmed that this was my chance to make a dent.

A committee under the Sugar-Cane Act held a meeting, which was chaired by the DM. I was not a part of the committee, yet the DM requested my presence. I witnessed a lot of resistance from all quarters in that meeting. But I must give huge credit to Krishnaiah, who stood firm on this decision.

For the first time in the history of Bihar Police, an exercise was conducted to prove a link between the production of black money and the proliferation of crime. I was getting more and more convinced through the results of my experiment. Our method literally freed the challans from the control of powerful people in the district. Every little incident that used to happen at the mill gates—the cash robberies, the kidnappings of agriculturists on the way back to their village—just stopped because of the absence of cash from the entire scene.

Back in those days, I had the foresight of understanding the impact of a cashless economy on day-to-day crimes. Black money and crime are almost like two faces of the same coin. I derived and followed this concept even as the DGP of the state later on.

∽

People may realize that the government today is trying to bring about a cashless society with the backup of a digital economy. We tried to introduce this way back in 1993, while demonetization was tried much later in the country. The farmers were happy, though the powerful lobby in the district, including public representatives, were very uncomfortable.

They got the CM to come to Bettiah to cajole the DM into rescinding his order. The DM stuck to his stand, arguing that this worked for the farmers, as none had complained of any difficulty so far. He made it very clear through his actions that no amount of pressure tactics would work.

I, too, kept on attacking black money in the district unabated. The next visit of the CM was designed by the local deputy minister who perhaps, for reasons best known to him, wanted to get the satisfaction of getting me reprimanded in public. This is a usual ploy used by the people in power to demoralize a conscientious officer in the presence of a crowd so that his self-esteem is hurt and he begins to fall in line. The first attempt was made with me in a closed room of the Circuit House in the presence of public representatives. Another time, in a closed hall full of people. This visit was planned after both these attempts had failed.

Common man is the best shield for honest officers

The CM had planned to hold a public meeting on the campus of the collectorate. The place was not large enough for this purpose, and on top of that, I was given an insufficient two days to make preparations.

A minister in this district had a deep-seated grudge against me: that I did not give him enough time while the common man was showered with it. This bothered him so much that he even complained about it to the CM. The public meeting was perhaps planned to show me my place.

The CM started off his speech on a stage. I was stationed below the manch[6], alertly watching the activities both on the manch and in the crowd. Suddenly, I noticed the minister on the manch taking out a pair of scissors from his pocket and slicing the wires of the mike. The public address system was lost. I quickly sent an officer to tape the wire. This took about two minutes. In the meanwhile, the CM chose to shout at me from the manch.

---

[6]Stage

A PROBLEM WELL-STATED

I was feeling quite upset about the incident. Just then, I saw something unbelievable happen. A poor, ill-clad destitute had climbed up the bamboo barricade in the ground and yelled in the local language at the CM, 'CM sahab, you cannot speak even one word against our SP.'

There was pin-drop silence on the ground for a few moments until the CM resumed his speech. I realized that this was indeed the biggest shield I had against politicians in power. I had never met that person before or after this incident, but he showed me the power and magnanimity of the aam aadmi.

∞

The third big source of black money in the district was the large-scale felling of trees from the best natural forest in the state of Bihar. For many long years, the dense forest of this district had faced the scourge of felling trees, which had become a big business. This gave birth to another illegal business of sawmills. These mills provided good quality timber to people. Almost all of them were running without a license. I ruthlessly stopped this business.

This sale and purchase were being carried out by the moneyed goons of the district as if it was an authorized activity. I remember one of my predecessors in the district had even requested me to get him wood on payment. When I told him that under my orders, it would no longer be possible, he was shocked.

I went into the law and logistics of this illegal business, and geared up my department to conduct raids on illegal dumps of timber. Consequently, most police station campuses became timber dumps. According to law, the police needed to submit the reports to the divisional forest officer (DFO) to first seize and then auction these. In a few cases, I found that the timber was released to the accused by the DFO himself. I immediately appealed for such cases before the DM, followed up and got orders reversed. The illegal business of timber was brought to a halt, which started showing its good impact on kidnapping.

Illegal mining of pebbles in the shallow rivers that criss-crossed the district was the fourth source of black money in the district. The pebbles from this mining activity were used in the crushers, creating a great avenue for the criminals to generate huge sums of black money.

I had observed that the pebbles were being carried out of the district in rakes. I sent my officer to the headquarters of the DRM of that area to collect data on which parties booked what quantity. To my surprise, I found that most of these were regularly being booked by the powerful families who had connections with the kidnapper gangs. The government was losing millions in revenue through royalty, cess and sales tax. This was reported to the government so that it could get a thorough enquiry conducted. Just by collecting data from the office of DRM, I was able to stop illegal mining.

I requested the DM to depute his district mining officer to inspect the crushers. The officer backed out, pleading his safety. I assured him of all police support and got the probe carried out. All these efforts helped.

The fifth and final source of black money came from smuggling across the Indo-Nepal border. I shared a lot of data with the appropriate agency, called Customs, and together we organized many raids to successfully curb this.

This strike on black money, made decisively through a planned approach, whittled the power of rich families and the kidnapper gangs in the district. Every powerful lobby was arraigned against us. The only group in our support was the aam aadmi. The powers that be knew that if they transferred me ipso facto, there would be a huge protest. The government decided to promote me prematurely and posted me as DIG (Military Police) at Patna.

That was the end of my journey as an SP, the time when I really experimented with all the ideas that came to my mind, even half-baked ones, without any fear of consequences to my career or life. I had learnt that too much planning is a lot of redundancy. A bit of insight into the plan and pure intentions are good enough to begin. Rest is taken care of by the Almighty.

WHAT MAKES A GREAT LEADER

The greatest leader is not necessarily the one who does the greatest things. He is the one that gets the people to do the greatest things.

—Ronald Reagan

DIG (BMP) (15 June 1993 to 12 June 1996)

I felt elated. Stars on my official vehicle, and the shoulder badges were heavier than before. Gravity in the rank hierarchy was setting in. I got a feeling that I was now in the echelons of policymakers.

During my SP days, I never got to experience working as a commandant of any battalion. This made me feel concerned. I realized that these men looked towards their commandant as a guardian figure, unlike in the district police, where the relationship with the SP was mostly mechanical. In fact, the world of the constabulary began and ended with their commandant. I struggled to figure out a place for myself.

I needed to redefine my role in this new assignment. Benevolence towards and welfare of the men became my priority. Waking up the commandants from slumber if they had slipped into one was another. Discipline couldn't be enforced without welfare.

My office was part of a sprawling campus that housed three battalions, almost self-sufficient in all respects. I had lived here for a year as a schoolchild during my father's tenure as the AIG. Back then, this campus used to be vibrant with life. When I joined here during my service, I was somewhat depressed to see that most of the activities had disappeared. Added to this was the fact that the children of the constables did not have facilities for education. They behaved like indisciplined vagabonds, moving around aimlessly on the campus, at times, unintentionally damaging the order of the campus. I immediately decided to set up a school inside the campus for them.

※

Unnamed school in the military barracks

I started looking around for a building. The campus had a large number of barracks, most of which remained vacant because of the continuous deployment of the armed forces. I picked up two adjoining barracks. My next task was to find the teachers. I suddenly remembered that a majority of the constables were highly qualified; some of them had done their bachelor's and master's as well. I summoned a group of such constables and interviewed them. Finally, five of them were selected; four for teaching English, Hindi, arithmetic and general studies, while the senior-most was made the principal.

The school was inaugurated. It had all the trappings of a school except a name. Name, it doesn't have even today. It started functioning immediately. I would also try to find time to teach the young children.

Later, when I became ADG (BMP) and DGP, I went back to the school, and I would feel so satisfied to see that it was functioning and doing well for itself. Many lowly paid constables and even class IV employees benefitted, as their children did well in life. The school even helped the girls who were not getting an education, as they were not sent out of the campus due to security reasons. I was later told that some commandants of the battalions were keen on getting the barracks vacated but faced resistance from the constabulary and had to withdraw.

As DGP, whenever I addressed them, I would point towards the school and tell them that it embodies their development. Their life had stagnated at the point where they were, but this school symbolizes and shows the path of development for their family. The school is now 25 years old, still without a name, but the output it has produced can make any prestigious school proud.

This, I think, had laid the foundation of my passion for spreading education in poor classes of society, which finally found an expression in Super 30 later in my career.

◈

I noticed the unhygienic condition in which the constables lived in the barracks. Cooking food on woodfire was rampant, which produced a lot of smoke. I ordered LPG cylinders and initiated the process of setting up a gas agency. With some effort, we succeeded and named it 'Amar Jawan Gas Agency'. It catered not only to the campus but to all the members of Bihar Police.

It was an instant hit. It also became a huge source of their 'welfare fund'. This fund is a private fund created by the battalion itself to help its members get loans when in need. Their life was changing for the better for all times to come, and I was able to see discipline descend through the route of benevolence.

The MMP battalion did not have any source of this fund. I found a novel way to solve this problem for this neglected battalion.

◈

Would you go to your wedding in a police vehicle?

The MMP, with its headquarters at Arrah, lay in my jurisdiction. I had planned an inspection of the campus one day. I went around the campus where the horses were kept and looked after. Just then, I saw, in one corner, which was littered with the waste of the office, sat a palki not in a very good state but it appeared to have belonged to someone wealthy. Out of curiosity, I enquired about it. I was amused at the answer I got. The officer said, 'This palki belongs to the Maharaja of Dumraon. This campus also perhaps belonged to him in earlier days, and therefore, this thing found its way here. Since it is of no use to us, it's been lying here in the junkyard.'

I immediately got an idea. I asked the men to take the palki out, called someone from the market to refurbish and make it into a chariot. I selected two of the old horses who were no longer fit enough for police duties and made them the chariot drivers. I passed this order in my inspection note and came back to Patna.

A month later, the head of the MMP informed me that the chariot was ready and wanted to know what he was expected to do with it. I asked him to send it across to Patna. Once it arrived, I let it be known in the city that it could be loaned for the marriage season, which was just around the corner, to be used by the grooms for their baraat.

I was informed that the chariot was heavily booked for the entire season. The money that the MMP got through this activity created a corpus for their welfare fund. The demand, in fact, was so high that one chariot was not enough. I had to get another one of a similar design made from Varanasi. The men in the MMP battalion were extremely happy.

∞

I noticed that the barbers appointed by the government for the battalions used to do their work in a very cavalier fashion, which appeared unkempt and unhygienic, to say the least. I decided to set up three salons on the campus. This brought about a semblance of decency and hygiene on the campus, further raising the quality of life of the constables.

Things were now falling into order. The constables had started feeling my presence in the role of their guardian, who they could look up to. Had I not built this confidence in them, it would have been very difficult for me to get their honest and unwavering support in all the police operations during my tenure.

There was a phase when Naxal attacks on police pickets had become the order of the day. Armed forces were getting killed in large numbers, so much so that all official functions had to be cancelled. This caused huge concerns and embarrassment for the department. One such incident occurred, and the bodies were brought back to the campus. Emotions were running high. The DGP planned to visit the campus for the last salute but cancelled it last minute, as his sources indicated that he could face the wrath of the constabulary. I knew that his absence would only worsen the situation. I somehow convinced him to visit and assured him that they would not misbehave. I kept my fingers crossed. He came, and nothing unseemly happened. The constables later told me that they had kept their emotions under check only due to the respect they had for their DIG, who always sought their welfare.

Meanwhile, I was called one evening to the police headquarters and received an order to move 20 companies of armed force without delay to Kokrajhar in Assam. Bodo insurgency had erupted there. I came back to my office and talked directly to my men. In one voice, they said they were prepared to go anywhere on my command. The next evening, all the 20 companies were off to Kokrajhar on a special train. I was there at the railway station to see them off. Just when the train was about to steam off, a constable came running to me, saying he had just returned from leave and would like to go along with the rest. I was moved to see the camaraderie among my battalions.

The armed force was not accompanied by any doctor. Two out of the three commandants who were meant to lead the force reported sick with cancer, which was hitherto not known. I lost no time in starting off in my vehicle in the evening itself, drove without a stop and reached Kokrajhar almost along with the train. I stayed with the force to give them the confidence that I was with them under all circumstances. Ten of my men laid down their lives due to malaria. It was a very difficult deputation.

A sensational murder incident took place in Jamshedpur. I was asked by the DGP to form a team and investigate. I had no business investigating cases as I was in the Armed Police. Anyway, I formed my own team and moved to Jamshedpur. It was a trip to remember. The movement of the team was done by my official car from Patna. I stayed in a worn-out state government dak bungalow, although Tata Iron and Steel Company (TISCO) offered their best guest house for our stay. The special investigative team (SIT) was formed at the request of TISCO itself. I called a company commander of a battalion under me and requested him to prepare food for the team in the mess of the constables, for which each team member would pay.

We took a team of Forensic Science Laboratory (FSL) scientists from Patna to assist us in this investigation. The team did a marvellous job. While recreating the place of occurrence, they could identify the exact location of the suspected car. This car had already been serviced by the time we took over the investigation, yet the FSL team inspected the car bit by bit and recovered four more exhibits, including bullets and tufts of hair, even after so many days of the incident. This was an eye-opener for me. I could see how shallow the police inspection of the place of occurrence is as against that done by the scientists. We were able to recover the pistol and the bloodstained clothes from the house of the suspects. We were on the verge of the final exposé of the case when it was abruptly transferred to the CBI.

I convinced myself that I had no business to investigate that case anymore, and therefore, I should not take any further interest in this matter. However, I had learnt many professional aspects of a scientific investigation, which I used positively during my tenure as DGP.

My DGP had confidence in me. He would call me to his chamber and quietly pass on files for scrutiny and advice in sensitive matters. I had never gotten a chance until then to look into the functioning of the police headquarters, except for maybe the intelligence department. He exposed me to this, but discreetly. I could see the mess created by the so-called blue-eyed IPS officers of the government of that time. Ultimately, posterity pays for all of this, as such people are too short-sighted to understand the damage they create and the far-reaching consequences such idiosyncrasies have on well-established systems.

LIMITATIONS OF THE LEGISLATURE

Till I got to the National Police Academy, I had not been exposed to the activities of the legislature beyond textbooks. In the initial days, the Acts and Rules passed by the legislature would overawe me. I would get inspired by the content of the Acts and their interpretations by the judiciary, to the extent that I would try to use them in finding solutions to problems in policing. When I stepped into practical policing, I could see gaps in the implementation of the intentions of the legislature. To my dismay, with time and experience, I could see that these gaps just kept growing bigger and bigger.

One evening, in my early days as the SP of a district, I was sitting on a lawn surrounded by quite a few learned people. A young legislator, who perhaps was attempting a jibe at me, started advocating the killing of criminals by police. I nonchalantly asked him if he was willing to bring a private member's Bill in the House to this effect. He scorned me, saying he didn't want to lose the next election. This struck me. There are members who do not believe in a Bill and yet vote for it to make it into an Act. I felt concerned, not just as a policeman but also as a citizen.

In my SP days, legislators would come to me complaining about the actions of junior policemen. I would take their complaints seriously and try to address them in the most legalistic manner possible. Administrative solutions would be my last resort. In one incident, all the legislators marched together into my office. I assured them of an administrative redressal of their issues. As per my understanding, legislative bodies were meant to debate issues plaguing society to seek solutions through statutes. But when I suggested the same to the legislators, I clearly noticed that this did not find favour with them. They were just content that they had brought their matter to the notice of SP and three more echelons above him in case he did not act upon it.

During elections, an inadvertent narrative often keeps popping up about choosing legislators who can ensure the development of their constituency. My question is: aren't legislators meant to create laws that can ease problems of the common man? If the objective is development, then it has to frame laws that facilitate development, but the actual work should be left to the executive.

The overlap between the two bodies is too big to maintain the 'separation of powers', thereby rendering the spirit of the Constitution meaningless.

The year 2006 saw a very powerful period in the annals of the history of the Indian police, especially the legislative part of it. The Indian police till then was being governed by the Police Act. I had joined the police department when this Act held unchallenged sway over the functioning of the department, in both its form and content. We had become used to its presence. It was ingrained so deeply in us that thinking differently was nothing short of blasphemy. I had even used its quaint parts (after all, the law was more than a quarter-century old) to my advantage in many situations.

Then came an order of the Supreme Court. The states were given some guidelines and were directed to create new police acts for themselves. The CM of Bihar formed a committee to draft the Bill for the new Act. As the ADG (HQ), I was made a member of this committee, with the chief secretary as its chairman. This was going to be my first legislative experience.

The two major issues that needed to be addressed as per the guidelines were regarding political interference and the decisions taken by the chief political executive in postings and transfers of the DGP of a state.

A young lot of IPS officers came to me in groups canvassing

LIMITATIONS OF THE LEGISLATURE 213

for independence from political interference and similar things. Perhaps they thought this was their opportunity to get more 'powers' for the police. I asked them a simple question, 'How is your general image in the eyes of the people? Have you, as IPS officers, acquitted yourself so well that people have implicit faith in you?' Silence descended, and they retreated.

What most IPS officers fail to understand is that if the police wants more powers and independence, it will have to have an impeccable public image. When that happens, people themselves will push for such legal powers. The much-talked-about political interference has, in fact, become an inevitable part in the functioning of the police, only because the police has not been able to earn complete trust of the common man. This interference exists in a tenuous equilibrium, one that should not be disturbed in any manner for fear of breaking it.

An obvious debate pops up: which should come first? Image of police or its independence?

People's acceptance of the police will go a long way in achieving what the Supreme Court wanted. In my career, I have myself experienced how people's acceptance could kill the venomous desires of political powers; they couldn't touch me with a long bargepole. I indeed feel humbled and obliged to dedicate this book to the people of Bihar.

At a very personal level, having had the opportunity of interacting with all shades of legislators, from the most-educated to the not-so educated, I could see a clear demarcation into two broad categories. The first category feels that their best bet is the executive, hinting towards the officers and not the law. Hence, they do not attribute the cause of critical problems to a deficiency in law. The other category strongly feels that all problems can be solved by creating new laws.

These two groups lie on two extremes of the spectrum. The result is that there is a surfeit of laws but a dearth of efficacy. As soon as the legislature notices a social problem, they translate it into a Bill almost immediately. They completely overlook the fact that the existing laws are powerful enough to provide solutions if we try to interpret them in a conducive manner.

When I had proposed the creation of Special Auxiliary Police (SAP) for the Bihar Police, I was asked whether a new law needed to be enacted. I had categorically clarified that law provides for constables and that it is the prerogative of the government to decide the source of the appointed men. This was how we created a whole new concept in Bihar Police without creating a new law!

To the second category of legislators, this was almost blasphemous.

When I sat down to draft the Bihar Police Act, my primary addition to the existing Act was to purposefully introduce a few enabling sections, whereby technical personnel could be inducted into the police to enhance its performance. This was passed by the House without any debate.

I so fondly wish some visionary in the government could make use of these enablers to enrich police through advanced technology. In the first 10 years of the new government in Bihar, both the top politician and the political combination had largely remained constant. I was consulted on a number of occasions regarding the creation of new laws to make the police more effective. In a vast majority of them, I held on to my view that police has a very sound legal basis, which had been historically tested. Therefore, what was required was the intelligent, novel use of existing laws and not the creation of new ones.

There was only one exception. I wanted to get a new dimension to policing in the state government's control over the creation and use of black money. I sadly admit that I failed in this attempt of mine towards controlling crime. I was told that there is a lack of legislative competence to make it happen. Although, I still feel that if the law wasn't ultra vires and didn't militate against the PMLA, a state law against black money could have passed the test of legal scrutiny.

LIMITATIONS OF THE LEGISLATURE

The government has created various departments that run under its administrative control. Education and health are two of the most important ones that have a greater impact on the common man as compared to the police. Yet, these two are not a creation of statute, whereas the police is. As a result, the executive, namely the IAS officers and the ministers, take the liberty of controlling the structure and dynamics of these two without caring about the legislature. The police, however, gets shielded from such caprices of the government by virtue of its creation and control by law directly. Its anatomy is created by an Act, and hence, can be changed only by law, not by executive orders.

As I grew up in police, I realized that the executive drafts the Bills, and the legislature clears them. My textbook knowledge told me that there was a separation of powers amongst the legislature, the executive and the judiciary. What I saw, in reality, was that the executive was feeding the legislature its most sacrosanct function of 'legislating'. As a result, there was hardly any Bill that was not tabled by the executive and passed on party lines.

No wonder Acts that get passed in a hurry require amendments in a hurry!

The legislators raise issues that are pure narration of incidents that take place in society and seek intervention by the executive. Never have I seen a debate where the legislators tried to define the problem in its systemic perspective and seek legislative structural solutions. Only if the legislature could be an erudite body of debaters, who could discuss, debate and in the end lay their finger on the real reasons behind the problems plaguing the society, then they would be able to suggest solutions that could be woven into powerful legislation that would stand the test of time.

What happens instead is that the agenda is usually set up by the media and debated in the media on the basis of meagre reliable data and historical perspective of the problem. The government of the day decides in its wisdom to legislate on the issue. The members of the executive are tasked with the job at hand. They do it with legislative, technical finesse sans objective content. The Bill is tabled and almost pushed through.

It is not surprising that such Acts fail to affect the lives of people or at times even get rejected by them. The judiciary, too, finds it difficult to glean arguments from the debates in the House, stifling them from deciding meaningfully on constitutional issues raised after the enactment.

The culmination of the legislative machinery into such Acts, which reflect the thought process of bureaucrats and not the legislators, fails miserably in reflecting the need and will of people.

CHANGE THE WAY YOU LOOK AT THINGS

When you change the way you look at things,
the things you look at change.

—Max Planck

DIG/IG (Wireless) (13 June 1996 to 17 February 1999)

After three years in the BMP as its DIG Central Zone, I was sent to an assignment called DIG (Wireless). In Bihar Police, this was considered a 'shunted' posting, one of the most obscure. I, somehow, did not feel that way, though the politicians in power who ordered my transfer might have felt a sense of achievement. The best an IPS officer would do here was to keep transferring the 500 employees of the department, whose primary job was to transmit wireless messages of the police and government officials from one place to another. From the AIG below me to the ADG above me, there was no dearth of officers who would carry out this job.

I had to define my role very precisely in order to make my assignment meaningful.

All other IPS officers posted in the department during that period were from humanities background. I was the odd one out. I, therefore, decided to focus my efforts on the technical part and left the personnel component to the others. To be honest, I had no interest in the personnel management of this wing of the police. What excited me the most was the thought that my background in physics would finally come to use in a job that had drifted me far away from it. I wanted to make the most of this opportunity to improve the wireless communication of the Bihar Police.

There were three communication systems functioning in the police: VHF, high frequency (HF) and dedicated telephone network. The first was a wireless system to cater intra-district, while the second was an inter-district wireless communication. The third one was popularly known as 'hotline', which was ridiculed by everyone as 'cold line'. A large number of the communication equipment in use dated back to the Second World War. In fact, the 'hot tubes' that were functioning as diode and triode valves would make any person feel as if he had walked through a time machine.

I felt I had a lot of room to play around. Two officers were adequately qualified to become a party to my experiments. Both were in the rank of DSP one with an MSc degree in physics from Patna University, and the other with a BTech from BIT Mesra in electronics and communication.

For the gadgets in use, a technical wing of the department looked after their repair in workshops. I spent a substantial part of my time in these workshops with the staff there. I would even intervene in their work with my suggestions and solutions to their problems. I remember once I was watching a technician repair a set with a malfunctioning oscillator. The circuit was a little too complicated for him to repair. He was almost on the verge of declaring the set unserviceable and throwing it away as deadweight. I asked him to get a set from the same deadweight pile in the workshop whose frequency matched with the set he was trying to repair and extract the oscillator from the dumped set. This could then be jettisoned with the set at hand. He immediately understood what I was suggesting. The next day, he happily reported that the problem was solved except that the set looked slightly ugly. I felt happy that we had managed to salvage a set from being thrown away as garbage.

Wealth in the debris

Immediately after taking charge, I went to the technical workshop. I spent hours with my men to discover, to my joy, that they not only had the technical skills but also had enough theoretical understanding. I was thrilled that Bihar Police had a segment that understood the niceties of physics.

The purchase of spare parts of damaged wireless sets used to be done annually as a routine exercise. Because of my constant and close interaction with the technicians in the workshop, they were now confident of my genuine interest in the department and had begun to open up to me. One day, they told me that there were vintage sets belonging to the Second World War period lying in a godown a little distance from the office. These sets had become unserviceable but could be cannibalized for their workable parts. They suggested that if we used those parts instead of buying new spare ones, it could save the government a lot of money.

I loved this idea. I gathered all my technical staff and drove down to that godown. It was quite big and was covered in a thick layer of dust. The condition of the place soon faded out for me as I started tracing the circuit diagrams, locating the oscillator, modulator, demodulator with childlike excitement.

While I was lost in my own treasure hunt, suddenly one of the technical staff came running to me and, almost panting in excitement, said, 'Sir, there is silver in here.' In his hand was an old HF set, inside of which was an oscillator made of silver. We carefully removed the dust lying over it. Shining silver gleamed through.

There were many sets of this type lying in the godown. I got all of them collected, extracted the oscillators and asked a local goldsmith to check for their purity. His rough and ready method suggested very high purity of the silver. I then got it officially checked by the FSL of Bihar Police, which too confirmed the same result. A committee of various ranks in the department was formed to weigh the recovered silver and then seal it. The entire lot was deposited in the treasury of the collector of Patna district, and the information was recorded in writing.

Fifteen kilograms of pure silver from government's waste!

※

In one instance, I was reading through a file wherein close to 500 sets were to be sent to a company for capital repairs. This company, also the supplier for these sets, was charging ₹1,500 per set for repair. This amount was to be processed by the operation wing, which did not understand the technical functioning of the sets. I took the file to the workshop, called a meeting of the technical wing and asked them to get one of the sets that had to be sent for repair.

Upon examination, it was concluded that the battery of the set had died out. They opened up the 'power pack' of the set right in my presence, and we found that the battery was nothing but a neat collection of 10 pencil batteries in series. I ordered the purchase of 5,000 pencil batteries for the 500 sets. This simple, straightforward exercise saved us about ₹5 lakh.

The technical wing was a bunch of competent people who had solutions to many a problem. All they needed was encouragement. They did wonders during the period in which I was there.

In a world that was ignorant of the concept of mobile phones, I developed a simple patching device between VHF and hotlines to facilitate direct communication between the senior functionaries from interiors of one end of the state to another. A Range DIG, who once was in the interiors of a jungle handling a Naxal operation, needed to communicate with the DGP in his office at Patna. This patching device came to his rescue, and he could establish direct communication via the wireless set in his car from the jungles of Palamu with the DGP over the hotline. For

Bihar Police, this was nothing short of a marvel. The DGP called a meeting of all his officers functioning in the police headquarters to witness what he called 'magic'.

Bholwa and Kurdeg were the farthest police stations in the state of Bihar. The VHF link from these locations to the district headquarters at Ranchi used to be a problem. The wireless department had made multiple failed attempts at fixing this. I tried to link them to the state headquarters through a patch up of the VHF and HF network. In our experimentation of patching three channels, the hills of Bihar came in handy, and we could successfully use three high range hills to do this work. This was acclaimed as an achievement.

On one occasion, the DGP wanted to know if direct communication between Bistupur Police Station mobile in Jamshedpur and Kowali Police Station mobile in Patna was possible. Not only did I confirm its possibility, but I also made him listen to that conversation. This demonstration thrilled him no end.

By now, the dual tone multi-frequency (DTMF)[1] technology on the mics of the latest VHF sets had arrived. I set up codes for the VHF sets of each police station to enable them to talk to each other without being heard by any other police station.

In Naxal attacks on a police station, VHF sets had started getting looted. This was becoming a serious issue. I approached the manufacturers of the VHF sets to create a software that could disable the sets that were looted even in remote areas. This was successfully done, and we could stave off massive security threats.

The Pentium age was yet to arrive. Processors were still in the 486 age. I was probably the first and the only person who tried putting these archaic computers at the two ends of the hotline to establish text communication between two ends of the state.

---

[1] A touch-tone signal to the telecommunication providers generated through a touchpad of keys on a phone, replacing the rotary dial.

It became an exotic topic of discussion among the officers when the first message was sent from Muzaffarpur to Patna through these old-age computers.

I had conceptualized a very ambitious 'radio canopy' project during my tenure. I wanted to have seamless communication all over the state, not just geographically but also between all ranks of men in the Bihar Police. I had floated a global tender to the US, describing the problems we faced and recommending the technology that could be used to solve them. The data I had provided included a clear indication of the financials of the project too. This was the first time that Bihar Police had done anything like this. The response to this tender was very encouraging. Top telecommunication companies of the world came forward.

However, I could sense that a serious effort was being made by the government to thwart the project, and they finally succeeded in doing so. One of the biggest regrets I have even today is my failure to get Bihar Police under one canopy of a seamless communication system catering to voice, data and picture with a huge bandwidth. I remember when I used to tell people that one day, we would be the owner of the bandwidth of our communication system, they wouldn't even understand the magnitude of this. They would remain stuck in calculating the tower cost in the project.

When decision-makers have tunnel vision and little understanding of technology, the future of institutions gets seriously jeopardized.

At one point in time, the purchase wing of the police, headed by a senior officer, tried to ridicule my tender for analog VHF sets in the presence of reputed manufacturers. I could smell his lack of education, which made him believe that digital technology was better than analog. I felt hurt at the way my tender was being ridiculed. After he was done with his learned discourse, I politely told him that in carrier frequencies in the VHF range, digital technology, which is seen in the UHF and microwave range, was yet to appear. I offered myself to even explain to him the reason behind this difficulty. The teams of the top manufacturers present there seconded my submission. The senior withdrew, but the way he had approached the subject without understanding the technology had left me smitten.

I felt I was able to do justice to my role in this so-called shunted posting due to my long years of training in physics in my student days. This, in turn, also helped me later when I became the DGP of the state. I could take quick decisions, all on my own, by going straight to the workshop and discussing directly with the technical staff, bypassing hierarchy.

MY POWERS ARE ORDINARY

*My powers are ordinary. Only my
application brings me success.*

—Isaac Newton

IG (Training) (23 March 1999 to 6 March 2000)

Training was a routine exercise for the Bihar Police, never its forte. In the last decade of the twentieth century, constables were recruited in huge numbers. The level of mismatch between this number and the resources needed to train them was such that it shook the management of the police department.

With the division of the state into Bihar and Jharkhand, all police training institutes and schools went to Jharkhand. Such perfect timing for me to get posted as the IG (Training) in Bihar Police! The sheer number of untrained police personnel was mind-boggling. I knew I had an uphill task. I accepted the challenge.

My attention went to the resources available in terms of both place and people in the district Police Lines. I proposed that each district SP make arrangements for a makeshift training establishment in his own Police Lines and put to work his own people as instructors. Such a thing had never been witnessed in Bihar Police. This experiment was an instant hit.

The district SPs realized that they had recruited these men, they were the ones who were training them, so ultimately, they would be the final users of their product. This created a tremendous sense of responsibility in them. They felt empowered with the authority to use their trainees in times of urgency without seeking any permission from the police headquarters.

This project was criticized severely by the IPS officers of my vintage, so much so that the DGP who had approved of it became sceptical about it. They felt that I was diluting the standard of training.

A project that started as a no-taker soon metamorphosed into a successful experiment. I did everything without any government sanction and budget allocation.

I had noticed that in service, the training of men and officers was falling into disuse. There were two striking reasons for this:

1. Long duration of training courses which did not find approval with the trainees as well as their SPs.
2. Dislocation of officers from their base hampered them, both personally and professionally.

I changed the format of the in-service training programme and reduced it to a very short, typically a one-day course at the district headquarters for a small set of critical skills. I got the inspiration for this idea from the 'distributed intelligence' concept of computer network theory. This proved to be a big hit.

The DGP tasked me with the training of IPS probationers, although this is supposed to be handled by the police headquarters. I took it in my characteristic style. I would send questions and assignments to the probationers once every month, eliciting their answers. One time, I asked them to write a paragraph on 'A man on bail is a man in custody.' Almost all of them were baffled. After a series of questions and answers and a few hints, they could finally catch on to its meaning.

Throughout the training exercise, my only intent was to provoke these young minds into thinking. I wanted them to think differently and not fall prey to the rut and rot.

The department was falling short of men to tackle a large

number of incidents that kept happening every now and then. Some of these were creating riotous situations. The DGP called me up and asked me to raise an anti-rioting force in the state police. I applied a very similar concept. I made each district SP raise his own force. I held a meeting of old officers who had preserved all their old manuals and could impart training with only a minor bit of editing. Every district got their own company of state Rapid Action Force (RAF) to tackle riots with no government sanction and no financial requirement.

I had realized quite early that in assignments such as wireless, training, BMP, I had to function as a service provider to the mainstream police department. I needed to adjust to the changing requirements and purpose of these demands. I did exactly that.

I AM THE MASTER OF MY FATE

It matters not how strait the gate,
How charged with punishments the scroll,
I am the master of my fate,
I am the captain of my soul.

—William Ernest Henley

IG (Provisions) (23 November
2000 to 22 December 2003)
IG (Economic Offences Wing) (22 December
2003 to 31 March 2005)
Zonal IG Patna (1 April 2005 to 21 May 2005)

A new DGP had just taken charge. I was summoned immediately. In a very solemn voice, he expressed that he was planning to give me a new responsibility in the police headquarters as IG (Provisions). He felt that this segment of the department had become infamous because of its vulnerability to corruption at an unimaginable scale. Everyone, right from the constable to the DGP, knew this as a fact. In fact, a CBI case, popularly known as wardi ghotala¹, had already made things murky. The DGP seemed wary of this backdrop. He wanted me to head this segment and ensure that nothing which brings a bad name to the police, happens.

---

¹Uniform scam—a scam in Bihar Police in the years 1983–84 in the procurement of police uniforms and other amenities

I politely told him that the government might not agree to this proposal, as I was not in the good books of the chief political executive. He smiled at me and said that I shouldn't worry, as that had already been taken care of.

The next day, I was in the police headquarters as IG (Provisions).

It took me only a day to understand why this part of the department was the way it was. The rules laid out for purchases in government were being followed to the letter but not in spirit. A regular inspection of the office might not reveal anything improper. But if one looked under the hood, one could see corruption clearly. Cartels had been formed, and all orders were being placed only with a few local supplier firms year after year.

I feel my experience in the CBI helped me in handling this assignment. I formulated processes whereby the local supplier firms who pocketed everything were naturally edged out.

I asked the office to explain to me why the information about ITR filing was being sought from tenderers. I got a prompt answer putting all the blame on 'government instructions'. I picked up a random file and showed them a supply order worth ₹5 lakh, while the total ITR filed by the tenderer showed only ₹20,000. This, they could not counter by any logic. A new condition was introduced in the tender process that the total turnover in the ITR of any tenderer should be at least 10 times the supply order to ascertain the financial viability of the supplier. Only this change eliminated the local suppliers and broke the cartel.

At a very young age, which is proverbially called impressionistic, while working with the CBI, I had seen many standard ways in which corruption prospered. One of them was tailor-making of tenders. Corrupt officers would define the specifications in an order so smartly that it would almost automatically eliminate all other parties except the one of their choice.

At one time, a large number of ambulances had to be ordered, and I was to determine the technical specifications for the order. I suddenly got an idea. In the meeting with my staff, I unabashedly announced, 'I am neither an expert on ambulance technology nor can I become one. I can define my problem and the purpose for which we need ambulances. I will do only that in the tender document. The manufacturers are free to contact the police headquarters and seek any other relevant data they need.'

This type of tender was the first for the department. In the technical tender meet, each manufacturer was asked to present his case to convince us about his product. During the presentation, I asked one of them about the length of their stretcher. When they answered my question, I enquired whether they knew the average height of the constables of Bihar Police. They immediately packed up and withdrew.

We made this approach the norm. Probity in public life and transparency in all dealings are the keys to trust.

Bulletproof jackets were to be bought for Bihar Police. An understandably lengthy and cumbersome process had begun. At some stage, there was a technical cum legal snag, and the process had to be stopped for good. The supplier firm went to the high court, pleading that they had already invested a lot and the decision was unfair to them.

The DGP got summoned by the CM, who told him that the complaint appeared to be genuine. The DGP came back for a discussion with me. I told him that if we accede to this request, it will bring us to a legally weak wicket in court. We need to be consistent on our stand, especially since we had done this with due diligence and after proper deliberation. I believe these are the hallmark of a good administration. The DGP then went and explained this to the CM, who, in the end, agreed.

The Provisions wing of Bihar had a massive warehouse, which the IG (Provisions) would rarely visit. Even if he did, it would be a prearranged event with a lot of drills. I made it a point to pay unplanned visits to this warehouse almost always and quietly watched all activities inside. I observed subtle yet glaring gaps in the distribution of supplies to the units of state police. For instance, a new vehicle allotted to a district would not be given all ancillaries like a tool kit. This, though it appeared petty, cumulatively amounted to a huge sum of money. I created procedures that stopped such malpractices.

Upkeep of weapons was my charge. On inspections of the central armoury, I realized that arms in huge numbers had become unserviceable, unnecessarily occupying a large space. I was at a loss. Even the very old hands in the store had no clue. I turned to the Police Manual and, to my surprise, could find a simple solution. Following a provision that said that such weapons could be melted in the blast furnace, I got all of these melted in the Bokaro Steel Plant furnace. This had never been done earlier. This brought about a quantum change in the output of the department.

All complex problems have a simple solution

We were making arrangements for the general elections to the Bihar Assembly. The charge of the weapons was placed with me. A serious problem of shortage of about 2,000 weapons in the form of 303 rifles emerged. I discussed this with the DGP, R.R. Prasad, who asked me to seek help from neighbouring states. I shot off letters to my counterparts, but quite obviously, I did not get a positive response, as each state was also preparing for their respective elections.

I went to the experts. I called a conference and placed the problem before the armourers, basically the constables and the havildars. They came up with a really out-of-the-box solution. There were weapons in the R1 or Repair 1 category. Issues like a broken butt or a jammed bolt were all repairable but for the fact that the weapons were so archaic that the ordinance factory did not manufacture their spare parts anymore. When I got to grips with the problem, I could understand the solution.

The weapons that had become unserviceable were all brought in. Their usable parts were used to repair the R1 weapons. Carpenters from the battalions were immediately summoned for repairing the wooden part of the butt. It was a eureka moment for me. I grinned to myself. I galvanized the entire armourer cadre of the Bihar Police, asked all the SPs to send their R1 and R2 weapons to the arms headquarters and got them repaired. This exercise was done on a war footing and, finally, we got a huge number of repaired and functional weapons, many more than was required for the elections.

The cadre of armourers is quite small and often neglected by seniors who focus mainly on the large army of constables and officers. I needed these armourers for getting my work done, but I couldn't do any good to them because I was not their cadre-controlling authority. I immediately drew up a proposal before the DGP to make a change in this and hand it over to the IG (Provisions). My proposal was accepted, and all issues of the cadre that were hanging fire were resolved. I now had an army of satisfied armourers, making my output many times better. The happier your men are, the better they will perform.

One day while sitting in my office, I suddenly felt uneasiness in my chest. Sensing a problem, I very slowly came down the stairs and lay down on the rear seat of my car. I asked my driver to take me home. My mother saw my distraught face and probably sensed something wrong. We did not communicate, but she lost no time to put a Sorbitrate pill under my tongue. The family had seen a similar episode with my father in the past. My wife, who is a doctor herself, arranged for a cardiologist, who advised hospitalization. There I was in the hospital being treated for cardiac infarction. Everyone was all praise for the way I sensed my problem at the earliest moment, which saved my life.

It took me about four days in the ICU to stabilize and recover.

After I came back, I even went to the UK on a training trip which, I feel, helped boost my confidence.

In December 2003, I was transferred to the post of IG (Economic Offences Wing), an innocuous cell within the CID. Historically, it was created to look into scams in the cooperatives department. After going through the documents explaining the tenets and the purpose of its creation, I understood that I could expand its application to other departments as well without seeking any government nod. I studied the functioning of the revenue-earning departments in the government and found the loopholes in each one of them.

I picked up sales tax as my first project. I took the secretary into confidence and organized joint raids on warehouses where revenue loss was in crores. My experience of income tax raids from my CBI days came in handy. These raids were a massive success; criminal cases got registered. The secretary told me that revenue collection had gone up manifold. It was quite amusing how the senior sales tax officers were now taking out time to explain their laws to the IOs.

My next target was the Excise and Transport departments. Things looked up. A defunct unit of CID, which even the CID chief would not acknowledge as his priority, became a force to reckon with. The police department, however, did not appear as enthused. Ideas were sown in my mind, which flowered and blossomed later when I became the DGP of the state.

President's Rule had been imposed in Bihar in March 2005 owing to an inconclusive outcome of the elections that had just been held. Rumours said that the chief secretary picked me for the post of Zonal IG of Patna. I was to handle a field assignment after a really long break. I decided to get into my old groove, though I knew it would ruffle many feathers.

I realized that data analysis had grown up as a technique in investigations. Data analysis of call detail records had picked up in many states, while Bihar had been left far behind. I had been sidetracked in the department to the extent that I never knew when such techniques came into existence. I conceived a project around this and raised its standards using my statistical prowess through predictive mathematical modeling based on big data analysis. I had put in a personal effort towards this. Bihar Police was enabled to get real-time data for my model. Every district developed its technical and human resources and could arrest criminals as early as the stage of preparation of the crime. Cases could be detected with minimal invasion just via a brainstorming session within a group of police officers.

This became so intoxicating for the district SPs that they would compete against each other. The CM was eager to equip the police with this weapon. I drafted a note for the concerned minister in the Department of Science and Technology. A Cabinet decision was taken to this effect, but it never saw the light of day.

I held this post for a brief stint of hardly two months. It was almost after about 13 years that I was meeting people in my office in huge numbers, as many as 200 a day. This time, I decided to change my approach towards this activity. I did away with name slips from my SP days. I felt that such slips created more hurdles for people who came to me for help. I would instead ask people to walk in and raise their concerns with me directly. I would categorize the problem immediately, put it through a legal channel there and then, wait for the process to be completed and ensure an outcome.

SP abducts a truck

A gentleman walked into my chamber. He was tall, well-built and had an air of confidence. I looked at him, and he started narrating his complaint. The SP of a district had seized his truck and parked it in the police station. It had been around five days, and now he was being asked to pay an illegal sum of money for the release of his truck. I got upset because the allegation was against a district SP. I needed to verify it first.

Very impulsively, I made a call to the concerned SP. The conversation I had with him is so etched in my mind that I still remember every word of it.

'The trucks that ply on the national highway in your district, are there gangs who hijack them on and off?'

'Yes, sir, there are such gangs in the district.'

'When these gangs hijack a truck, do they give a seizure slip to the truck owner that the truck has been abducted by them unlawfully?'

'Sir, criminals never give a seizure slip, and why would they?'

'There is a truck at your police station campus that you have seized without giving a seizure slip to its owner.'

'Sir, that truck had hit the SP's vehicle. Hence, we seized it.'

'What is the difference between you and the criminal gangs then?'

I hung up.

I spoke in a very calm tone throughout the conversation, and I could hear his shocked and trembling voice from the other end. My message was clearly conveyed.

The man who had come with this complaint was still standing in front of me. Once my call with the SP was over, he left my room only to come back two minutes later saying, 'Sir, I have got a message on my mobile from my driver. The truck has been released.'

I received a letter from the new DGP one day, demanding an explanation on some decision I had taken as IG (Provisions). The officer who was now holding that charge came to me with the file and suggested that I should go and meet the DGP to settle the issue. I took all the relevant data about the issue from him and thanked him for his advice. Post that, I submitted my explanation in writing but never tried to meet or talk to the DGP. I have always followed that if someone creates a muck in his head about me, it's his job to clear it up. I will not be his scavenger. This principle has worked almost always. Wherever it did not, no harm finally came by anyway.

My style of working was becoming indigestible for the department. There were times when my successors faced the consequences of my doings. My seniors were at a loss to even understand my plans and my actions.

An IG is also an SHO

'Officer-in-charge, please register a case.' This used to be one of my pet orders right from the day I started as a probationer in the police. It made me feel that the police is not expected to inquire into incidents but only expected to investigate into matters. So, whenever I needed to pass orders on a petition, I would ask for an FIR to be registered and an investigation to be carried out.

As the Zonal IG, I would send hundreds of petitions directly to the police stations with orders to register cases and start investigation. I hated putting problems under the carpet. As a result, the number of cognizable offences increased tremendously.

My successor complained about this in a conversation with the DGP while we were sitting in his office one day. He said, 'How can a Zonal IG send matters directly to the SHO, bypassing functionaries like the DIG and the SP of the district?' He expressed that he felt it was administratively improper. The DGP quizzically looked at me and asked, 'Could you answer this Abhayanand?'

I said, 'Yes, sir, I can. As the Zonal IG, under Section

36 CrPC, I am also the SHO. I could have got the case registered in my office itself if only I had the FIR register of all the police stations. This was my only constraint, or else under the law, I could get the investigation started directly from my office.'

'Why should the aggrieved person lose time in sending petitions to the DIG first and then the SP and then maybe the DSP and finally the inspector? It will take infinite time for the grievance redressal. I don't see any wrong in getting orders sent directly to the SHO. As it is, I've ordered merely the registration of a case. The SHO can put the FIR through the process of supervision and investigation, and then take appropriate action.' After hearing my explanation, the DGP concluded that my approach was right and, in fact, even recommended it to others.

Because of my background in science and an understanding of technology, I didn't take time to catch up with the new techniques. What I also noticed was that certain smart IOs had monopolized this skill. I was strictly against such knowledge hoarding and spread this skill amongst as large a base of IOs as possible. This really helped in better investigation of cases.

During this posting, I was exposed to the ways of functioning of some senior officers, which left me aghast. The activities that they were involved in were beyond my imagination. In fact, I had to order for registration of a criminal case against the wife of a DM in one such episode.

DM's wife thinks she can run her own court

My jurisdiction extended to 10 districts of Bihar. The doors of my office remained open to people every day to ensure that people with grievances have the first access to a senior police officer.

On a particular day, I was faced with a very unusual complaint. The man who came in with a written petition was living in a rented house and had certain disputes with his landlord. One day, the wife of the DM, along with a posse of armed force, arrived at his house and tried to 'settle the dispute', which included almost an order to vacate the house. I was extremely surprised because never had I heard of such an incident in my entire career.

On the petition, I wrote to the SP ordering him to register an FIR against the wife of the DM and asking him to start an enquiry against the officer in whose order the deputation of the armed force was done. I gave the petition back to the petitioner, asking him to kindly give it to the SP of his district.

The next day, the DIG of that region called me up, literally pleading that he would ensure that such things don't happen again and that I may please pardon the local administration. He also requested that I meet the DM and his wife, who wanted to plead pardon.

The next day, both of them arrived in my office with folded hands and tears in their eyes. In a very stern tone, I raised legal questions to them, for which obviously they had no answer. Something told me that I should give them a chance, and I pardoned them with sufficient warnings. I kept wondering what makes such senior officers involve their wives in such illegal activities. What does it all even mean to them? I couldn't think of a definite answer. I checked up on the issue a month later and found that such activities had been halted immediately in the district.

I was told that a law and order problem had occurred in the market. I rushed to the place to find that the DSP was behaving roughly with the shopkeepers who were trying to close down shops. I talked to the shopkeepers to find that the goons working for an influential politician were collecting levy regularly, and the police was doing nothing about it. I ordered for tables to be laid out on the roadside and FIRs to be registered for all incidents, including those that had occurred in the past. Law had to be enforced irrespective of who was involved.

No wonder I was promoted and transferred within a few months.

Richa, the elder of my two children, had got into IIT Roorkee, followed closely on her heels by Shwetank, who got into IIT Delhi. Thanks to my so-called shunt postings that I could find time to teach my children. This also had another unintended consequence: the birth and evolution of Super 30.

While in their respective colleges, they had come home during a vacation. My father asked them about their plans after finishing college. Both answered in one voice that they were not sure about what they would do but were very clear about what they would certainly not do. Hearing such a reply, my father grew curious and asked, 'What won't you do?'

They said, 'For two generations, this family has kept its brains as girwi[2] with the government, and we are not willing to do this anymore.' My father was a little shocked. He looked at me, but when he found that I was unmoved, he could understand that no more questions were needed.

---

[2]Mortgaged

THE INTERREGNUM CALLED SUPER 30

My children had got admission into the prestigious IITs one after the other. I continued to serve in the peripheries of the police department as per the wishes of the government. During this period, I chanced to meet a young man named Anand Kumar in the room of the editor of an English daily in Patna. Anand appeared to be a man of average means, who was coaching students in mathematics at the intermediate level in his coaching institute named Ramanujam School of Mathematics. We got introduced, and our interactions began as he started visiting me in my office and at my residence. Mathematics would be our common talking point. I also got an opportunity to teach physics in his classes; an activity I hadn't experienced before but ardently wished to.

I always believed in the power of education, especially in the lives of poor families, and I had seen that it was their only ticket to prosperity. From my early days, I felt a deep sense of gratitude towards society. The feeling that I owe a lot to the people around me overwhelmed me. I could now see a path getting carved out. With some confidence after teaching my children and seeing them emerge successful in their competitive exams, I decided to try my hand at guiding poor talented students for IIT-JEE.

I sought the help of Anand Kumar. In 2002, my idea was set into motion when we decided to select 30 bright students from his classes, all belonging to financially weak families, and started guiding them for JEE. Super 30 was born.

We did not have a chemistry teacher. Students were enthusiastic and managed without one. As I started interacting closely with them, I soon realized that these students needed us not for helping them gain knowledge of the subjects but more for instilling confidence in their abilities. I took physics classes every day, even on holidays.

The classes were held in a remote corner of the city, where even connectivity via a concrete road did not exist. I remember it used to be a walk of about 100 yards through narrow alley, literally with a handkerchief over my mouth and nose to prevent an attack from flies and insects. All of this faded against my passion for teaching the students. The result of the first effort was satisfying quantity-wise, though not as much quality-wise.

As this journey progressed, I discovered my deficiencies. Not being a professional teacher had both its advantages and disadvantages. Introspection helped. The results started improving every year, from 2003 to 2005. The coaching world of Bihar had woken up to a new phenomenon, one that was becoming a household name.

The 2005 general elections had brought in a new government that decided to put me centre stage with onerous responsibilities. My teaching time was being snatched away by State obligations. I was now not able to monitor the Super 30 activities on a daily basis, which I had managed so far in the first three years. At the same time, the results of Super 30 had started positively impacting the commercial output of Anand Kumar's classes, which were his source of livelihood.

By 2006, this experiment had caught the attention of international media. By 2007, I figured that things in Super 30 were not going as per the original intentions.

I reckoned that this was essentially a clash between profession and passion. For me, this was a passion, but for him, this was his full-time profession. We had diametrically opposite missions, and therefore, couldn't run in tandem. I parted ways with Anand Kumar. I even declined to be a part of the celebrations of the results that year in Patna, where the CM of Bihar was the chief guest.

Our last public appearance together was in an award function titled 'Real Heroes' organized in Mumbai by Reliance Industries.

I had never tried to find out how the expenses of Super 30 were being met by Anand Kumar. I only knew that my contribution was absolutely non-financial and purely academic. In my mind, Super 30 was a philanthropic effort that was never to be made commercial.

The concept did not die out though. Many people approached me to carry it forward. Each child who has benefitted from this experiment is a story of the transformation of lives of thousands of poor families overnight, not through corruption but through education.

In 2008, I had withdrawn from teaching activity completely after getting disillusioned. One day, I received a sudden request from one of my acquaintances seeking time for a meeting on behalf of somebody named Maulana Wali Rahmani in my office of ADG (BMP) for a serious dialogue. I acceded to his request. A sober-looking old man in white attire and white flowing beard came into my office. His demeanour impressed me. He put forward his request. He said that he had seen me help many poor students find their feet in life through education. He wanted me to do the same for his community, which he felt was educationally not up to the mark, especially in the field of science and mathematics. The candid and forthright manner of the Maulana left me no option but to accept his request with great pleasure.

Rahmani 30 came into existence instantly because all logistical arrangements were made by him without any delay. I was amazed at the fervour the community showed for their future generations.

What followed was a decade of association with the Maulana. Although he was essentially a politician, he always respected my principles and never talked to me about anything apart from education in the Muslim community. He never discussed Bihar politics with me, though he knew fairly well that I had access to many important facts as the DGP. Similarly, the political chief of the state, too, knew that the Maulana, who enjoyed a pride of place in Muslim matters, held me in high regard. Yet, he would not get his political feelings conveyed through me. May the soul of Maulana Wali Rahmani rest in peace.

Rahmani 30 grew in stature with age. Today, it is a strong organization that has kindled the flame of education in its community without state support. They are competing with other students in all national-level competitions without seeking any type of concession.

Hailing from Gaya in Bihar, I got an invitation from the people of my native place to set up a Super 30 for the poor children there in 2009. This effort was led by a businessman named Dalmiya. Vagaries of old age had caught up with him, yet he literally begged for resources from society, even though he could fund it all by himself. His motto was '*Samaj ke dwara, samaj ke liye* (By the society, for the society).' It resonated with my views.

This is how Magadh Super 30 came into being. It was managed by a local journalist, Pankaj Kumar, who is now seen as a father figure for the hundreds of families whose economic status has been transformed through education.

Although Shri Dalmiya is no more, today, his efforts, in the shape of Magadh Super 30, is a modern-day living example of our traditional gurukul. One has to see it to believe it. This experiment contributed in its own novel way in containing the menace of extremism that had hit the Magadh region hard. This was a silent, bloodless revolution.

S.K. Shahi, who was running an NGO in Delhi called the Centre for Social Responsibility and Leadership (CSRL), approached me in 2009 to help set up a Super 30 at Kanpur under the aegis of Gas Authority of India Limited (GAIL). He brought along with him a request from the chairman as well. I thought this was worth exploring. The board of GAIL had very direct and blatant questions about my methodology. I explicitly

THE INTERREGNUM CALLED SUPER 30

put forth the concept and the USP of Super 30 without weaving emotional stories. By 2008, Super 30 had cleverly been made to look like an intricately beautiful fairy tale. After speaking to me, when the board was able to see through this clearly, they were very keen on bursting this bubble.

They requested me to come on board. I agreed on one condition: 'I will not have any financial links with the project. My involvement will only be academic.' I travelled to take in-person classes on long holidays and would teach online on other days.

This was the beginning of a long list of CSRL Super 30s, the count of which I fail to keep.

Other PSUs, too, noticed the promising results of GAIL Super 30 and contacted me. My model of engagement with them remained the same. This activity yielded improved results every year. The number of such centres increased markedly and got noticed by universities across the world.

The activity still goes on, but I watch it grow from a distance.

In the year 2010, one day, I received a letter from the Andaman government addressed to the Government of Bihar, requesting my help to set up a Super 30 outfit for the benefit of the educationally backward people of their area. I was delighted to see this.

Within a few days, I got a letter from the Bihar government seeking an explanation about this activity without government permission. I was amazed at this, more so because the head of government had attended the celebration of Super 30 results publicly in the past. I sent a reply nevertheless, 'I do not need anyone's permission to teach physics and mathematics to poor children in my free time. I am not making money from this activity.' The matter did not arise again, but I realized I couldn't carry out this activity on a large scale.

After my retirement in 2014, I devoted all my time to teaching. Transparency in every aspect of this activity pierced the veil of secrecy that had hitherto been worn on various grounds, most importantly security.

Well-meaning people gravitate towards Patna to understand the concept of Super 30. Each one edits the story in his own way. Each has his own version of the truth. Projects that don't have any hidden agenda thrive, and those that have vested interests fall by the wayside.

Many individuals and organizations continue to approach me for help. I have but one thing to say, 'I don't have money to run such institutions. I can hand over, for free, the "software" I have developed and handhold you for a few years. Your institution will learn to mature and become independent, while another Super 30 is born somewhere else.' This approach has worked. Super 30, today, has proliferated into every part of the country, helping poor and talented students. Numerous such Super 30s today are delivering the benefit I always desired them to. The carriers, who joined me on this journey at different points in time, kept changing. It has been heartening to see that after I initiated Super 30, a noticeable number of officers started chipping in with similar efforts to help poor children.

If a mathematics teacher teaches mathematics, it is no news to the world. If a coaching organization that avowedly makes arrangements for students to help them qualify for IIT-JEE, tells the world that a large fraction of its students succeeds each year, the world will not sit up and take notice.

It is akin to saying that if a dog bites a man, it does not make news. However, if a man bites a dog, it catches attention spontaneously. This is exactly what happened during the period 2003 to 2007. People observed that a top cop who was busy tackling the menace of crime in the 'badland' of Bihar took time off to teach and guide students with a genuine intention of transforming society through education. His efforts were noticed as 'never before'. The man was seen as 'biting the dog'.

There was nothing extraordinary about the results that Super 30 produced, as there were many institutes in this country that gave better results both qualitatively and quantitatively. I feel it was the 'Top Cop with a Chalk' image that made Super 30 exotic.

This explains why the international media lost interest in this experiment after I announced my exit from the system in its first form. Inertia at the national level carried it on for a few years. Unfortunately, no one tried to probe into the tall claims made by the organization and how it was being run. Transparency steadily became a casualty till Super 30, in its original form, died a natural death. The essence of the experiment, however, survived.

The king is dead, long live the king!

THE ELECTIONS OF 2005

A ny democracy stands on just one pillar—fair elections. Before I delve deeper into this statement, a few noteworthy incidents need a mention.

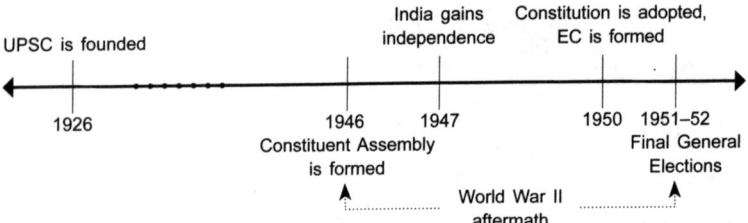

This timeline is quite intriguing. The concept of UPSC was kindled as early as 1926, much before the country had defined its fundamental law and administration structure. When the Constitution was adopted in 1950, this commission was constitutionalized. The Federal Public Service Commission was renamed UPSC as we know it today.

The Second World War had just ended, taking a toll on the country's resources. Consequently, corruption bubbled up at the surface, starkly visible to the naked eye. The Constituent Assembly became wary of this. They felt the need for strong and sturdy pillars to hold the weight of the country's day-to-day administrative responsibilities. The All India Services (AIS) was conceived under Article 312 (2) of the Constitution.

One can imagine the prestige and the position that was bestowed upon this segment by the lawmakers. The brightest minds were handpicked for this job. I would not hesitate in saying that the AIS officers formed the most elite group of people in the country. In fact, if you look around, you would discover that nowhere else in the world are such highly capable and qualified men and women put on these jobs, specifically, in the police.

With such intellectual pedigree and such privilege of authority, there is absolutely no tenable reason why they should not be able to fulfil the purpose of their creation.

UPSC and the Election Commission of India (ECI) are amongst the few institutions that were designed to function with autonomy and freedom as permanent constitutional bodies. Such was the level of trust placed on them. Their existence can be called meaningful only if they can protect the fabric of democracy.

An election is the biggest celebration of a democracy.

The other fact that stands out is the formation of the ECI in 1950, although it became visibly present only towards the end of the century.

Up until 1990, the IAS and IPS officers understood the ownership that was expected out of them. They were successful in earning the trust of the people and had gained the reputation of being able to uphold the ideals of administration. They, quite literally, formed a network of distributed authority at their respective levels to ensure that elections were conducted in a fair and free manner.

Around 1990, ECI started becoming an audible voice in the electoral processes after being a background score for almost 40 years. The role of the IAS and IPS officers in conducting the elections got circumscribed. They now became adeshpaals[1] of this constitutional body. AIS was shaken. Political interference was allowed to seep in through the cracks that got created. A torrent of excuses for under-delivery gushed.

Without going into the chicken-and-egg debate, I would still say that no reason is good enough for the AIS to have become a let-down.

---

[1] Peon

In the Representation of the People Act of 1951, enacted just before the first-ever general elections, the concept of a 'returning officer' came to life. There is no legal compulsion on who should take up this post. Yet, somewhere someone created a tradition of appointing the DM or the SDM for carrying out this job. Was it due to mere convenience or something else? I do not know.

Officers from the civil administration, under whichever nomenclature, would not have any implicit or explicit interest or association with the contestants of an election outside their home state. Imagine if we imported such officers and nominated them as returning officers, the fairness of elections would become as clear as day.

Now the question is: what is a fair election?

While preparing for the UPSC examination, I happened to read quite a few good books on humanities. What I understood was that the absence of faith in the fairness of any election, right from the level of a panchayat till the president of the country, is a guarantee of the demise of democracy. The structure survives, but the spirit sleeps and eventually dies.

The first glimpse of the strength of a system lying in its fairness was when I got a chance to take independent decisions during a by-election as ASP Sasaram. I could literally feel the massive moral support of the majority when I knew that the people in power loathed my decisions. I had got my first clue.

In the early part of my career, I had no occasion to countenance the ECI. Their observer would visit us, but we never felt his nagging presence. We would take it as our duty to ensure that the election was conducted properly, benchmarking the satisfaction of the people as the ultimate test of our performance.

By the time I reached the position of a DIG, my first interaction with the ECI had begun. My perception of my role in elections changed completely. I was no longer the owner of the process. I lost all creativity and would just look up to this body for instructions at every step.

During the Bihar Assembly elections of the early '90s, I was the DIG of Armed Police. I had been entrusted with the job of only force deployment. This was a clear indication that the whole concept of 'fair election' was being confused with 'peaceful election'. The state was flooded with paramilitary forces.

One particular evening, the divisional commissioner of Tirhut division went on air to say that there wasn't enough force for him to conduct fair elections in his area. All hell broke loose. The chief election commissioner, who was known for demanding reports by the clock, in hours, minutes and seconds, asked the chief secretary of Bihar to submit a report by 9 a.m. the next day. I submitted details of the forces deployed in the concerned jurisdiction. A meeting was convened at 6 a.m. in the chamber of the chief secretary. The meeting started on a very solemn note. In a gruff voice, the chief secretary said, 'There is more force in your area, Divisional Commissioner, than was deployed in the Battle of Dunkirk.' There was laughter in the meeting hall. The matter was closed. The ECI had mistaken Bihar elections as a battle that had to be fought. I was a witness to the way the elections were conducted. Despite the war-theatre backdrop, the elections witnessed violence, IED explosions and silent rigging.

The losing party cried hoarse over rigging, and the people's demand for President's Rule was dutifully raised.

The sanctity of elections held in this country has been questioned frequently. Unfortunately, this frequency has only increased monotonically. Systems have carried the blame most times. Things do improve when systems are tweaked a bit, but the gains are very ephemeral.

By now, I was clear on what a fair election meant to me—an election where there are no grievances from the losing party after the results are declared.

It was finally in 2005 that I got a chance to be a part of what was called a 'historic election' in Bihar. The ECI nominated me to the team from the police side to handle quite a few distinct responsibilities. I got a free hand and did not have to look up for instructions. I freely experimented with new ideas. For the first time, I could see the concept of 'distributed intelligence' in play, with ECI sitting at the centre of it all.

What made the elections of 2005 historic?

The activities carried out during the 2005 elections were unique in many ways. Every action of mine had only one objective—a fair election. I would like to list just a few techniques I adopted that made a massive impact on the entire electoral process.

Voter's list: Fake voters had crept into the voter's list. Out of a voting population of about five crore people, as many as 20 lakh were identified and removed. These included many dead people who had been deftly added to the list over a long time.

Booth allotment: Deputation of the police force as well as the officers at the voting booths was done using a process of randomization through computers, thereby eliminating the scope of any manual intervention.

Repeat voters: In a vast majority of booths, voters were photographed while polling. This data was run through an imported software using facial recognition technology to identify repeat voters.

Force deputation: The data of votes polled at each booth in the election that was held six months ago was put through a software that used the inclusion-exclusion model to develop a coefficient indicating the extent of booth capturing. This was used to decide the deputation of force instead of the subjective report of observers.

Booth captures: A booth-wise detailed analysis of the booth captures was done. Cluster maps were made to identify the reasons behind booth captures. They were elaborately identified, and tough legal action was taken indiscriminately against them.

Rotation of IPS officers: Cadre IPS officers who had chosen to run away from state government at an early stage and hide in the anonymity of the vast sea of Government of India were brought back to conduct elections. They were rotated throughout the state to standardize the preparation and remove all possibilities of any kind of biases.

Black money: Black money plays a very important role during election days. A committee headed by the chief secretary of Bihar was created with all state- and Central-government agencies to closely monitor the raids conducted to curb this aspect of elections.

This was the first and probably the only time in the history of elections in Bihar that such initiatives were implemented at this scale and in such detail. The results spoke loud and clear.

The 2005 elections that were held in October–November concentrated on the purity of voters list, identifying miscreants at the booths, applying appropriate law to each such person and following up at the micro-level. This laid a more serene backdrop that lulled the political parties into sleep regarding the strategy being adopted by the ECI. Whatever was being seen by the media was not even the meat of the strategy that was made.

A fair election was finally conducted in Bihar after almost two decades.

THE ROAD LESS TRAVELLED BY

I shall be telling this with a sigh
Somewhere ages and ages hence:
Two roads diverged in a wood, and I—
I took the one less traveled by,
And that has made all the difference.

—Robert Frost

ADG (Special Branch) (17 December 2005 to 9 April 2008); ADG (Headquarters) (17 February 2006 to 9 April 2008)

Year 2005. President's Rule had been imposed in Bihar. The Assembly could not get constituted based on the results of the elections held earlier in February. Re-election was conducted in October of the same year. An era of non-Lalu raj was heralded in November.

After being kept in hibernation for 15 long years in the peripheries of the police department, I was brought centre stage. Many of my colleagues had undergone a similar fate in these years; some had even lost their equanimity. I somehow managed to retain my sanity by engaging myself in academics, not just as an indulgence but also with a desire to make myself socially relevant in this domain. I said to myself, 'So what if the government is not interested in me? Society is.' I found my rescue from getting into a morass and decaying. As a consequence, an alternate image of mine was created in society, one that was much larger than that of a police officer.

I was keenly observing the political situation emerging in Bihar during the past few years. In the early part of my career, I had worked on the field across several districts, witnessed electoral processes firsthand, and hence, had a fair idea of how things worked back then. Elections before 1990 and those after, I felt, fell into two distinct categories. Post-1990, since I was not in field postings anymore, my understanding of the electoral processes remained limited to and constrained by newspapers and magazines. I got my hands on erudite reports of senior journalists whose pieces were more than scholarly and capable of sparking intellectual debates. As an officer who had been intentionally shelved from the mainline of administration, I did not feel satisfied with just the media analysis. My scientific mind demanded that I separate the grain from the chaff.

The question that kept haunting me after each election was: why doesn't the losing party accept defeat gracefully? This question was almost always absent in the elections prior to 1990.

As soon as polling would end, talks on rigging would become quite voluble. This became more marked as the decade progressed. According to the media, 'rigging' was associated with violence during polls and maybe just before or just after. I could not accept this definition. Another noteworthy development in this period was that the returning officers had started getting rewarded immediately after the formation of the new government.

Thus began my quest to find out that 'one thing' that was the central cause of unfairness in elections. I knew it could not be violence. Violence was just a distraction to hide the main culprit. The word 'djinn' gained currency in this decade. I wondered what was its relevance, more so, in the context of elections?

It had taken me more than a decade to clearly define and find a simple solution to this problem. Just when I was able to crystallize my thoughts around this, I got the godsent opportunity to be a part of the re-election in 2005 in Bihar, the election that literally started the second innings of Bihar's politics.

Out of nowhere, I was summoned by the chief election commissioner, B.B. Tandon, to meet him in his office. Agenda of the meeting unknown, I was at a loss to comprehend why I had been singled out. As soon as I reached there, I got ushered in and was asked to take a seat. Then, out popped the million-dollar question, asked forthrightly, 'How can a fair election be conducted in Bihar?'

༄༅༅

Fair election in Bihar?

This question is quite genuine. The track record of the sanctity of elections in Bihar had been appalling ever since 1992. All elections had been branded as rigged by the losing party every time. The people of the state raised a hoarse cry for President's Rule almost incessantly, which did not appeal to me at all. I felt that a fair election is a primary requirement in a democracy, an answer to all democratic issues.

So, when this question was asked to me, I was not taken aback. I could understand that the bogey raised and the noise created in the last 10–12 years in Bihar would have definitely been noticed by the chief election commissioner, whose concern was quite justified.

I did not have a well-defined plan in mind, but my impromptu answer somehow appealed to him. I said, 'Sir, an election is as fair as its voter's list. If the voter's list is corrupt, the election cannot be fair.'

He asked me, 'How will I be able to say that the voter's list is corrupt?' Based on the data I had collected from the media over the past few years, I had concluded that the number of voters in the voter's list far exceeded the number in the census data. I explained my observation to the chief election commissioner. He seemed to like the way I was placing things.

We went into some details, and what followed was a purging of ghost voters from the list. It turned out later that this exercise had influenced the outcome of the election way more than any other move.

∞

Perhaps the djinn had been identified.

We had defined the problem, we now needed to ensure that the execution did not fail. What could be the most important gear to make this machinery work? The answer was obvious. It had to be the officers on whom the entire onus of conducting the election lay.

∞

Only fair officers can conduct fair elections

The chief election commissioner asked me another question, 'Does your department have SPs who can think independently and can implement the instructions given by the Election Commission?'

I was painfully aware that the best of the officers of the cadre had left on central deputation and didn't seem to have any plans of coming back. I improvised an idea at that very moment and made a suggestion to him.

The chief election commissioner could make a request to the Government of India, asking for the services of these officers directly under the ECI. I noticed that this idea clicked instantly, and right in my presence, he dictated a letter on behalf of the ECI to the prime minister, requesting for the services of 11 SP rank IPS officers from the Bihar cadre who were then on central deputation. The list that was mentioned in the letter was based on my recommendations during our discussion. The letter was shot off immediately. I was really impressed and surprised at the speed with which the decision was taken and executed.

A week later, I came to know that nine of those officers had been relieved by the Government of India for Bihar election duty. During the election preparations, these officers were transferred and posted in districts in a phase-wise manner and rotated throughout the state to ensure that the instructions of the ECI were carried out in letter and spirit. The impact of this methodology was just too emphatic. Had this been extended to bringing in returning officers from outside the cadre, the sanctity of the entire election process would have been many times higher.

In the election that ensued in October–November, I must say, I experimented with a lot of my ideas in association with the chief electoral officer of Bihar.

Police will follow a machine's orders

I had witnessed the first election of my career as a probationer in Ranchi. Since it was a novel experience for me, I would go to every arena of election preparations, participate in the activities from the periphery and observe things keenly. With each observation, I would question myself: how free and fair is the election going to be with this process?

There was one issue that irked me constantly. I had seen that the representatives of most parties and candidates moved around in the Police Lines arena, trying to influence the members of the police team in the process of deputation of policemen to the various booths. Whenever I got an opportunity, I would physically be present at the Police Lines to prevent this from happening. Yet, I was not satisfied because I wanted to develop a system whereby even if a senior police officer wants to interfere in this process, he will not be able to do so.

I had done an experiment in the early days of my career as SP Nalanda. In the age before computers became a household name, I had devised a method whereby policemen were deputed to electoral booths through a process of randomization, without any manual intervention. Incidentally, the DM who had worked with me at Nalanda was functioning as the chief electoral officer of Bihar in 2005. We, therefore, had no problem replicating my older successful experiment with better software this time around.

When this decision was communicated to the policemen in the field who were responsible for the deputation of the forces, they were quite intrigued. I had to bring them to Patna to get them trained on that software. I, too, was slightly nervous about the new process because this had a state-wide impact. Any failure anywhere would put complete responsibility on me for my single-handed decision.

There were certain hiccups, but fortunately, all of them were resolved much before time. The DGP, who was very sceptical of the process, called me one evening after seeing the process functioning smoothly at the Police Lines of Patna and felt that there was no threat of human bias anywhere in the process. I felt happy that the doubting Thomases had been satisfied. This change in the booth allocation for elections did wonders. Today, it has become one of the strongest features of the electoral process.

Simultaneously, the issue of violence in elections was not ignored. Deputation of armed forces was done to ensure that booth capturing and violence did not occur. The ECI was supervising every little detail.

When you're hitting a wall, focus on one brick

The ECI planned to come to Patna and address all the police officers, right from the DGP to the SPs, DIGs and the Zonal IGs. This meeting was being held in the conference hall of the secretariat of Patna. The ECI had, by then, already passed an order saying that the ADG (Special Branch), i.e. I, would be monitoring the election arrangements from the police side.

After the team addressed all the officers in the room, the session was opened for discussion. One of the DIG rank officers, who was an eloquent Hindi orator, made an emotional speech about how the Bihar Police Men's association would hamper and create hurdles in the path of election processes and how the state police administration would be put into difficulty by their actions. It was a sufficiently long, extremely moving speech with a suggestion that the ECI should scrap this association. At the end of the speech, I noticed, to my surprise, a huge majority of the officers present there started thumping their tables, as is seen during debates in the Parliament.

The meeting ended on this note, and the officers started leaving. I heard the chief election commissioner calling out my name, asking me to stay behind for some discussion. All the three members of the ECI were huddled at one place, tension visible on their faces. It was not difficult to understand that the speech and the response it got had left them quite upset and concerned. I was asked to advise.

Calmly, I said, 'The Election Commission is here to get the election conducted in a free and fair manner. It should not get involved in peripheral issues like the Police Men's Association. This association has been there since my father's days, it is there today, and will very likely remain in the future too. My suggestion would be that we should concentrate on the preparations as per the plan. As far as I know and understand this association, they know that if they do anything silly to obstruct the elections, it will turn out to be suicidal for them. A tiff exists between them and the officers, but they are mature enough to understand where to draw a line.'

I could see that after my reassurance, they felt relieved, and the tensed wrinkles on their faces started receding. They wanted me to find out why had this speech been given in the first place. I told them that generally, the association has a running fight with the senior police officers and this speech was only its manifestation; the ECI should not get bothered by this. Their concerns had been addressed.

∞

One of our primary focus areas was a whole-hearted drive against black money, which plays a very important role during election days. Under the orders of the chief election commissioner, a committee headed by the chief secretary of Bihar was created with all sate and central government agencies. These were the agencies that dealt with black money, like customs, central excise, income tax, Economic Offences Wing of the state police, the IB, the CBI and the local police Special Branch. The committee held meetings every third day to monitor the progress of the raids conducted and to review the intelligence inputs gathered.

All these measures created an environment for a fair election in the state.

24 November 2005. Bihar assembly poll results had been announced, and the coalition of the Janata Dal (United) and the Bharatiya Janata Party had won by a convincing margin. The losing parties accepted their defeat gracefully and were trying to figure out the causes for their defeat. The chief election commissioner called me up the same evening just to express his pleasure at the way the elections had been conducted. He had reposed a lot of faith in me and felt I had fulfilled my role quite well. We had worked as a team and brought about a lot many modifications in the process of the election.

Soon after its formation, the new government was struggling with certain serious and critical problems that needed to be resolved at the earliest. Traditional methods and solutions would easily take five years to fruition, and that they could not afford. People of the state were expecting instant results because they had voted on the promise of better governance. There was a general feeling amongst the top politicians of the two ruling parties, including the CM, that crime would just melt away, and criminals would flee as soon as the change of political guard would take place.

This did not happen.

In less than a month's time, a kidnapping took place in Patna, and on the first day of the New Year, a massacre happened in Vaishali, where people were locked in a house and burnt to death. These incidents visibly shook the faith of the new government.

Some of the top ministers of the Cabinet started feeling that the development of the state would have to be kept pending till law and order and crime situation came under control. They would keep asking me, *'Law and order kab tak thik ho payega* (By when will the law and order situation be set right)?' How could one answer such questions? I preferred to keep quiet but was repeatedly reminded that everyone was in a hurry to get this sorted. We needed to innovate if we wanted instant solutions to prolonged problems.

An air of expectations hung all around. People had a list of top priorities in their minds for the new government to work on. The new government had to deliver. I knew that something had to be done that could create a macro-level impact and sustain on its own once the wheel was set into motion.

The pressure of a promise

Soon after being sworn in, the new CM called a meeting of the police department. The police headquarters gave a presentation, communicating that the department lacked all types of resources, both animate and inanimate, and that there was interference in its functioning that needed to stop if we wanted results. The demands that were raised were quite huge. I was on personal leave for a trip to Delhi and had no clue about that presentation.

When I returned, I was summoned by the CM for my view on the matter. The first thought that came to my mind was, *'Na nau man tel hoga na Radha naachegi*.'[1] The police department had basically told the CM that either the government give them all the resources or be ready to face the consequences of not being able to live up to his promises made during the election campaign. I could empathize with him.

He wanted to know if there was any method by which an impact could be made immediately. Before I could even respond, he suggested, *'Police ka rutba bahaal karwa dijiye* (Restore the status and power of the police), and things will improve immediately.' My retort was, *'Police ka rutba aur wardi ki gundagardi mein bahut fark nahi hota hai. Rutba hoga to kanoon ka.* (Enforcing the power of police is no different from exercising hooliganism in uniform. Power has to be only of Law, not of police).'

I made it very clear to him that police had to work within legal limits and could not create its own laws. Problems keep changing from time to time, but laws don't. In fact, it is the job of the top police officer to interpret and use the existing laws to tackle different situations. This is where his ability will count.

He said, 'As head of the legislature, I can get laws that are deficient either created or amended. As the head of the executive, I can also get the police department the money

---

[1] It is a Hindi proverb inferring a situation where someone places impossible demands for doing a task.

that they require.' My brief answer was, 'I need neither, as laws are in plenty, and policemen and judicial officers are in sufficient numbers.'

In matters of crime control, resources are not the rate-limiting factor[2]; it is the mental capability of the administration that decides who wins or loses the chase with the lawbreakers. Implementing the law doesn't require huge capital.

∞

I had my next move conceptualized—an idea which gained popularity by the name 'speedy trial'. People invariably ask me why I chose Arms Act cases to begin my speedy trial mission. My reasons were threefold.

1. Almost all crimes of violence are committed using firearms.
2. Almost all criminals are arrested at least once in their lifetime with an illegal firearm.
3. All the witnesses of such cases are policemen, so trial becomes very easy.

This simple logic helped me push through Arms Act cases in the courts to secure a conviction.

∞

Illegal weapons become police's weapon

I realized that instead of frittering away my energies in all directions, I would need to find that one point that could create multiple impacts. My mind got stuck on the concept of illegal firearms. With more than 25 to 30 years of practical experience in police, I was confident that any criminal of

---

[2] It is the most critical variable in a process, which has the maximum impact on its progress.

some standing could be arrested with illegal firearms under Section 25(1)(A) of the Arms Act at some point in his life.

By itself, this section is not very heinous, but it enveloped almost all criminals. The witnesses in these cases would be the policemen in the raiding team who unearth the illegal firearms, the IO and two private individuals, called seizure witnesses, who accompany the police during the raid. According to the CrPC, the seizure witnesses need not be produced in court except when the accused demands or the court desires them. This was a great relief.

I felt this was my best bet. However, the IPS officers had absolutely no understanding of trial procedures. They had been taught chapters on investigation in the academy, but their input into trial procedures was not satisfactory. I debated within myself and realized that if I start training them, this project will get pushed to eternity. Conscious of the little time I had, I decided to teach them over the telephone by pointing them to the relevant sections of CrPC. The officers picked up this process faster than I could have imagined.

Charge sheet in Arms Act cases along with the sanction of the DM were to be submitted within two days of the arrest. I had instructed that the arms seized and the accused should be immediately produced before the CJM so that the defence does not take the plea that these arms are planted. As a result, witnesses queued up before the court, which as per the law, needed to give them a date for the very next day. The courts would have no option but to examine them without any delay. In all, the trial could be completed within 10-15 days of the seizure, and the final order could be passed within 20 days. In many cases, a conviction was secured within a week of the recovery of the firearm. This method started yielding results. The SPs had now begun to get the hang of how trials were conducted.

It was the first day of the year 2006. SPs were being instructed on mobile phones on the process to be followed. The target was to take up only incidents of 25(1)(A) in the first phase. By 31 January, about 25 cases had ended in conviction in record time. Informally, I called all the reporters who were on the lookout for any news from police headquarters and shared this data with them. There was a mixed feeling of surprise and happiness on their face. I vividly remember one comment, 'For the first time, we have been given the detailed output of a project without prior announcement of any plan.' I smiled and left my room to brief the CM.

He expressed a very similar feeling. He asked me intriguingly, 'The media is not giving this any attention?' I quipped back, 'This should not worry the government. They may call me a freak, but I will not create any hype about this. I will show a consistent result for a year and let the results speak for themselves. I am sure it will be too large for media to ignore.'

This is exactly what happened. Everyone started talking about speedy trial. Every victim of crime wanted it. Even today, this is a 'go-to' weapon for the government when faced with any law and order crisis.

I wondered why a CM becomes impetuous to showcase even routine achievements. I saw this tendency increase with time. Talking of plans became more fashionable.

It is noteworthy that the concept of 'speedy trial' had taken shape in my mind; nothing was ever written down on paper. There were no written instructions from the police headquarters. I used to personally monitor it every night from nine till midnight. All the SPs were expected to be ready with their data and update me about their progress. I felt satisfied seeing how they discussed the technicalities amongst themselves and created a very healthy competition. Each one of them wanted to get as many convictions as possible to make their district look the best in the state.

Hundreds of thousands of illegal arms seized as a result

of this exercise were gutted in furnaces and remoulded into farm tools. All this was done legally under the supervision of magistrates. Nothing like this had ever been done before, and this gained huge popularity among the people. We were turning the tools of destruction into tools of creation and development. The farming tools made from life-threatening arms would now produce food to feed the hungry. Who would have thought such symbolic messages could be conveyed through as trite a process as law?

Fear started gripping the criminals; fear that was of LAW and not of POLICE.

The message of certainty and speed of punishment could be heard loud and clear. Do whatever you can; not even God can bail you out if you are caught with an illegal firearm.

When speedy trials for Arms Act cases had started running smoothly, I opened up its ambit to all types of cases, especially those involving professional criminals and cases in which solid evidence against the accused persons could be identified.

I was aware that there could be unscrupulous police officers who may falsely implicate innocent people and bring a bad name to my game plan. Sure enough, this happened. In fact, I was waiting for this to happen. I got into action and got the officer dismissed with similar speed. It became clear to the police officers that any such behaviour would subject them to consequences without delay.

The public prosecutors were taken on board. SPs were instructed that any professional crime, especially the ones that got detected immediately, should be personally monitored on a minute-to-minute basis. A competent prosecutor had to be attached with the investigating team to conduct the trial as well as to document the court proceedings, ensuring no legal loopholes. This was one important ingredient of speedy trial that generally went unnoticed by senior police officers and remains so even today.

I had this clarity from my days in the CBI, where I had

seen that the prosecutors were a part of SP's office, an aspect missing in the state police. Prior to the 1973 update of the CrPC, prosecution used to be handled by the State. In speedy trials, I would ensure that the SP had sufficient functional control over the team of prosecutors. This was done to deprive the accused of any advantage at the trial stage. The IO and the prosecutor were made to work in close unison. Charge sheet used to be laid in record time, and procedures in court would be pushed really fast. The SP would monitor the progress of the cases, and I would monitor their work daily.

∞

When stuck, get back to basics

In our daily sync, the SPs would discuss the practical on-ground problems they were facing while implementing speedy trials. In the early stages, they reported a problem they faced with the courts. After the witness was examined, the magistrates and the judges would give a date in the distant future, sometimes as far as two months ahead, due to which the concept of speedy trial would go for a toss.

I was really worried about this problem. I picked up the CrPC to read through the relevant portions, and I hit upon Section 309. In principle, this section envisages day-to-day trials if the witnesses are present and have given their attendance in court. The adjournments can be given only after recording reasons by the magistrates/judges and that too at the cost of the opposite party. Thus, if the accused sought an adjournment, he would have to pay for it.

I convened a meeting of the prosecutors and the SPs and instructed them that they should get their witnesses, all in one go, make them appear before the court, file their attendance and then apply Section 309 CrPC. The magistrate/judge would have to impose a cost and justify reasons for an adjournment from their side. This process hit the bull's eye immediately. The judiciary felt that the prosecution was going full throttle to ensure speedy trials using the legal framework. Results started coming in as fast.

∽

The higher judiciary in the state noticed this and grew not only inquisitive but also interested in this innovation. I was summoned formally by the senior-most judge of the Patna High Court. He complained that the bottleneck in a trial was the non-attendance of IOs and doctors. I committed to him that I would develop a software application that would provide the presiding court with real-time visibility of the IOs and the doctors posted in the cases. The proposal found favour with the high court to the extent that the development and training of the app was personally supervised by three judges of the high court in my presence. It became functional in a month's time, with tangible results.

The judges confessed that it was only because of the right intentions of the State that they were willing to associate with the execution of the speedy trial programme. I was warned that if they sensed any bias, personal or political, they would withdraw immediately. I, in turn, had noticed that the judiciary was in sync with the State in administrative matters relating to trial but not in substantive matters. I realized that I had taken up a Herculean responsibility of ensuring fair play and justice at the stage of investigation to build trust with the judiciary. I took up this challenge for almost seven years, partly as ADG (HQ) and finally as the DGP with the help of Advocate General Prashant Shahi, who I consulted regularly and who would always give me sane legal advice.

This was the period when all wings of the CJS worked in unison in the interest of the aam aadmi. The magnitude of this was difficult for most to comprehend.

∽

Every action needs to see a logical end

An overwhelming queue of appeals filed by the convicted individuals in the higher courts was an undesirable by-product of the speedy trials. On top of this, I had no visibility on the status of these appeals.

I started moving around in the district headquarters and conducted meetings with the public prosecutor with all the additional public prosecutors. Initially, I tried to understand the process through which the appeals are tackled. I saw that there was no record of which appeal was pending with which additional public prosecutor and what was the latest status of that appeal. In fact, I was quite surprised that it was completely left to the discretion of the public prosecutor as to which additional public prosecutor he would choose for a particular appeal. As a result, the allocation of appeals amongst the various additional public prosecutors became skewed.

With the help of the DM, who is theoretically the head of the CJS of the district, I started getting this process rectified so that the distribution of appeals was in an equitable fashion. After this was done, I ensured that the moment an appeal was filed, the corresponding additional public prosecutor would file a written reply immediately. The court, therefore, would no longer be able to grant adjournment citing the absence of the additional public prosecutor as a reason.

This change sped up the appeal processes noticeably. This was the beginning of the concept of speedy appeal, which in conjunction with speedy trials, created a huge impact on the crime situation of the state.

※

I was amazed at the way things had evolved. I had never seen such smooth functioning of law earlier, not even in the CBI. The key concept behind all this was *mutual trust*.

I made a suggestion to the Advocate General to organize a seminar with all stakeholders, including the CM and the Chief Justice of the state, on one platform. I believed this would do a lot of good to our cause. He assiduously pursued this with the Chief Justice. The proposal was accepted and executed in the Central Hall of the capital. The seminar was followed up by joint workshops of judicial officers and policemen, over the next three days, where they were addressed by the Chief Justice and his brother colleagues. There was one request, though, which I had made to the Chief Justice for the seminar, that he turned down forthrightly. Legislators were not invited.

This effort proved to be a grand success. I saw it as the pinnacle of the much-touted and least-understood word 'speedy trial'. The right signal in the right measure to the right quarters of society was instantly sent. The segment of society that benefitted most was the common man, who always feels that he is living in a 'justice-deprived' system.

The various parts of the CJS in this country don't work in harmony. This is the root cause of dissatisfaction for the common man, who is only bothered about the final outcome and not the nuances of the process. He has nothing to do with the complex ego fights amongst the various stakeholders. Unfortunately, the common man is always left out of the equation, which plays out in the dynamics of the working of the system.

Bringing about harmony amongst the various players was easier said than done. Later on, when things were said or written about speedy trial, I felt as if the 'body' was given more weight than its 'soul', which was invariably missed.

Though the legislators were not allowed to be part of the seminar, it was this group of the ruling dispensation that reaped the biggest harvest. Satisfaction of the common man ensured a thumping majority for them in the 2010 Assembly elections where the Opposition did not even get enough seats to justify their standing as Opposition. This was completely unprecedented.

After speedy trial, I tried my hand at a section in law that had been completely put into disuse by almost every state police. I had tried this during my ASP Sasaram days but did not get a chance to use it later on.

Old is gold

Section 110 CrPC is to be handled by the executive magistrates. Since it had not been used for almost the past 50 years, nobody had any idea about its implementation. I chose five district SPs, talked to them on the phone and explained to them the nuances of this section. I asked them to pick the hard-working and intelligent executive magistrates in their districts and get them involved in executing this section.

This section has an individuality in the sense that this is the only section of law where the character of an accused is treated like relevant and admissible evidence. The second advantage is that the inquiry of this section is not necessarily held in a prescribed court but can be done in any public place. In all the five districts, the SPs had arranged for shamiyanas[3] on crossroads in full public view for conducting the inquiry against the criminals. The witnesses would go there and depose about the bad character of the accused person.

This had such a serious impact on the psyche of the criminals that they became completely demoralized. The people who watched the proceedings felt happy that these criminals, who everybody was scared of, were being shown their place in front of the aam aadmi. The aam aadmi was feeling superior to the dreaded criminals.

One SP told me that in his district, criminals had started fearing this much more than the trial itself. He went on to say that during one such proceeding, an old man came up to him

---

[3] Cloth tent house

and said the last he saw this was during his childhood days after the independence of this country. I really do not know why such an effective legal process was given up over time.

∽

Another big issue was the huge vacancy in the constabulary. There was no easy and fast solution to this problem. The scale of this problem was so large that even if the government started recruiting, it would have taken ages to just complete the recruitment process, let alone getting them trained and then deploying them for anti-gang and anti-Naxal operations.

Suddenly, an idea flashed in my mind. Retired army jawans, who were trained in weapons and could take on organized armed groups, could be taken into Bihar Police on contract. I discussed this idea with the CM. He was a little hesitant, as nothing similar had ever been tried earlier. His main point of concern was that it would raise a question on the sanctity of the government, whose most sacrosanct function is the protection of the citizens of the state. The idea of almost outsourcing this function on a contract brought some discomfort. After a detailed discussion of the plan with me and confirmation of its viability on legal grounds by the then Advocate General, the idea took off. With not even a word on government records, the CM declared this as his plan before the Assembly. The bureaucracy looked sideways to find if anyone had any clue about this project. SAP was created.

∽

Bihar Police recruits army men

I went to the local cantonment at Danapur, to the office which looks after the rehabilitation of retired army men. When I met the colonel there and explained what I was trying to do, he was extremely happy. We worked out a whole scheme and prepared a list of army personnel of a particular age group who were in the fighting unit and who had good records. These men were called to attend a parade. A committee of DSP rank officers was set up to select the best from the lot. The first batch of the SAP was created.

The brigadier of the cantonment, the DGP of Bihar and I, the ADG (HQ), were all present in the stadium for the induction. It was a great moment for the Bihar Police. In one shot, we were able to fill the gap of almost 5,000 trained men from the army, who were ready to take on the organized gangs as well as the Naxals in Bihar from the very first day. The army personnel were also very enthusiastic as they felt satisfied that they were being employed by the state.

This idea was so well-appreciated that the then Defence Minister Pranab Mukherjee wrote to all state governments recommending its application. The neighbouring states like Jharkhand and Chhattisgarh, and maybe a few more, eagerly took it up. This experiment still continues in Bihar.

෴

SAP was an instant hit. Organized armed gangs started fearing it. With the success of both speedy trial and SAP, a perception of safety started descending on society. These two initial projects showed how things could move without getting enmeshed in bureaucratic tangles.

When SAP was being brought up before the top civil servants of the government for the first time, the home and finance secretaries were called over to the Assembly and briefed about it. They had their own concerns and requested some more time to examine the issue, as there was no formal proposal mooted by the police headquarters to the state government. On the other hand, the political leadership seemed to be in a hurry to go ahead with critical decisions because people's impatience was palpable and delivering on the promises was the top priority.

The CM made his intention abundantly clear, so there

was no question of the civil servants, especially the finance secretary, wriggling out of it on the pretext of the absence of any documentation. All issues and obligations were discussed in real-time. The finance secretary raised objections on the salary figure proposed by the CM, comparing it with that of other government servants. When I was asked to respond to this, I almost instantly said that if the others with whom these salaries are being compared could rid the state of kidnappers, we could abandon this proposal. The CM immediately overruled the objections and chose to announce the creation of SAP as a government decision in the Assembly in his address.

This was symbolic of the urgency the government was in, which even reflected in their work at the beginning of 2006, immediately after its formation. The first principled decision that set a lot of things right was that policing had to be done within the four walls of law, but freedom would be given for creativity within this boundary. In executive procedures, across-the-table discussions became the order of the day. Decisions were being taken without even a rough piece of paper for the bureaucracy to ruminate on; the documentation that followed up would be only for record rather than anything else.

October 2006. A discussion on some serious issue was going on in the residential office chamber of the CM. During lunch break, I got an impromptu invite to accompany him upstairs in his room. I could gauge that he wanted to discuss the political situation in the state, and I was right.

As his ADG (Special Branch), I gave an unconventional response to his questions. I said, 'The fight between the elephant and the crocodile was not won on physical strength but the turf on which the fight took place. Your turf is development and better administration. Your adversary's turf is caste. Your victory is certain if you stick to your turf in the political arena.'

Later in 2008, when I was moved to BMP, my transfer notification read HQ to BMP, with no mention of Special Branch.

Understanding the background of my transfer, I handed over the charge to my immediate junior and stopped advising on intelligence-related matters.

I had a few more obligations to fulfil. My daughter Richa's marriage had been arranged with Pritesh Ranjan, who was a graduate from IIT Delhi and had followed up with an MBA from IIM Ahmedabad. The wedding took place on 13 December 2006 in a festive though solemn ambience. Immediately after the ceremonies were over, they all left for Delhi. For the first time in my life, I felt that I had lost a part of myself. I tried to put up a bold face after her departure but finally broke down in isolation.

Late Dineshwar Sharma, my samdhi ji[4]

In 2005, I was looking for a suitable groom for my daughter Richa. The prospective groom was an IIT-IIM graduate working with a big multinational company. His father, too, was in the IPS, working with the IB as its joint director. I liked the alliance and began talking to the father, who was posted in Delhi. I got to know that he was to come to Patna on an official visit. I was eager to receive him and requested him to tell me the details of his travel. He politely said that his officers would be there for him, so I need not really worry about it. Yet, I decided to go to the railway station in the morning to receive him. The train came to a halt on the platform, and I looked around, trying to locate him. Suddenly, I spotted him carrying a bag in his hands, coming out of an ordinary three-tier bogey.

Such was the personality of Dineshwar Sharma. Grounded, simple and unassuming. My humble shraddhanjali[5] to Dineshwar ji, my samdhi ji, who breathed his last on the

---

[4]Father-in-law of one's son or daughter
[5]Tribute

4 December 2020.

The period from 2005 to 2010 is considered as one when people of Bihar felt that the promises made in the 2005 elections, mostly on the law and order front, were fulfilled. This phenomenon is extremely rare in a democracy that has gained infamy for forgotten election promises of almost all political parties.

This was possible only because the dynamics of the government in that period was anything but bureaucratic. Innovations in law, adoption of quick executive procedures in critical situations were events of a 'rate-limiting' nature. Various agencies, which would never come together on one platform, were now willing to unite. All this was happening because the intent of government expressed through its policies and functioning was clear and evident.

The biggest beneficiary was the common man, who showed his affection to the political dispensation by giving them a mandate that they could have never got. The government had managed to synchronize all varieties of agencies towards the common goal of serving the common man, without bothering him with sad songs during election campaigns.

The year 2006 to 2007 saw how fast decisions could be taken and implemented without demur. People and politicians, particularly from the Opposition, would come to see me on some pretext and would inevitably talk about the changing perception about life and security in the state. A phrase that had caught on to the masses was: 'Now anyone can travel at any time, anywhere in Bihar.'

In fact, my wife one day challenged me, saying that she would very much like to test the veracity of this feeling. The test that she prescribed was that only the two of us go to a night show at a local cinema theatre in our personal car without any policeman guarding us. I accepted the challenge. After the show was over, as we were driving back home, I motioned to her towards the sight of a newly married couple riding a rickshaw back home after the show. She conceded that this was the ultimate, and Bihar had passed the litmus test.

Local and national media had gone into raptures over both the concepts of speedy trial and SAP. Articles were written in large numbers giving credit to these two innovative ideas for changing the entire crime scenario of Bihar.

I made transparency in the functioning of the police department a hallmark of the police headquarters. Officers were made to realize that they would have to answer questions asked by the common man, without hiding behind any legal or administrative shield.

On one occasion, the police headquarters was conducting a recruitment test for constables all over the state under my direct supervision. The CM chose to ask me in the presence of a mixed group of persons if the recruitment process was going on properly. I immediately asked him if he was getting any sort of complaints in his Janta Darbar.[6] When he answered in the negative, I said that he could then conclude that it was being done without any issue.

One evening, during an informal communication with the CM, he expressed his concern about corruption eating into the fruits of development. I said that if he was serious about this issue, it could be addressed fair and square. He looked at me questioningly. By then, in a flash, I conjured up an image of an organization very similar to SAP. I told him that we could hire retired SPs of CBI who had risen from their rank and worked as IOs. We should give them the task of collecting details about the properties of departmental heads and registering appropriate DA cases. I took care to exclude abuse of authority cases because that would start questioning decisions taken by the officers, which, in turn, would stall other developmental work.

The CM seemed to like the idea. I was ordered to keep it

---

[6]Open-house session for the common people to raise questions and complaints

confidential. On the Independence Day that was approaching, he put it across in his speech to the people of Bihar, the only part of his speech that was not drafted by the bureaucracy. There was thunderous applause from the people, and a shock wave could be seen in the official gallery. On the same evening, I was asked to implement this idea. The documentation was being done by the vigilance secretary.

The Special Vigilance Unit (SVU) was set up in a month's time and started showing results within two months. SVU was another example of a big project that came into existence first, while paperwork and formalities followed later.

The first two accused were senior IAS and IPS serving officers, followed by top officers of other departments. General people were feeling redeemed; corrupt officers had begun to feel the heat. Certain officers who felt uneasy chose to leave on central deputation.

By now, the informal lobbies that had always been powerful, no matter the government, the ones who enjoyed power without any responsibility, had become restless. A theory was being concocted that the police headquarters was getting divided into groups, one of which was led by me. One day, the CM raised this question outrightly to me in front of others. I immediately answered, 'Yes, there are two groups. I am the lone member in one group, and the rest belong to the other group.' There was no further question asked.

In about a couple of years, the speed was slowing down. I was transferred and posted as ADG (BMP). I handed over the charge no sooner than I got the transfer notification. I proceeded to the nearby temple and offered prayers. The moment I came out, I found a battery of media personnel waiting with their questions for me. 'Why this transfer, sir?' and similar barrage.

I told them that I wouldn't know the reasons for my transfer, but whatever it was, I was there to thank God for it.

BRAVE HEARTS DARE TO CLIMB THE STEEP

'Tis not the softer things of life
Which stimulate man's will to strive;
But bleak adversity and strife
Do most to keep man's will alive.
O'er rose-strewn paths the weaklings creep,
But brave hearts dare to climb the steep.

—Ernest Lawrence Thayer

ADG (BMP) (10 April 2008 to 8 March 2010)
ADG (Training) (8 March 2010 to 31 October 2011)

There was one small and shabby government hospital with three doctors to cater to 3,000 men of the Bihar Military Police (BMP). The way this hospital functioned was abysmal, but I was in no mood to write typical letters to the police headquarters with detailed proposals and wait till eternity.

I asked myself: why does the constabulary have to be so dependent on the government in matters of their and their family's health? They should not beg the indulgence of the government on this and instead take charge themselves.

The problem with this self-righteousness was the low salary structure of the constables. They would get a paltry sum in their salary as medical allowance, while the privileged class of IAS and IPS received hefty amounts for their healthcare. Not only that, while working in the police headquarters, I had also seen how scandalous the medical claims of these privileged employees could be.

This made me aware of the bias that government policies showed against the constabulary in matters of both health and education. In my earlier stint as DIG (BMP), I had set up a school on their campus. This term, it had to be a hospital.

If not the government, who else could help in this direction? I figured out that the cumulative strength of the constables was the answer. It was epitomized by their association, which could be the agency for this change. It took me some time to make them see that together they were a financial force that did not need any begging bowl.

Fractures existed in the association, and people in various seats of power entered these 'crevices' to manipulate, use and abuse the constabulary. Yet, the association united for this noble task. It geared up and galvanized its function, worked its finances with complete transparency and converted the government hospital into a 15-bed modern hospital with the best facilities. In this new mission that I had undertaken, I made them function as one. It had a modern operation theatre to top it all. Unlike the school, this hospital was given a name: Command Hospital.

The hospital was ready to be inaugurated. I chose the member of the BMP family who was the senior-most, not in rank but in age, as chief guest for the ceremony. This man happened to be a sweeper of a battalion and was retiring the next day. The function was held in the same grand regalia as is the tradition of armed battalions. Even today, the plaque of the hospital bears the name of chief guest with his designation as jhadukash[1].

Such is the power of self-belief!

I was on an evening walk in the stadium of the battalions of BMP. From a distance, I saw the sports coaches busy with their

---
[1] Sweeper

teams. I summoned them immediately for a meeting. An idea had flashed.

I gave them the task of selecting the children of the constabulary who had potential in sports and coaching them. This activity yielded fabulous results. These children turned out to be sportsmen and sportswomen of repute at various levels.

Unfortunately, this activity did not last after my retirement.

The administration of BMP can be handled through collective decision-making, unlike in the field where every moment is a crisis. I observed that the association of constables would recommend transfers and postings whenever carried out on a large scale, making life uneasy for the ADG. I experimented with a novel idea. In the name of collective decision-making, I appointed a committee of the office bearers of the association and did not become its chairman. This solved a lot many problems.

I had started enjoying my work in the BMP mainly because it gave me enough time to move around the state, trying to unearth problems that were, until then, being ignored.

The role of the MMP unit of the BMP had been reduced over time to that of a ceremonial showpiece. I took it upon myself to restore it to its past glory. By the end of my tenure, I had succeeded in re-establishing the identity of the MMP as an armed unit in its own right, and it had also started competing with the army and winning medals in the national equestrian meets. From a piece of decoration in ceremonies to bringing medals in open equestrian meets was a jump that thrilled me no end.

I was on a visit to Kanpur during a personal leave. It was 3 December 2009. Suddenly, I got a call from my mother informing me that my father had passed away peacefully in his sleep in the morning. I took a flight back from Lucknow to Patna. I had, in the meanwhile, requested the DGP, Anand Shankar ji, to visit my house and arrange things till I reach in the evening. I boarded the same flight that was carrying my son-in-law and daughter from Mumbai, who had taken the first flight from Mumbai via

Lucknow. All along my journey, I felt the comforting presence of both of them. Perhaps for the first time, I felt that children could be of great solace during times of crisis, just like parents are to them. There was gloom all over the house. My mother was insisting that her grandson, who was in the USA at that time, should be in Patna before the arthi[2] is lifted. Fortunately, Shwetank, my son, could make it just in time to shoulder the mortal remains of his grandfather.

I had located a point at the confluence of the Ganges and Triveni rivers. A small island emerged at this confluence, which was a 20-minute ferry ride from the bank of the river in Sonepur. This was chosen as the ground for lighting the pyre. The Bihar Police had arranged for the last farewell to their ex-DGP. The local villagers helped us in all our religious rites, and when at the end of it all, I offered them their remuneration, they politely refused and humbly reminded me of a story from the Ramayana about Rama and the kewat[3]. I felt very emotional and requested them to attend the shraadhh[4] in Patna.

The beacon light that had shown me the path in difficult times had been sniffed out, but his aura was still there.

Adding to my already long list of transfers so far, I got transferred again to the training section as ADG. I redefined my role and started working according to my own plan because neither the police headquarters nor the government had any design for me. Before I could really settle down, a well-respected senior, Manoje Nath, was posted as the DG (Training). I was happy to have him as an experienced guide. He would hear my plans and keep encouraging me. The government decided to post a junior as IG (Training) under me. He didn't even have a room to sit in the office that was there. I offered him my room that we could

---

[2] Bier
[3] A boatman. A character in the Ramayana who helped the exiled Rama, Lakshmana and Sita cross the Ganges on his boat.
[4] A Hindu ceremony performed in the honour of a dead ancestor.

share by shifts. Such an amicable solution in the police is usually unheard of.

Life in Bihar Police was getting painfully slow to the extent that I started feeling cramped for space. In Delhi, one day, sitting in the office of my samdhi Dineshwar Sharma, who was the then joint director in the IB, I shared my feeling with him. He advised me to meet the Union home secretary to explore opportunities that could pull me out of the stagnation I was in. I followed his advice and sent in my request to the home secretary. I was called in immediately. We had not known each other from before, and our conversation was quite matter-of-fact. He suggested that I come on deputation to the Government of India. This was an offer I could not reject. The next day, even before I could return to Patna, the cadre clearance request of the central government had reached the Government of Bihar. I had not seen or heard of such speed earlier. I wondered why.

I was refused cadre clearance by the Bihar government. I appealed to the chief secretary to help me. He unapologetically washed his hands off, telling me that this call had to be taken by the CM and not him. I sought an appointment with the CM to plead my case but was denied a meeting for a fortnight. Finally, when the audience was granted, I was given more than an hour to plead my case. I tried my best but failed.

Perhaps I was destined to end my career in the place from where I had begun, in my state, Bihar.

O CAPTAIN! MY CAPTAIN!

> *O Captain! My Captain! our fearful trip is done;*
> *The ship has weather'd every rack,*
> *the prize we sought is won…*
>
> —Walter Whitman

DGP Bihar (31 August 2011 to 24 June 2014)
DG (Home Guards) (25 June 2014 to 31 December 2014)

It was the evening of 25 August 2011. After finishing my office work, I was teaching physics to my students at Rahmani 30. My mobile phone rang. It was a call from the CM, who informed me that he had just approved my promotion and posting as the next DGP of Bihar. I was supposed to be taking over on the 31 August when the present incumbent, Neelmani, was to retire. I requested him to grant me an audience, as I wished to thank him in person. I was summoned immediately.

It took me just 10 minutes to reach the CM's office. He was alone in his room. His only request was that I should take over the complete responsibility of crime and law and order so that he could give undivided attention to the development of the state. My request, in turn, to him was that since I was not very conversant with the political happenings, he should tell me frankly when I become a political liability for him so that I could file in my papers and quit. This was followed by a typical reaction.

I then made a request seeking a day to visit Singheshwar temple. The short meeting ended, and I was seen at the local

Mahavir temple with my wife, with a battery of journalists waiting to ask questions.

Come 31 August. There were formalities galore, farewell parades and get-togethers. Even before the formal transfer of charge took place in the evening, I was mentally engaged in a communal situation in Araria district on the borders of Nepal. I remained in constant communication with the SP of the district, getting updates on the situation there.

Immediately after assuming charge, I had to address a press conference that teemed with many questions. I gave a brief address to my staff officers and then proceeded to meet the CM at his residence. The most obvious question popped up, 'What will be your priorities as the DGP of the state?'

I, in my mind, had my priorities fixed.

New priorities with the new chief

My topmost priority was scientific investigation. I was painfully aware that Bihar Police had based all its investigation on oral statements of witnesses, what was called bayaan[1]. Oral statements are slippery grounds, as the witnesses have an increasing tendency of retracting from their earlier statements. I had decided that I would transform this through forensic evidence in the biggest way possible. I told the CM that my top priority was to transition the methods of police investigation: 'bayaan se vigyaan ki ore (from statements to science).'

My second priority was to expand the definition of crime from offences against body and property to corruption and cheating people through Ponzi schemes. While the traditional function of the police of tackling crime and law and order had to remain, corruption had to be brought within its purview, as I always believed that corruption is as much of a cognizable

---

[1] Statement

offence as murder. Till now, this had been confined to agencies like the anti-corruption bureau, which was not good enough.

The CM gave his nod, and I proceeded. Within a few days of my joining, I was summoned by the Patna High Court and was asked to answer questions on the huge number of viscera reports that had been pending for ages. The FSL did not have any wherewithal to conduct the viscera examination, and I did not have a clue as to what was happening. I could only assure the court that FSL was my priority, and I would certainly find a solution. Within the next three months, I brought down the pendency of viscera reports to a bare minimum, galvanized my procurement section and ensured that people who were in charge of investigations that relied on the FSL kept sending exhibits.

For my second priority against corruption, I created an Economic Offences Unit (EOU) and gave it a special status. DA cases against senior government servants started getting registered directly with the police department.

These two dimensions brought out an entirely different paradigm of policing in the state.

∽

My innings as the DGP began with a series of small communal incidents spread all over the state. Each incident had to be tackled in the firefighting mode. It would take us a couple of days to douse the fire of one incident before another would erupt somewhere else. The CM would deploy the local politicians of that area, while I would employ policemen from neighbouring areas to handle the situation.

In one such incident in Sheohar, things were on the verge of getting out of hand. I was out of ideas and requested my batchmate V. Narayanan, who was an ADG rank officer, to help me out as he had worked in that area in the past and knew the people and the place quite well. He responded to my request positively and promptly. He camped in that area and moved tirelessly to bring things under control. I thanked him profusely.

In the 37 years of my tenure in Bihar, I had never experienced communal riots and consequential curfew in my jurisdiction. I always felt that curfew is the peak of failure for any policeman because in the first place, not only was he not able to prevent it, but he also failed at tackling it. Just before the 2014 parliamentary elections, when the state government decided to clamp curfew in the Nawada district, one can only imagine my feeling of defeat.

I remember many nights when both the CM and I would sit together in his office, trying to connect to people who could help us in sorting out these problems. This happened on numerous occasions. For a person who had worked in Bihar all through, this was a very disturbing situation. I had faced similar situations in the past, but during those three years of my DGP tenure, the frequency was unusually high for some reason.

By 2013, I was seriously concerned about the nagging communal problem in the state. Although the intensity of these incidents was never quite high, they kept emerging with regularity. I requested the CM that I wanted his political perspective on my studied analysis of all the communal incidents of the last two years with a view to finding out the reason behind them. We sat down to discuss, only to conclude that neither of us could lay a finger on any possible root cause.

A few months later, in November 2013, in the DGPs' conference held at Delhi, this issue was brought up for discussion in a room full of DGPs from all over the country. I was sure that with the prevailing situation, Bihar would be called upon in the panel of five states on the dais to discuss the issue. To my shock, this did not happen. Bihar was not counted in the list of states affected by the communal issue. When, a few months later, the 2014 election results came, this incident, in retrospect, seemed to be in synchrony.

In the year 2013, the Union home minister too had organized

a meeting of the extremist-affected states. The CMs were attending along with their DGPs. Bihar CM wanted some advice from me on the content of his address. I had observed that in every extremist situation, the only antidote used was an armed reaction to an armed action. Most meetings I attended at the so-called 'high levels' had the narrow format of comparing the number of Naxals killed to how many policemen/civilians were killed. To me, this always seemed too simplistic. Hence, I requested him to talk about how Bihar was using various legal means of restricting extremists from eating into the state's revenue, thereby crippling their financial strength. At the same time, I also suggested that we request the Union government to use its economic intelligence agencies to identify the channels the extremists used to siphon off the black money. The point made by Bihar was well taken but not carried forward.

With more years of experience in the police, my understanding and my approach towards tackling the Naxal problem also matured.

∞

Kill two birds with one stone

One day, I got information from my sources that the Naxal leaders had held the lands of certain people as benaami[2] property and were practising farming on them. They would take away the produce of the agricultural land for their personal use.

This gave me a clue. I got a survey done in certain villages where this was happening. Through the DM of the district, I was able to confiscate those pieces of land and the agricultural yield under the Police Act. This crippled the Naxal leaders financially. Similarly, I tried to identify their properties and applied the UAPA, wherein the money and the property gained through such activities could be confiscated under

---

[2]Unnamed

the law following the orders of the home commissioner of the state.

This plan of action, I felt, unnerved the Naxal leaders much more than any armed force operations against them. More petitions were being filed, and a lot of hue and cry was being raised. This method seemed effective on two counts: One, the leaders were getting unnerved, as they got deprived of their financial power, which was needed to carry out all Naxal activities. Two, they were now compelled to fight out their matters in a legal process. This completely damaged their theory of running a parallel government, and they had to submit to the law of the land.

∞

I had, by now, started working on my motto of *'bayaan se vigyaan ki ore'*. I get reminded of one of my very first inspirations behind this whole concept that came from a couple of IPS officers who I had met even before I joined the IPS.

∞

Subconscious inspirations

When I got selected for the IPS and was preparing myself to join the training at the National Police Academy, I had the occasion of talking to a few senior IPS officers who were juniors to my father. I recall two experiences shared with me by two promotee SP rank officers.

One incident was narrated to me by late Upendra Sharma when he was SP Saharsa. He recounted that a spate of dacoities had taken place in his district during his tenure. None of these cases could get detected through the usual techniques, yet he had managed to supervise all of them and even found a common feature across all. There was a 12-bore fired cartridge found at the place of occurrence in each of these cases. He told me that he kept on seizing these cartridges diligently. Finally, one day, somebody was caught with a 12-bore gun somewhere in his district, and just out of curiosity, he sent the weapon that was seized from this person to the FSL in Patna. He requested the lab to match the weapon with his cartridge collection. Those were the days of comparison microscopes, which were manual instruments, unlike the modern computerized versions available today. It took the FSL about a couple of months to perform all the comparisons. In the end, the results that came astonished everyone. All of the fired cartridges that he had collected were found to be fired by the same seized weapon. He was extremely happy that his effort had paid off and he was able to detect all the past cases in one go through a scientific but patient approach.

The second incident is associated with late K.D. Singh, who later became my Range DIG when I was SP Madhepura. He told me about a dacoity that took place when he was DSP of Bihar Sharif. He had supervised that case and had painstakingly taken detailed statements of all the inmates of the house. He was not able to detect that case through the usual police process, so he kept reading the statements of the witnesses. Suddenly, his mind stopped at one of the statements given by a lady in the house. She distinctly remembered that one of the dacoits had a foot that was unusually large. She had, in her lifetime, not seen a foot as big as his. He picked up this clue. In those days, there were no big brands that manufactured shoes. People got their shoes made to order from shoemakers. He went to one such shoemaker in Bihar Sharif to place an order for his shoes. He noticed that the shoemaker was noting down all measurements in a notebook. He leisurely started flipping through it and found the page of a customer whose measurements seemed unusually large. The statement of the lady witness from the dacoity case flashed before him.

He carefully noted down the address of this person from the shoemaker's notebook and quietly sent a team to that address. In spite of the fact that the person did not even belong to that state and was from a neighbouring state, he was able to locate him. The case was detected successfully.

⁕

I had observed that the Bihar Police monotonously believed in the recording of statements of witnesses in case diaries and the submitting of notes by senior officers. The quality of investigation was determined by the length of details in the statements. If the place of occurrence was described in detail with a sketch map, the investigation would get a special mention. Recovery of something material relating to the crime became the ultimate pinnacle of investigation.

As I grew up seeing this state of our quality of investigation, I was pained by the deficiency that was so blatant, especially realizing that forensics had made galloping progress in the world around us. We, in the Bihar Police, had clearly missed the bus. The laboratory we had was an apology both in terms of human and material resources. I knew that any effort towards improving these two resources would open up the next gate of problems immediately. Training the policemen and supervisory officers in the technical aspects of forensics had been bid farewell a long time ago. I had only three years, and there was a lot of ground to cover.

There was hardly any day that I did not spend an hour in the forensic laboratory, standing on their ground with the scientists, understanding their processes. I remember once a scientist was examining each piece of fake Indian currency note during an analysis. When I asked her why was she not sampling the notes to save time, 'court's demand' was the answer I got. I immediately made a suggestion to the director of the lab to write to the HOD of the statistics department of the Patna University, asking him to recommend a sampling process based on the principle of randomization. The cumbersome process became easy and gave their reports scientific validity too.

This incident gave the scientists the confidence that they could discuss their technical issues fruitfully with their DGP. I would often bring along the young district SPs to the laboratory and show them around. I felt this was the best way to create awareness amongst the police officers about forensic investigation techniques. This obviated the need for an additional training exercise. In important cases, I would arrange for a dialogue between the investigation team and the scientists to encourage brainstorming to get more value on evidence.

∞

Scientists become investigating officers

The FSL, as well as the scientists, were putting in their best to make my project a big success. I arranged a fleet of about eight police vehicles for them. Their director was instructed to fix a TV in his room and keep an eye on the local news throughout the day to catch any crime incident in the state across all districts. As a result, all eight police vehicles were in movement from one scene of crime to another, almost round the clock. They would land at a place of occurrence without any invitation from the local police with their own kit box. They would even help the local police by training them in lifting exhibits when they visited crime scenes.

In the year 2012, a very gruesome murder of two people had taken place in the Sheikhpura district of Bihar. These men belonged to Uttar Pradesh and had come to Bihar on a business trip. The local police had arrested a suspect, a local from that area, based on information from a source. When the forensic team reached there, they examined the place of occurrence and found it smeared with a lot of blood. They also heard the local villagers talk about the incident, which indicated a very close physical battle between the assailant and the deceased.

The officer-in-charge had really lost his temper and was about to manhandle the suspect when the forensic science team intervened. They asked him to arrange some hydrogen peroxide from a nearby chemist shop so that they could help him by assessing whether he had caught hold of the right suspect or not. He got hydrogen peroxide procured immediately. The scientists scrubbed off some debris from the nails of the suspect, put it on a paper and examined it with the chemical. After their analysis, they told the policemen that they had found blood below the nails, but they could not tell yet whose blood it was. The moment this was declared, the suspect broke down and confessed his crime. The police then found it very easy to collect all the relevant evidence of the murder.

The case was detected cleanly because of the forensic scientists' presence of mind. They helped me detect a lot many cases and had those gone undetected, Bihar Police would have definitely faced a hard time.

∞

Within a very brief span of time, the activities of the forensic scientists became a matter of curiosity for the common man. It amused me when some reports suggested that the public demand for the presence of the team of scientists was becoming more frequent than the demands of getting the DM and the SP at the crime scene.

The CM, too, was liberal in sanctioning equipment to improve the quality of the forensic laboratory. No 'babu'[3] could throw in a spanner. I remember, during this period, the term of a few scientists was to expire on a particular day. I had requested a formal meeting

---

[3] Word used for government bureaucrats, usually in a derogatory sense.

on that day for granting an extension. The time was fixed, and the government officials chose to be absent from the meeting. I was fuming because I knew that if these scientists got terminated, a few wings of the laboratory would shut down. I went straight to see the CM and put my issue across to him in the same mental condition. He calmed me down and asked me to leave. The next day, the government order of their extension was in my hand.

The ultimate equipment that gave us an edge was the DNA lab that we had set up. We could detect and get a trial done for cases where we had no witnesses, or even worse, hostile witnesses. This, I felt, was remarkable.

∞

Science brings justice against all odds

Year 2012, Buxar district, Rajpur Police Station. Early in the morning, the SP of the district reported to me over the phone that a minor had been raped by a close relative of hers. The case had been registered, and the SP was proceeding with the investigation and supervision. His analysis thus far told me that the case appeared to be true.

Statements of the child and her parents had been recorded. The SP had smartly done his work without losing any time. I congratulated him and asked him to proceed with the investigation quickly and ensure that the charge sheet is laid before the court within the next 48 hours. The trial started within five days.

The SP called me up on perhaps the eighth day, saying that the prosecutrix had turned hostile, and the next day, her mother did the same. He was really apprehensive that the case may fail in court. I advised him to send the exhibits of the case, i.e. the victim's clothes, to the FSL and pray to the court to wait for FSL's report. I simultaneously instructed the FSL director to speed up their process.

The report came within about 10 days. The DNA of the stains on the clothes of the child matched with those of the semen of the accused. The court was perplexed with this report because there was just no recorded oral evidence, but on the other hand, there was the highest form of scientific evidence. The judge was in a fix for almost a month. He finally concluded that the charges had been proven in spite of the fact that all the witnesses had turned hostile. He convicted the accused and gave him 10 years of rigorous imprisonment. This was one of the first cases under the Protection of Children from Sexual Offences (POCSO) Act, 2012, where a conviction had been procured and that too without any oral evidence.

Modern techniques in modern times

The branch manager of the Punjab National Bank in Bihta left for his home in Patna on his motorbike after finishing his job for the day. In the twilight of that day in the year 2013, we got the news that he was overtaken by two men on another motorbike, somewhere in an isolated place on the highway between Bihta and Patna, and was shot dead. The local police, including the SSP of Patna, went to the place of occurrence and carried out the usual necessary actions. A delegation of very senior officers from the Punjab National Bank met me in my office and obviously demanded detection of the case and the arrest of the murderers.

The local media was ablaze with this incident. I called the SSP Patna and enquired about the progress of the case. I got to know that only routine work had been done, and if the case was left at this, it would just end in a no-clue case. At best, the police could wait for some source to come up with some more information.

I decided to sit down with the IO, all by myself, to analyse the case. Like a movie in my head, I visualized the branch manager being tracked by the two motorcyclists right from his branch to the deserted place, where they overtook him and fired a shot at him. I was sure that if I started investigating the case with an approach to find motives in the initial stage itself, I would get lost, as motives could be too many. The strongest clue of any incident is always found at the place of occurrence and the exhibits thereof. These two should never be lost in any investigation.

Keeping this in mind, I drew up my mental model to track the movement of the deceased from the bank to the place of occurrence. There were three mobile towers catering to the mobile network along this route. We got the activity dump of all the three towers and analysed it through a software that was created for this purpose.

Next, we noted the time between the event of him leaving the branch and the next event of him reaching the place of occurrence. These two events were mapped on Google Maps, and an average speed was calculated. We fed this information to the software, which churned out all the mobile numbers that met the following conditions: (i) the number should be in motion for the entire route from the branch till the place of occurrence, (ii) average speed should match that of the victim, and (iii) there should be two changes in the tower for that mobile number during this duration.

This turned out to be a very effective model. I still remember, I had fixed up a meeting with the IO in a secluded place in the night and had called in for the services of a software teacher from a computer coaching institute. The teacher helped us code my logic into the software. He went on to refine that logic more and more with each attempt, and after putting in an effort for a few hours, we were able to shortlist 17 relevant mobile numbers.

We were quite satisfied with this progress. The next day, we placed all those 17 mobile numbers on surveillance. Within 24 hours, we could refine the list to two numbers based on their conversations. These two numbers had frequent discussions, mostly about this incident and how far the police was getting near them. They sounded happy that the police had not been able to find any clue thus far, while we were extremely happy that now the case would be cracked.

These two men were residents of Bihta itself. The police raided their houses. I had instructed the FSL team to be present during this raid since I always felt that scientists did a better job at examining the place of occurrence than policemen. This opinion of mine was reaffirmed that day. While examining the house of the suspect, they found a motorcycle parked inside a garage. A careful examination of the motorcycle brought out a blood mark on its mudguard. Suspecting that the blood mark could be of the deceased, they lifted the motorcycle and seized it for forensic examination. It was reported to me after a complete serological and genetic examination of the blood that it was a perfect match with that of the deceased.

After successfully identifying the criminals, we went into the motive of the case. We sat down with the members of the branch to locate that these two persons were friends and had taken a loan from the branch. There were some issues with the branch manager on the repayment of the loan, which culminated in this incident.

Had we started by first trying to figure out the motive and then trying to find the killers, it would have been a wild goose chase. The case was wonderfully detected. We could arrest the killers and put them on trial.

∞

For cases of hanging, drowning and burning, where post and ante-mortem reports are always under dispute, we solved the problem for good through a new histopathological lab.

Doctors in the police department

Did death occur due to hanging or was he hanged after being killed? Did death occur due to burning or was he burnt after he was killed? Did drowning occur before or after the death?

These questions always haunt the police while investigating such cases. I, too, throughout my career, had to contend with them, and whatever conclusion I would draw at the end, would be with a great deal of difficulty. These disputes were of a very acute nature, and figuring out the right answer was very difficult for anyone. Most of the time, we would have to infer it from circumstantial evidence and the statements of witnesses, which I have always held as very unreliable.

During my tenure as the DGP, an IPS officer named Paresh Saxena, who was essentially a doctor by training, was working with me. He came up with a brilliant idea one day. He said that on the body of the deceased, the cells at the site of the ligature mark or burnt skin or at the lungs where the first signs of drowning can be seen, are the best places to get categorical evidence from. These are the places from where very clear pieces of evidence of post-mortem or ante-mortem injury can be obtained. He explained that the logic behind this was the same as that in the case of living or dead people suffering from autoimmune diseases, where identification of the disease can be made only from the cells of the organ that have been directly affected.

I felt that this idea was wonderful. I requested him to teach the FSL scientists how histopathological slides of the cells from the site of the injury can be processed, put on a slide and fixed permanently. That slide could be examined by pathologists to find out the changes in the cells to arrive at a definitive conclusion. The idea was so exceptionally good that I decided to set up a laboratory for this in my FSL. We called this the histopathological lab, where the cells would be preserved on slides and then sent to the pathological department of the local medical college for their opinion.

We put this to test and found that we could get objective conclusive evidence of the death reasons, and we did not have to wait for unreliable oral evidence.

∽

In short, our quality of investigation had improved considerably. Trial courts and the high court had taken notice. The common man, too, had started observing this change. The media had begun to carry stories on visits of forensic teams and convictions based on forensic evidence.

Finally, the CM chose to blame me for not inviting him to the laboratory, which was, by then, hogging the limelight from all quarters. I apologized and arranged for his visit. It turned out to be a big event. He chose to visit every segment of the laboratory, spending two hours moving around, seeing all the new equipment that he remembered sanctioning for purchase. He then addressed a meeting of intellectuals who were invited along with the press.

The FSL was not only born in Bihar but had come of age in a short span of time. The only aspect in which I couldn't succeed was to get a top-level forensic scientist of national repute to lead the laboratory. This would have rid me of the responsibility I was discharging in this direction. All thanks to the civil servants and their holy rules, which came up from somewhere each time in different hue and colour to become roadblocks.

There was a sudden spurt of crime in 2012. I tackled it through an experiment that no state police had ever carried out. It worked wonders and became a grand success. The problem was solved much sooner than I could imagine.

∞

My experiments with law

All my experiments with law had started showing results. Finally, it appeared to me as if we had succeeded in belling the cat. Suddenly, a noticeable rise in crime took place. I put on my thinking cap, gathered data on all recent crimes and applied 'data mining and modelling' techniques to analyse them.

I was summoned by the CM and was asked to explain the reason behind the situation and obviously the remedy thereof. I requested him to convene a meeting of the chief secretary, the home secretary, the law secretary, the Advocate General and people who mattered, to get their opinion on this matter. The meeting was promptly arranged. In the discussion, the only suggestion that I heard in the room was the mundanely obvious one: increased visibility of the police, which essentially means more patrolling and even more patrolling. I was amused at the length of the tunnel of their vision.

It was my turn to speak. I said, 'I have been collecting data of all the recent cases, some of which have been detected too. The criminals in almost all these cases are the ones who have been convicted by the lower courts and who have come up in appeal to the higher courts, mostly the high court. On filing an appeal, they have got bail, and at the moment, they are out on bail committing crimes.'

The assembly looked askance at me. The CM wanted a solution. Bail cancellations and speedy appeal was my answer.

The Advocate General and law secretary agreed that the suggested method was a valid legal process, but it had not been tried by any other state in the country. It was decided that Bihar would be the first state to try this legal experiment.

To simplify the task for the Advocate General, I suggested that he kindly allot one district per government advocate in his panel. It would become a one-to-one relationship between the government advocates and the district SPs.

In the meanwhile, I summoned all my SPs, gave them the principle behind bail cancellation and taught them how the proposal had to be drafted and how facts had to be collected. Once this was done, proposals started streaming in from all district SPs to their respective government advocates. The advocates vetted these proposals, and then the filings in the court began.

I fixed up fortnightly meetings with all the government advocates in the chamber of the Advocate General to discuss the progress of the process. In the first meeting itself, I was told that the honourable judges were angry at such proposals. They felt that the state was asking them to cancel the bail orders that they themselves had granted. They were so offended that they wanted or rather warned the state to withdraw such petitions. I told the Advocate General that there was no question of withdrawing the petition. If the court wanted, it could cancel and reject my petitions, but withdrawal was not an option. This message was communicated, and soon, the judges were willing to listen to the petition and even issued notices to the accused persons.

This became hot news. The newspapers in the state were literally littered with this. The Patna High Court had issued notices to a huge number of accused persons. It created a dent in the confidence of these criminals. The crime breakout was contained within two months. The state police had acquired a new legal weapon in their arsenal.

⟡

My next agenda was to envelop corruption into the gamut of policing. I had decided to create an EOU directly under the DGP.

Within 10 days, the CM asked me to present the concept at a conference of police officers. The primary message that I conveyed in this presentation was my thought that the generation of black money through any source, including corruption, weakens the state. Crime flourishes in a weak state. Hence, EOU was meant to be a very powerful unit in my mission to attack black money and thereby mitigate crime.

The very next day, all required notifications of the government were issued. The unit started functioning with a set of chosen officers who were known for their integrity and investigative acumen. Within a couple of months, the EOU was making waves. Newspapers were replete with success stories. It was registering at least two cases per week. The Anti-Corruption Unit of the state raised an issue saying that corruption cases could not be registered by the EOU. I was amused at this stand. The Advocate General turned down this plea, as it was not in consonance with law.

This concept was a hit during those three years.

I took this forward by approaching the ED to register cases against criminals who had amassed wealth. We were perhaps the first state to start such a process. The EOU became the nodal agency for this purpose, and attachment of property of criminals under the PMLA started. The job of the police is to bring the recalcitrant before the process of law so that they recognize the might of law, not of police.

'Where does Bihar Police stand in the field of intelligence gathering using digital technology?' asked the director of IB, who was himself a Bihar cadre officer. My answer in a word was 'primitive.' I explained to him how I had just started getting equipment, but convincing decision-makers was a big hurdle to cross. He promised me all help. I introduced to him my young IPS officer who had a computer engineering background from one of the IITs, who he called upon for a meeting in his office in Delhi. This young officer was overwhelmed from his trip and, on his return, told me that the director had personally taken him around and showed how things worked. After his trip, I gave him this task and empowered him to use technology in an evolved way. It had begun to add value to our investigative outputs.

The Chief Justice of the Patna High Court was gracious enough to grant me the privilege of a meeting whenever I needed one. In one such meeting, I took the opportunity to tell him that there were a huge number of cases whose appeal had been disposed of as dismissed, but the accused had not been remanded to judicial custody because the high court administration had not sent the lower court records to the trying court. He looked into this matter and started an exercise to resolve this. I couldn't follow up on the matter but felt the inadequacy of the CJS decisively.

A honest young officer, who was somewhat erratic in his behaviour, had committed an act that got to the notice of the Chief Justice personally. When the latter consulted me, I assured him that I would get the officer transferred but requested against any explicit action against him, as it would bring to nought the career of a budding young IPS officer. I called the officer to my residence and gave him a lesson. He was transferred, and the matter ended without any escalation.

In addition to the leaps in the investigation techniques that Bihar Police saw during this period, there were many arenas where it found its footing for probably the first time ever.

The year 1955 had seen the first All India Police Science Congress organized in Bihar at its capital, Patna. Thereafter, Bihar never hosted another Congress event for 58 long years even though the event kept happening every year. In 2013, as the DGP of the state, I volunteered to host this event at Patna. I succeeded in organizing the event very well, inaugurated by the CM and the valedictory ceremony done by Justice Aftab Alam of the Supreme Court. All sessions in the event had active participation. A large number of retired seniors congratulated and thanked me for bringing them a chance to witness such an event during their lifetime.

Another event that Bihar had never hosted was the All India Police Athletics Meet. During my tenure as the police chief, I was happy that I could make this happen. Just for this event, I got an international standard synthetic athletic track prepared, which was inaugurated on the opening day of the meet. All such events of national importance that Bihar had missed out on were organized in a short span of time and in a facile manner.

The 2014 parliamentary elections were round the corner. Just then, I got to know that a huge number of door frame metal detectors (DFMDs) and hand held metal detectors (HHMDs) were damaged and needed repair. With the approaching elections, this took the shape of a veritable crisis, as these gadgets were required for the security of VVIPs. I was chasing tight deadlines. We approached the manufacturers who started quoting exorbitantly high rates. Just then, I got an idea. I stepped into the workshop of the Police Wireless and gathered the technicians whom I already knew. I gave them the task of repairing these gadgets. They were quick in identifying and fixing the issues, even when the circuit diagrams were not available. I even got a few of the retired technicians on contract for this purpose. This scheme worked so well that, in record time, all the security gadgets were repaired at a nominal cost.

My overall principle about elections, as always, remained the same: a fair election is a basic necessity in a democracy.

∞

Fairness in elections above everything else

The election had not yet been announced. The CM and his Cabinet colleagues were on a trip to the different areas of the state. As per protocol, I was accompanying the troupe.

A halt of three days was planned in the itinerary. One of those evenings, a Cabinet colleague of the CM requested me to come to his village for dinner the next day. He told me that the CM would be attending it with all his Cabinet members and important functionaries of the party. I showed acceptance and told him that I would certainly be there. However, I did not go.

When the minister met me the next day, he confronted me. I politely explained to him that the elections were going to be announced, and I should not do anything that would make people lose faith in the sanctity of the elections. No matter how impartial I appear in conducting the electoral process, if I, as the chief of the police, have dinner with the functionaries of a particular political party, it will not be taken in good spirit. For me, this was extremely important.

∞

After the 2014 parliamentary election results were announced, there was political turmoil in the state. The CM had just resigned and was about to nominate his successor. I got posted as the DG, Home Guards, which I was handling as an additional charge anyway.

My son Shwetank's marriage also took place in 2014. Major obligations that I had, were over.

My stint as DG, Home Guards, was too brief. The only notable contribution I made during this period was not to Home Guards but to Fire Services. The day I joined, I asked for the Act by which my state was governing its fire services. While going through the Act, I found that it was designed for fire in thatched huts. I smiled to myself.

I proposed a new modern law to amend this. It was passed by the Assembly and approved by the governor. However, it is yet to be notified by the government. We still live in the age of thatched roofs with multi-stories climbing tall all over the state.

Came 31 December 2014, my day of superannuation. The traditional parades were done. I handed over my charge at around 4 p.m., changed out of my uniform in the washroom of my office, never to wear them again. I had requested my wife to come to my office in our personal car. I left everything official in the office itself and drove back home in our car, as a *free* and *unfettered* man.

I had resolved to forget the P of police and carry on with the P of physics. I also wanted to now understand why at all did I lose my health. From the next day on, a new journey started.

A STORY THAT WAS NEVER TOLD...

Results of the parliamentary general elections had just been declared. JD(U), which had decided to go alone in the election hunt, had put up a dismal performance. The CM took a decision to resign, apparently to give a message to the world that he was taking moral responsibility for the defeat.

He was definitely piqued by the fact that in spite of his best efforts to seek votes in the election campaign based on his superlative performance, particularly on the law and order front, which had always been a central issue for the people of Bihar, they chose to vote for the BJP at the hustings.

The political dynamics of everything was being churned out at a very fast pace. Seeing the turn of events, I sat in solitude for a few hours with eyes closed, lost in deep thought. Almost like a video clip, I could see the future of Bihar playing in my mind, one with a lack of strong administration and correct decisions. I could see that my position as the DGP could no longer be as effective with the emergence of a fractured and uncertain political condition. In such a murky politico-administrative future, tiny political parties would get a chance to demand their pound of flesh for supporting the minority government in the Assembly. Most of the demands were being made on the police department. I immediately took my decision.

I lost no time to drive down to the CM residence and told him point-blank that it may not be possible for me to perform my function as the DGP any further. I requested a transfer to head Home Guards. A conversation ensued for a couple of minutes, which was more from the throat than from below it. I was in no mood to reconsider my decision.

I had requested the CM when he had chosen me as the DGP to tell me plainly when I become a political liability so that I could relinquish and quit. I felt betrayed that my request hadn't been respected. I knew that I couldn't alleviate the political miseries of the CM, but going by my own political sense, I sought the shift myself.

Jitan Ram Manjhi was elected as the new CM. He called me and wanted to confirm whether I had sought the change. When I said yes, I felt, I saw an expression of relief on his face.

It took the government about 15 more days to decide my successor. The moment I was informed by the home secretary that I had been shifted to the Home Guards, I relinquished my charge as DGP without even trying to know who my successor was. I left the room, never to visit it again.

Before I was relieved from the post of DGP, the secretaries who huddle around the CM tried to get some transfers 'signed off' by me. I plainly refused to oblige. Since I was anyway awaiting my shift, I felt that they might as well transfer me first and then do whatever they wanted to.

The next day, Maulana Wali Rahmani paid me a visit. He had only one question: 'Did a specific political leader demand this transfer as a pound of flesh?' He had gathered enough facts himself and wanted to only confirm them. This politician who supported the minority government from outside had approached me earlier for certain favours. I had blatantly refused. His requests were granted immediately after I had relinquished my charge. The Maulana, perhaps, seemed to have drawn his own conclusions.

A couple of days later, the same politician called me up, profusely apologizing on behalf of a huge buzz that he was behind my transfer. My reply to him was, 'IPS officers of my age and seniority see the police department for 30 to 35 years at best. I have seen it for almost 60 years, out of which three years as the DGP myself. So, five months make little difference to me.' I told him that he should not be worried on my count and ended the conversation. I was later told by a senior journalist that the political leader had become wary of a segment of his vote bank.

I had retired and was leading a quiet life in my house outside the municipal limits of Patna. The new state government had been formed. The CM remained unchanged, but his political partner had changed. One day, on one of the TV channels, I heard the political partner of the CM telling the media that the outgoing DGP had lowered the morale of Bihar Police by not allowing them to use lathi. He did not name me, but the next day, a group of journalists from both print and visual media came to seek my reaction to this comment. I understood that my willingness to get involved in political controversies was being tested and refused to say anything on record.

EPILOGUE

As the book draws to a close and I laze in my rocking chair, recollecting incidents of the past and post-retirement life, some remnants pop up.

Gandhi Maidan serial blasts in October 2014. A harrowing incident by any standard for a state police chief. A typical intelligence input, which was neither here nor there, had passed through me as a usual one-of-the-many pieces of paper I glanced at every day. Somehow, I felt an unknown premonition, which left me uneasy.

According to my scheduled approved tour plan, I was to represent India as part of a contingent of three police officers at an Interpol meet in Columbia. This is a rare honour for an officer working in the state police. I approached the CM to rescind his approval of my trip. I had decided to stay back.

Those six hours felt like a storm. Seeing the blasts alive from the office, getting the incident investigated real-time and handling law and order with speed and alacrity required exceptional calmness of mind. Everything around me was breaking down, while I held my nerves, backing up my officers who were getting singed in the fire of the blasts.

Our efforts paid off. By the end of the day, the entire conspiracy was unearthed from Ranchi. Physical direct evidence was recovered at Hatia. Even the undetected blast at Bodh Gaya temple had been detected.

It was now up to the National Investigation Agency (NIA) to connect the dots.

Brahmeshwar Mukhiya was murdered in the wee hours of a morning in Arrah. When this incident happened, I was driving down from Bhagalpur to Patna for an important meeting. The plan was to return to Bhagalpur on a chopper, accompanying the CM on his onward journey to the Kosi division.

On receiving information about the murder and the panic that was taking over, I decided to proceed to Arrah without stopping at Patna as per the original plan. What happened at Arrah is a video-recorded incident. What is not recorded is the effort I had put in to convince the family of the deceased that since none in the family had seen the incident, an FIR should be truthfully recorded. If this had not happened, Bihar would have again got pushed in the same cauldron that it had been in through the '90s. I had to persuade them that the FIR should be based on true facts and not on their suspicions. An investigation should be objective.

What happened in Patna the next day is still talked about. I had debated the pros and cons of implementing a typical police action of lathicharge and/or firing in such situations. I could see what consequences it would lead to and single-handedly took a decision against it, in spite of huge provocation by the media. At the end of the procession, when I was talking to the agitated press, who wanted to know who was the man behind this decision, I unabashedly clarified that it was me. I was even prepared to answer the legal aspect of it. I had used my magisterial power from the Police Act, which had never been used by any DGP of this state.

The next day, the incident was covered in an eight-column first page and the entire centre spread of all newspapers. There was also a live video-streaming of the funeral procession. I could only imagine the amount of money that would have been required to get such extensive real-time media coverage. In my entire professional life, I couldn't recollect any incident in any field of public life getting such limelight.

I sighed, telling myself that my decision had punctured some 'unknown conspiracy'.

∞

I had completed the evening arghya[1] of 2013 chhath[2] in the pond at my home. I was changing from my traditional clothes when I saw news flashing on the television screen. A wooden bridge on the bank of the Ganges in Patna had given way, and a huge number of chhath devotees had drowned.

Within two minutes, in a half-dressed condition, I was in my car, rushing to the place of occurrence, while tying and buttoning up my uniform. Midway, the CM called up. He tried to narrate the incident to me, and I assured him that I was already on it and would do the needful. When I reached the place, the crowd was restive and milling. Instead of sitting in the police station, I was in the midst of the crowd, handling the situation and helping the people in distress. It took us the whole night to stabilize the situation, but the speed with which the police reacted eased out the sentiments and a major backlash was averted.

∞

Communal incidents had taken place in Nawada on the eve of the parliamentary elections of 2014. I was getting unnerved and drove off to Nawada without any delay. The district SP was new and had just joined after a change of cadre. On the way, I got a call from the CM, who advised me to camp in the neighbouring district of Nalanda. I asked the SP to come over to Nalanda with a map marked with the spots where the incidents had taken place.

He came prepared. As soon as I saw the map, the reason behind the incidents became very clear to me. I could link these incidents with the riots of 1989 that had happened in Nawada

---

[1]Hindu tradition of offering water to seek blessings of ancestors, gods and goddesses on an auspicious day
[2]Hindu festival in worship of the Sun God, observed primarily in the state of Bihar

itself. The reasons were economic. The sharp SP could see the connection very fast. I told him the names of the two rich people who I suspected could be behind this. They were handled deftly and remotely. The situation cooled down much faster than we had imagined.

Almost three years after my retirement, one day in 2017, my domestic help informed me that two sahabs from UP had come to meet me. I came out into the sitting area. They introduced themselves as home secretary and law secretary of UP.

They wanted me to share with them my 'formula' of handling crime and law and order situations in Bihar. I said, 'The methods will be as many as there are police chiefs, but the only principle that is a constant is that law is a solution to all problems.' I briefly shared some details which they sought. Finally, before leaving, they had two questions. The first question was, 'Could I give my standing orders on this subject?' They could not believe that I had never issued any standing order. I told them that the legislature and the superior courts churn out reams of printed documents which we call law. Why should the police be further burdened by adding more of these? My role as the DGP was to help my policemen understand the law and inspire them to work on its application. Lathi should not always be used.

Their second question was, 'If the UP government requested my presence in Lucknow, would I agree?' I politely refused this invitation saying that my age for working on '*pad and paisa* (post and money)', was over. Whatever is left of me, I would give to society but not through the state.

This book tries to bring out the story of the struggle that my family and I went through in all of those 37 years of my life as a policeman, which evolved painfully alongside its trials and tribulations. It will be naive to project that my children and their mother remained insulated from the heat and cold or the ups and downs of this life. There were days together when they would not hear about me. Children would sleep in the night and wake up the next morning to find me missing from the house. Every night was a nightmare.

With the non-existent means of communication in rural Bihar in those days, my wife faced a tough time answering their concerns about the safety of their father. To make things worse, the security personnel would often times feed them with horrifying stories. Yet, my wife would always put up a brave front and contain the emotions of the two children.

My only consolation remained in the fact that no unscrupulous element of any hue could confront me directly. I must have hurt all such people, from the richest economic offenders to the most dreaded outlaws, but never felt the heat frontally. The powers that be subverted my passage often, though one could never see it blatantly.

No wonder my two children decided to stay away from government jobs. They shunned such jobs like a pariah.

I used law as my weapon of offence as well as defence, never the lathi. Even today, I live in a desolate part of rural Bihar without any institutional support. I often wonder why the top public representatives who do so much good for the people they 'serve' need protection through statutes and institutions from the same people they profess to have served!

We, in the police, hurt the interests of powerful people, become so vulnerable and yet do not require any protection from the State.

My health had deteriorated a bit too far. Beset with too many difficult health issues, I started reading about them to find my own solutions. What I understood was that 'Food is the best medicine' and 'Body is the best doctor.' I was egged in this direction by my daughter Richa, who herself became a naturalist, shunning a coveted VP post at the multinational bank Morgan Stanley. I modified my lifestyle drastically, especially in terms of food. I realized that this had a more positive impact on my health and well-being than any course of medicines.

Teaching physics and mathematics had become my passion in the second half of my career as a policeman. Even after retirement, I never thought of converting this passion into a profession, though there were many tempting offers. I absolutely loathed the idea of earning money through the two subjects that I really loved. The passion is still alive.

People who don't know me feel that I have political ambitions. Unfortunately, to their dismay, I would never lose my self-respect by going around in the streets of towns and villages, begging for votes.

My prayer to the Almighty is that He absolve me of situations that require me to stand with folded hands before another human being, howsoever powerful, seeking something. The only place where I am made to bow my head should be in the presence of the Almighty Himself.

ACKNOWLEDGEMENTS

My respected senior, Mukund Prasad, who retired as the chief secretary of Bihar, had once advised me very seriously to write about my experiences in the police. I am thankful to him for sowing the seed of an idea that has finally culminated in this book.

After I retired, my wife Nutan and both my children, Richa and Shwetank, kept reminding me of this unfinished task. I am thankful to them.

Swami Samarpananand ji Maharaj, a great friend and a valuable guide, who has advised me at critical junctures, my thanks to him.

Prof. (Dr) Rajesh Chakrabarti has been a close acquaintance and a keen audience to my policing experiences. I acknowledge and thank him for his valuable advice.

Thanks to my editor Dibakar Ghosh and the team at Rupa Publications.

LAW LEXICON

Acts of the Parliament

Act Name	Act Title	Summarised meaning
Arms Act 25(1A)	Punishment for certain offences	Whoever acquires, has in his possession or carries any prohibited (not specially authorised by the Central Government) arms or ammunition shall be punishable with imprisonment for a term which shall not be less than five years, but which may extend to ten years and shall also be liable to fine.
DSPE	The Delhi Special Police Establishment Act, 1946	An Act to make provision for the constitution of a special police force in Delhi for the investigation of certain offences in the Union Territories for the superintendence and administration of the said force and for the extension to other areas of the powers and jurisdiction of members of the said force in regard to the investigation of the said offences. This legislation is the legal basis of the CBI.
Evidence Act	The Indian Evidence Act, 1872	This is an Indian legislation which contains a set of rules and allied issues governing admissibility of evidence in the Indian courts of law.
PMLA	The Prevention of Money Laundering Act, 2002	An Act of the Parliament of India enacted by the government to prevent money laundering and to provide for confiscation of property derived from money laundering.

Prevention of Corruption Act	The Prevention of Corruption Act, 1988	An Act to consolidate and amend the law relating to the prevention of corruption and for matters connected therewith.
Representation of the People Act	The Representation of the People Act, 1951	An Act to provide for the conduct of elections of the Houses of Parliament and to the House or Houses of the legislature of each State, the qualifications and disqualifications for membership of those Houses, the corrupt practices and other offences at or in connection with such elections and the decision of doubts and disputes arising out of or in connection with such elections.
UAPA	The Unlawful Activities (Prevention) Act, 1967	An Act to provide for the more effective prevention of certain unlawful activities of individuals and associations, and for dealing with terrorist activities, and for matters connected therewith.

Articles of the Constitution

Art. No.	Article Title	Summarised meaning
311	Dismissal, removal or reduction in rank of persons employed in civil capacities under the Union or a State	No person who is a member of a civil service of the Union or an all-India service or a civil service of a State or holds a civil post under the Union or a State shall be dismissed or removed by an authority subordinate to that by which he was appointed. No such person as aforesaid shall be dismissed or removed or reduced in rank except after an inquiry in which he has been informed of the charges against him and given a reasonable opportunity of being heard in respect of those charges.

312(2)	All India Services	The services known at the commencement of this Constitution as the Indian Administrative Service and the Indian Police Service shall be deemed to be services created by Parliament under this article.

Criminal Procedure Code (CrPC) sections explained

Sec. No.	Section Title	Summarised meaning
36	Powers of superior officers of police	Police officers superior in rank to an officer in charge of a police station may exercise the same powers, throughout the local area to which they are appointed, as may be exercised by such officer within the limits of his station.
82	Proclamation for person absconding	If any Court has reason to believe (whether after taking evidence or not) that any person against whom a warrant has been issued by it has absconded or is concealing himself so that such warrant cannot be executed, such Court may publish a written proclamation requiring him to appear at a specified place and at a specified time not less than thirty days from the date of publishing such proclamation.
83	Attachment of property of person absconding	The Court issuing a proclamation under section 82 may, for reasons to be recorded in writing, at any time after the issue of the proclamation, order the attachment of any property, movable or immovable, or both, belonging to the proclaimed person.

107 / 108 / 109 / 110	107. Security for keeping the peace in other cases 108. Security for good behaviour from persons disseminating seditious matters 109. Security for good behaviour from suspected persons 110. Security for good behaviour from habitual offenders	When an Executive Magistrate receives information that any person is likely to commit a breach of the peace or disturb the public tranquillity or to do any wrongful act that may probably occasion a breach of the peace or disturb the public tranquillity and is of opinion that there is sufficient ground for proceeding, he may require such person to show cause why he should not be ordered to execute a bond (with or without sureties), for keeping the peace for such period, not exceeding one year (or 3 years as in section 110), as the Magistrate thinks fit.
111	Order to be made	When a Magistrate acting under sections 107-110, deems it necessary to require any person to show cause under such section, he shall make an order in writing, setting forth the substance of the information received, the amount of the bond to be executed, the term for which it is to be in force, and the number, character and class of sureties (if any) required.
112	Procedure in respect of person present in Court	If the person in respect of whom such order is made is present in Court, it shall be read over to him, or, if he so desires, the substance thereof shall be explained to him.
113	Summons or warrant in case of person not so present	If such person as described in sections 107-110, is not present in Court, the Magistrate shall issue a summons requiring him to appear, or, when such person is in custody, a warrant directing the officer in whose custody he is to bring him before the Court.

116(1)	Inquiry as to truth of information	When an order under section 111 has been read or explained under section 112 to a person present in Court, or when any person appears or is brought before a Magistrate in compliance with, or in execution of, a summons or warrant, issued under section 113, the Magistrate shall proceed to inquire into the truth of the information upon which action has been taken, and to take such further evidence as may appear necessary.
116(3)	Inquiry as to truth of information	After the commencement, and before the completion, of the inquiry under 116(1), the Magistrate, if he considers that immediate measures are necessary for the prevention of a breach of the peace or disturbance of the public tranquillity or the commission of any offence or for the public safety, may, for reasons to be recorded in writing, direct the person in respect of whom the order under section 111 has been made to execute a bond, with or without sureties, for keeping the peace or maintaining good behaviour until the conclusion of the inquiry, and may detain him in custody until such bond is executed or, in default of execution, until the inquiry is concluded.

144	Power to issue order in urgent cases of nuisance or apprehended danger	In cases where, in the opinion of a District Magistrate, a Sub-divisional Magistrate or any other Executive Magistrate specially empowered by the State Government in this behalf, there is sufficient ground for proceeding and immediate prevention or speedy remedy is desirable, the Magistrate may by a written order direct any person to abstain from a certain act. The Magistrate may also take certain order with respect to certain property in his possession or under his management, if he considers that such direction is likely to prevent, or tends to prevent, obstruction, annoyance or injury to any person lawfully employed, or danger to human life, health or safety or a disturbance of the public tranquillity, or a riot, or an affray.
154	Information in cognizable cases	Every information relating to the commission of a cognizable offence, if given orally to an officer in charge of a police station, shall be reduced to writing by him or under his direction, and be read over to the informant; and every such information, whether given in writing or reduced to writing as aforesaid, shall be signed by the person giving it, and the substance thereof shall be entered in a book to be kept by such officer in such form as the State Government may prescribe in this behalf.

309	Power to postpone or adjourn proceedings	In every inquiry or trial the proceedings shall be continued from day-to-day until all the witnesses in attendance have been examined, unless the Court finds the adjournment of the same beyond the following day to be necessary for reasons to be recorded.
482	Saving of inherent powers of High Court	Nothing in CrPC shall be deemed to limit or affect the inherent powers of the High Court to make such orders as may be necessary to give effect to any order under CrPC, or to prevent abuse of the process of any Court or otherwise to secure the ends of justice.

Indian Penal Code (IPC) sections explained

Sec. No.	Section Title	Summarised meaning
144	Joining unlawful assembly armed with deadly weapon	Whoever, being armed with any deadly weapon, or with anything which, used as a weapon of offence, is likely to cause death, is a member of an unlawful assembly, shall be punished with imprisonment of either description for a term which may extend to two years, or with fine, or with both.
211	False charge of offence made with intent to injure	Whoever, with intent to cause injury to any person, institutes or causes to be instituted any criminal proceeding against that person, or falsely charges any person with having committed an offence, knowing that there is no just or lawful ground for such proceeding or charge against that person, shall be punished with imprisonment of either description for a term which may extend to two years, or with fine, or with both.

307	Attempt to murder	Whoever does any act with such intention or knowledge, and under such circumstances that, if he by that act caused death, he would be guilty of murder, shall be punished with imprisonment of either description for a term which may extend to ten years, and shall also be liable to fine; and if hurt is caused to any person by such act, the offender shall be liable either to (imprisonment for life), or to such punishment as is hereinbefore mentioned.
341	Punishment for wrongful restraint	Whoever wrongfully restrains any person shall be punished with simple imprisonment for a term which may extend to one month, or with fine which may extend to five hundred500 rupees, or with both.
379	Punishment for theft	Whoever commits theft shall be punished with imprisonment of either description for a term which may extend to three years, or with fine, or with both.
396	Dacoity with murder	If any one of five or more persons, who are conjointly committing dacoity, commits murder in so committing dacoity, every one of those persons shall be punished with death, or (imprisonment for life), or rigorous imprisonment for a term which may extend to ten years, and shall also be liable to fine.